IN SEARCH OF FLORENTINE
CIVIC HUMANISM

In Search of Florentine Civic Humanism

ESSAYS ON
THE TRANSITION FROM
MEDIEVAL TO
MODERN THOUGHT

HANS BARON

VOLUME II

PRINCETON UNIVERSITY PRESS
PRINCETON, NEW JERSEY

Copyright © 1988 by Princeton University Press
Published by Princeton University Press, 41 William Street,
Princeton, New Jersey 08540

Second printing, 1989

LIBRARY OF CONGRESS CATALOGING-IN-PUBLICATION DATA
Baron, Hans, 1900–
In search of Florentine civic humanism.
Includes indexes.
1. Humanism—Italy—Florence—History.
2. Florence (Italy)—Politics and government—To 1421.
3. Florence (Italy)—Politics and government—1421–1737.
4. Renaissance—Italy—Florence. 5. City states.
6. Political participation—Italy—Florence.
I. Title.
DG737.55.B35 1988   945'.51   88–2328
ISBN 0–691–05512–2 (alk. paper: v. 1)
ISBN 0–691–05513–0 (alk. paper: v. 2)

Publication of this book has been aided by a grant
from The Andrew W. Mellon Foundation

This book has been composed in Linotron Bembo

Clothbound editions of Princeton University Press books
are printed on acid-free paper, and binding materials
are chosen for strength and durability. Paperbacks,
although satisfactory for personal collections, are not
usually suitable for library rebinding

Printed in the United States of America by
Princeton University Press,
Princeton, New Jersey

CONTENTS

PART II

The Historical Setting and Influence
of Florentine Humanism

ELEVEN

Fifteenth-Century Civilization
North of the Alps and the
Italian Quattrocento:
Contrast and Confluence*

I

IN THE history of the events which changed the face of Europe around 1500, we must distinguish two interlocking developments. Besides the cultural transformation from which the term "Renaissance" has been borrowed to describe the whole period, there was the emergence of the states-system of modern Europe. During the last decades of the fifteenth century, England, France, and Spain, after long and complex preparation, had attained national unification under strong monarchies. In addition, a bilingual state had grown up in the rich borderlands of France and Germany—the state of the dukes of Burgundy. Since France, with an estimated fifteen million inhabitants, was potentially far superior to any of its competitors and, indeed, represented a type of great power not yet realized elsewhere (there were only about three million inhabitants in England, six million in Spain, and hardly more than six million in the state of Burgundy with the inclusion of industrial Artois, Flanders, and Brabant), France's neighbor states of necessity combined their resources. The German empire, France's only equal in population, could not serve as a piece on the new European chess-

* This introduction to Volume II, a comprehensive and comparative analysis of conditions in various European countries, was first published as a chapter in volume 1 of *The New Cambridge Modern History* (1957) under the title, "Fifteenth-Century Civilisation and the Renaissance." It is reprinted here with the kind permission of *The New Cambridge Modern History* and the Cambridge University Press. The reprint contains some stylistic changes.

board because it was a loose federation of territorial states and half-independent cities under the Habsburgs, who had little power as German emperors. In its Austrian and Alpine dominions, however, this house possessed the largest and strongest of the territorial states, and so the anti-French counterpoise was built upon a system of princely marriage alliances, first (1477) between Habsburg and Burgundy, and subsequently (1496) between Habsburg, Burgundy and Spain. The years around 1500, therefore, saw the encounter of two gigantic powers, or power combinations, such as had not been known to the medieval world; and when, beginning with the early 1520s, England endeavored to become the moderator of the balance between France and Habsburg Spain, the modern pattern of an equilibrium of states had been established on the European scene.

It was the same generation from about 1490 to 1520 that experienced the culmination of Renaissance art, Humanism, and a new historico-political science. (The growth of natural science did not reach a comparable phase of maturity until half a century later.) However, there exists a basic difference between this cultural revolution and the political transformation. It would be difficult to contend that outside Italy the new aesthetic values in art and literature, or the fresh views opened up in education and humanistic learning, had gradually matured in interrelation with the political development. Their roots were not in the soil of the west European countries; rather, they lay in a part of Europe which had not shared in the process of large-scale political integration but was to become the helpless object of the power politics of the new giant states: the Italian peninsula. This is not to say that Renaissance culture north of the Alps was merely an importation from the South. The art of France, Flanders, and Germany in the fifteenth century leaves no doubt that everywhere there was a fresh realism in the air; not only in Italy but also in the northern countries a growing individualism was striving for expression. Moreover, after contact had been made with Italy, the art and literature which finally emerged showed a different texture in every European nation, according to the native traditions. Yet the Renaissance artists, writers, and scholars outside Italy, from the late fifteenth century onward, were persuaded that the new era in art, literature, education, and scholarship had had its first and model phase in Italy; that their own inherited ways were hopelessly outdated; and that no future progress was possible in any field without deliberate efforts to absorb the best that had been attained south of the Alps. What were the factors in late medieval civilization, especially during the fifteenth century, that had produced this situation?

For many of the aspirations of the Middle Ages, a turning point was reached when the church councils of Constance (1414–1418) and Basle (1431–1449) succeeded in ending the schism, which had torn the unity of the Church but failed to satisfy the long-sustained hopes for religious reform and for the moderation of the strictly monarchical fabric of the Church. The frustrated program of reform had chiefly been elaborated by the medieval universities; the leaders of the party of reform had been the foremost minds of those great centers of Scholastic learning which had earlier been the source of bold political philosophies, and their proponents had incessantly explored and adapted to changing conditions the fundamental questions of the relation between church and state and of the mutual obligation between ruler and people. The intellectual vigor of Scholasticism in this whole area of thought was sapped when the outcome of the church councils put an end to all attempts at constitutional reform within the Church and made the power of the pope nearly absolute; as the ruler of the papal state in central Italy, the pope was soon to be drawn into the whirlpool of the politics of the Italian tyrant states. Nor were the considerable achievements of fourteenth-century Scholasticism in the natural sciences followed by comparable results after the middle of the fifteenth century. Life and teaching in the universities came to be characterized by lack of originality and sterile traditionalism[1]—the accusa-

---

[1] After much debate this is still the picture, as found for Oxford in H. Rashdall, *The Universities of Europe*, ed. Powicke and Emden (Oxford, 1936), vol.

tion which was so often leveled by later humanists against the learning of the Middle Ages as a whole.

It is also true that by the fifteenth century the day of medieval knighthood had passed. The military service of the vassal was nearly obsolete; and the economic position of the landed noblemen, dependent as it was on easy availability of agricultural labor, had been greatly weakened by the destruction of a third or more of the European peasant population through the Black Death and the lasting economic decline that ravaged most countries in the fourteenth century. Yet it would be erroneous to think that preeminence on the European scene was henceforth left to the bourgeoisie. The strengthening of monarchy in the course of building up the great European powers created fresh opportunities for the nobility, which together with the burgher class was indispensable in the new armies and administrations and could provide splendor to the princes' entourage. During the fifteenth century the balance between burghers and noblemen, between urban and chivalric culture, was largely to depend on the existence and influence of central princely courts; the outcome was different in each European country.

II

Except for Italy, the greatest strides beyond medieval feudal conditions in social and constitutional history were made in the English monarchy. English knights had been the first to lose the status of an armed military caste; in the course of the fifteenth century they merged into a gentry no longer separated by a gulf from the commercial world of the burgher class. They intermarried and socially intermingled with the leading London merchant families, and in the House of Com-

---

3, pp. 270f.; for Paris, in A. Renaudet, *Préréforme et Humanisme à Paris*, 2d ed. (Paris, 1953), 98ff., 158f.; for the German universities, in G. Ritter, "Via antiqua und via moderna auf den Deutschen Universitäten des XV. Jahrhunderts," *Sitzungsberichte der Heidelberger Akad. der Wiss.*, Philos.-Hist. Klasse (1922), Abh. 7, 95–99, 113–15.

mons the "Knights of the Shire" sat side by side with the bur-
gesses from the boroughs—a mark of social equality inconceivable in the meetings of most continental estates. It would
be wrong, however, to presume that in this association the
balance of influence gradually turned against the knightly element or was even equal. Since the first decades of the fifteenth
century, a growing number of the smaller parliamentary boroughs had sent gentlemen to the Commons, instead of the
merchants or members of the burgess class proper who had
been sent during the fourteenth century; the social composition of the English parliament was changing in favor not of
the bourgeoisie but of the gentry, until, by the time of Elizabeth, there were four gentlemen to every townsman among
the members.

We find a corresponding survival and even recrudescence of
the traditions of gentility in the cultural life of fifteenth-century England. As George Macaulay Trevelyan characterizes
the situation: If Chaucer's ghost had returned to the English
scene in the late fifteenth century he would have felt entirely
at home even though a century had passed. No fundamentally
new ideas or literary tastes emerged; the works of Chaucer
were still read as if they were contemporary productions. One
might go even further and judge that English literature had
not yet fully assimilated Chaucer's best achievements. His had
been a development in taste and interest from the days when
he translated the *Roman de la Rose* into English and acclima-
tized the allegorical style of French knightly love poetry to the
time of the fresh realism of his *Canterbury Tales*. Literary production in fifteenth-century England did include a realistic
trend, expressed chiefly in satirical and didactic writings; but
the elaborate literary works that reflected the intellectual climate of the period between 1400 and 1500 continued, rather,
the "aureate diction" of the allegoric and chivalrous love poetry of the early Chaucer. The favorite subject matter remained the knightly epic, which transformed past history into
a web of legendary tales of the descent of England's knight-

hood from Troy, Rome, and the "Round Table" of King Arthur.

To be sure, the century saw significant innovations and inventions. New schools were founded—among them Eton and Winchester—where the descendants of gentle and even noble families were educated along with the best talent from lower circles; as elsewhere in Europe, the period was at hand when a scholarly education became a normal part of the preparation for the man of the world. For the first time, letter writing was common in the higher strata of lay society. But wherever these letters allow us to observe prevailing cultural trends—as in the correspondence of the Pastons (yeoman farmers who rose into the gentry)—we find, besides an active interest in tournaments, that the medieval bookshelf was unchanged, comprising epics of knightly exploits, some religious works, and a few translations (not the original texts) of ancient authors. The coming of the printed book did not immediately lead to substantial changes in taste and outlook. When William Caxton, after a long life as a London merchant and representative of English commercial interests in the Low Countries, was engaged (during the 1470s and 1480s) in running the press which for England initiated the era of printing, the core of his book production, besides Chaucer's works, was the publication in English versions of the vast literature on the knights of Troy, Greece, Rome, Charlemagne, and King Arthur, the reading matter at late medieval courts. In translating and publishing a French work entitled *The Order of Chivalry or Knighthood*, Caxton, voicing the sentiments of the London merchant patriciate, did not hesitate to comment that this was a timely book to remind forgetful England of the rules accepted in all earlier periods when English knights were known for true chivalry, especially in the memorable days of King Arthur's, Tristan's, and Percivale's noble "manhood, courtesy and gentilness."

The historiography of fifteenth-century England proves that the spiritual world in which the contemporaries of Caxton lived was indeed a glorified knightly past. To be sure, instead of clerics writing in Latin, wealthy merchants now composed English chronicles of their cities, especially in London; and, as a consequence, many everyday events from the burgher's life were realistically observed and recorded in minute detail. But if the composition of the vernacular *London Chronicles* emancipated the burgher from his dependence on clerical writers, this change did not mean emancipation from the standards and prejudices imposed by the predominance of chivalrous culture. Among the scenes of city life found in the *London Chronicles*, none are described with greater zest than knightly tournaments and royal processions in the town; and no attempt is made as yet to look beyond external facts and pageantry, to consider causes and effects, the value of sources, and the need for selection and proportion—the features of the historiography which was to rise in the sixteenth century. In general historical works such as the *Chronicles of England*, published in final form in 1480, the background remains the fantastic tale—as told by Geoffrey of Monmouth in the twelfth century—of Brutus, the grandson of Aeneas, who founded the British kingdom after his victories over aboriginal giants; the chivalrous deeds of King Arthur and the knights of his Round Table are still accepted as historical facts and used as yardsticks in all judgments of the past and present. These deeds were also the theme of the greatest imaginative work of fifteenth-century England, Malory's *Morte d'Arthur*. When Caxton first published it in print, he urged his readers to believe that the stories of Arthur were not mere fiction; Malory's description, he said, had given a glorified account of the greatest age in England's history.

This unwillingness to break away from the world of medieval chivalry must be explained largely by social facts. From the fourteenth to the end of the fifteenth century, England, like many parts of Europe, passed through an extended period of economic stagnation. Although this time saw the emergence of the clothier, the wool manufacturer who built up capitalistic industry in a countryside unhampered by medieval city-guild regulations, the output of the English cloth industry remained almost unchanged until the great upsurge of England's economic life in the course of the Tudor era; the day of the industrial middle class still lay far in the future. The only social group of the bourgeoisie whose impact on culture could be significant in the fifteenth century was the London wholesale merchant class, which wielded the government of England's only metropolitan city and controlled her trade with the continent. But the exclusive and privileged "livery companies" of these merchants were in their nature less a harbinger of modern society than an epilogue to the history of medieval merchant guilds; nor did they represent a group keenly aware of its differences from the nobility, rather they formed a social stratum regularly passing into the landed gentry by intermarriage. Having acquired property in the country, the merchants merged into a half-feudal environment. Even as late as the time of Elizabeth, gentlemen of social and political importance led a seignorial existence on the land, surrounded by a crowd of retainers and gathering in turn around a patron in the higher nobility. If by that time the culture of the gentry and the nobility had largely outgrown the medieval chivalrous tradition, in many respects this was due to the influence of the new aristocratic education that had first flowered at the Italian courts.

It was not until the end of the fifteenth century, however, that any serious contacts between England and Renaissance Italy were made. Up to then, journeys to Italy had not formed a part of the education of the sons of the gentry or of the London merchant aristocracy. Before 1490, English travelers to Italy as a rule were clergy or officials in the king's service. Although these men occasionally acted as pioneers, in that they brought home rare humanistic manuscripts and a love for the new learning, Humanism was not to them a new education or a new world of ideas. On returning to England, they did not found new intellectual movements or groups opposed to Scholasticism. As a consequence, in spite of the stimulus of such pioneers, and in spite of the patronage of individual members of the English high nobility who persuaded some

Italian humanists to serve in England as secretaries or teachers, the only tangible result was the addition of a substantial number of humanistic manuscripts to English libraries and the inclusion of some Greek in the curriculum of the old schools and universities.

Before Humanism could mean more to late medieval England, the growth of Humanism in Italy had to reach the stage where the classicists' enthusiasm for ancient literature and art was balanced by renewed thoughts of religion and by endeavors to reconcile the classical legacy with the Christian tradition. After Lorenzo Valla, the great Roman humanist, made the first critical revision of the New Testament, scholars of the school of Neoplatonic philosophy revived in Florence, foremost among them Marsilio Ficino and Pico della Mirandola, set to work upon a new theology in a half-classical, half-Scholastic framework, drawing upon the religious literature of classical Antiquity. This heightened religious interest in Florence was reinforced for a while after 1490 when the preaching of Savonarola caused a widespread estrangement from the secularism of the early Italian Renaissance. It was during this religious-minded phase of the Renaissance that English scholarship established contacts with Italy. After a two-year visit to Italy, John Colet delivered public lectures on the Epistles of St. Paul in Oxford, from 1496 onwards, that represented a decisive break with the methods of Scholastic learning. Taking the paths followed by Ficino in those years, Colet interpreted Paul's teaching and missionary work against the background of the pagan and early Christian periods. Like Ficino, Colet showed a new psychological insight and understanding springing from a loving intimacy with the humane personality of Paul as a biblical teacher. In his exegesis of Paul's doctrine, Colet was guided by a simple piety and a confidence that faith in divine grace and the proper spirit were of greater account than the letter of the law or any rite. From this confidence sprang a striking unconcern for most of the abstruse problems of the theology of the Schoolmen.[2]

[2] That Colet's studies were influenced by Ficino is obvious from the simi-

Once this first bridge to the intellectual world of Renaissance Italy had been built, Humanism in England quickly became a movement which could spread beyond the walls of the universities. In metropolitan London, owing to Colet and Thomas More, there formed a circle of men whose minds, having been shaped by the new religious learning, were soon spurred on to social and political concerns; until, after the 1520s, in the latter part of Henry VIII's reign, Renaissance ideas on history and politics, on social problems and human conduct, were reaching England in an uninterrupted stream. When, shortly after 1500, an Italian humanist residing in England, Polydore Vergil, detected the fantastic note of medieval legend in the accepted accounts of Brutus and King Arthur and reconstructed the history of England in humanistic fashion, his criticism was still greeted with indignation and unbelief. Yet the seeds of doubt once sown would germinate, and from the 1530s onward the world of Geoffrey of Monmouth was gradually replaced by the historical vistas created by the Renaissance in Italy.

III

Across the Channel, the fifteenth-century balance between monarchy, nobility, and bourgeoisie had been different. The performance of monarchy in promoting political integration was more spectacular in the French-speaking countries than

larity of their approaches and has been accepted as a fact ever since F. Seebohm's *The Oxford Reformers* (1867). However, as very little is known about the details of Colet's Italian journey, evidence of personal relations between the two men has been lacking. Direct contacts have now been proved by the discovery of two intimate letters of Ficino to Colet; see R. Marcel, *Bibliothèque d'Hum. et Renaiss.* 14 (1952): 122f. Another difficulty in assuming Colet's debt to Ficino is the late date of Ficino's commentary on Paul's epistles—between 1496 and 1499, according to P. O. Kristeller's *Supplementum Ficinianum* (Florence, 1937), vol. 1, p. lxxxii. But since the commentary was preceded by lectures, its date is no obstacle to the conjecture that Ficino was already engaged in biblical studies, or even giving his lectures, at the time when Colet visited Florence.

anywhere else in fifteenth-century Europe. In the darkest hours of the Hundred Years War (1337–1453) and during the subsequent period of reconstruction, the crown had been the rallying point and the salvation of France; similarly, the state of the dukes of Burgundy was created solely by the efforts of a younger branch of the French royal house. In France, royal power was already becoming absolute; the États Généraux had practically lost the right of consent in matters of taxation, and the supreme judicial court, the Parlement of Paris, exerted only occasional checks on the omnipotence of the king. Royal centralized administration could not yet be extended to every province of the vast kingdom, and its place in Orléans and Anjou, Brittany and Burgundy was taken by princely courts and regional administration under branch lines of the royal family or other members of the high nobility. The work of reconstruction carried out by king and princes in the second half of the fifteenth century depended on the cooperation not only of the nobility but also of the bourgeoisie. Yet, although royal policy highly favored the industry and commerce of the towns, the urban element in France was not so much a respected ally as a submissive favorite, closely supervised by royal officials. The leading ranks of the townsmen did not represent a commercial or industrial class with a national horizon; they rather formed wealthy local aristocracies with merely provincial interests. Their most successful members were eager to purchase landed estates and associate themselves with provincial noblemen. At the French courts, therefore, the forms of social life and the spirit of literature and art remained almost untouched by urban influences; the legacy of medieval chivalry continued to be the dominating factor.

To be sure, within the framework of the princely courts we meet with still another element of cultural significance. Studies of the classical authors had always flourished among clerks in the French chancery, and in these circles, during the later Middle Ages, there existed a strong affinity of mind with the Latin classicism of Italian humanists. Frenchmen, like Italians, spoke a Romance language, and interest in surviving Latin literature had spread more widely in medieval France than in any other European country, including Italy before the coming of Petrarch. In the fourteenth century, the residence of the papal Curia at Avignon on the banks of the Rhône had brought the two countries into close intellectual contact; Petrarch had spent his formative years in a mixed Italian-French environment at Avignon, and during the first part of his life may have found better classical texts and information among his French friends than in his native Italy. In the first two generations after Petrarch (roughly the years 1360–1420), we find the secretaries of the royal chancery leading the typical social life of humanists: classical manuscripts were eagerly transcribed and letters and poems imitating ancient models were exchanged. But in the 1430s these activities began to decline, apparently having no permanent effect until Frenchmen began to travel in Italy and to be visited by Italian scholars in the second half of the century.[3] The explanation is not hard to find. A chiefly rhetorical trend of studies, confined to the narrow world of the chanceries and lacking important significance for contemporaneous French learning or for the values of those who were socially prominent, could not result in anything comparable to the organic development of Italian Humanism.

Although a mature humanistic movement could not develop on so slender a basis, the long influence of classical studies on France, as well as the proximity of Italy, caused interest in some favorite ancient authors to hold its own in the culture of the French courts. After the middle of the fourteenth century, the library of the kings added to its treasure of religious and chivalric literature a number of manuscripts of Greek and

[3] See A. Coville, *Gontier et Pierre Col et l'Humanisme en France au temps de Charles VI* (Paris, 1934), esp. 229–34. The decline of early French Humanism after the 1420s has been disputed by F. Simone in the Italian periodical *Convivium* (1951), 189, 193ff., and in his *The French Renaissance: Medieval Tradition and Italian Influence in Shaping the Renaissance in France* (London, 1969), 145–54), for reasons which in my opinion are not strong enough to confute the demonstration by Coville and also by Renaudet of a loss of humanistic energies in mid-fifteenth-century France.

Roman works translated into French at royal request. Livy's Roman history, Cicero's *On Old Age* and *On Friendship*, as well as the Aristotelian *Ethics, Politics*, and *Economics*, thus became available to courtiers ignorant of Latin and Greek; there were also some products of the early Italian humanists, especially Petrarch and Boccaccio. But these French versions made for princely libraries were very different from humanistic translations bent on reproducing the exact text, the literary form, and the historical atmosphere of the translated works; they were paraphrases and adaptations conceived in such a way that their content could be readily understood and borrowed by readers and writers eager to find an antidote to the decay of present-day chivalry in the hardiness, patriotism, and warrior virtues of the Roman "knights." At the court of Burgundy, cultural center of the French-speaking countries in the latter half of the fifteenth century, the legendary history of the knighthood of ancient Troy, Greece, and Rome became the framework for all ideas on conduct, education, and even politics. Ducal secretaries collected all available sources on Alexander the Great in beautifully illuminated manuscripts—translations of ancient historical accounts and medieval tales alike; the fabulous splendors of Alexander's court in war and peace served as a model and as a reflected image of social life at the Burgundian court. The knightly world of King Arthur's Round Table, still seen through the eyes of Geoffrey of Monmouth, and every available bit of information on Troy, whether wholly fictitious or from an ancient source, remained accepted parts of the picture of the past. Duke Philip the Good personally took a hand in the preparation of the *Hystoires de Troye*, the most splendid manuscript book among these collections; it was one of the continental works on chivalry later translated into English and published by Caxton.

In this atmosphere, classical works and Italian influences proved powerless to modify traditional ideals and the conduct of life. In the early development of chivalry, the knightly orders, the crusades, and the rise of the love poetry of the minstrel had been the crowning events; they had sprung naturally from the necessities of medieval conditions. Now these memories of the past were kept alive as parts of an elaborate system and ceremonial at the courts. The knightly orders of the Middle Ages had been free associations of knights devoted to the fight for Christianity in the East. In the late fourteenth and in the early fifteenth century, new knightly orders appeared, creations of the new monarchies which, with the help of the old chivalrous symbols and social forms, endeavored to integrate the nobility of far-flung provinces into the new state and provide new outlets in the princely service for the ambitions of noblemen. The first of these courtly orders was the English Order of the Garter; it was followed by the Burgundian Order of the Golden Fleece, the most magnificent and sumptuous of these foundations, continued as a Spanish institution after the union of the Low Countries with Spain. The rise of a French counterpart founded by Louis XI, the Ordre de Saint-Michel, and the subsequent creation of similar orders in countries as distant from each other as Savoy, Denmark, and Hungary, shows the significance of the Burgundian example for courtly society all over Europe.

In these new orders, the pomp and distinction of the ceremonial were intended to keep aloft the old standards of caste and honor. At least in Burgundy, even the memory of the crusades continued to play a vivid part. Plans for a new crusade were widely made in Europe after the Turkish conquest of Constantinople in 1453; in Renaissance Italy the humanist pope, Pius II, spent all his energies and resources on futile efforts. In the atmosphere of Burgundy the plans for the crusade assumed the appearance of a thrilling courtly event—a fascinating chapter added to the old epic of chivalry. At the end of a ducal banquet in 1454, famed in the annals of the period for its luxury, a symbolic figure representing the Church in her humiliation appeared, praying for salvation from the infidels; whereupon the duke, in a scene meant to revive the spirit of knightly valor, vowed not only to participate personally in a crusade but even to engage in single combat with the sultan— a vow outdone by the even more impossible vows of many of the knights of the Golden Fleece. Chivalrous love and poetry, too, were turned into a planned and organized institution at the French courts. From the end of the fourteenth century, *cours d'amour* were set up among the courtiers, formal meetings in which delicate problems of chivalrous behavior and love were judged and poems composed in the traditional manner of knightly love poetry were recited. These institutions were intended to similarly shape the minds of all members of the court, from the prince down to his bourgeois secretaries; all were joined together, yet carefully differentiated one from the other, in a solemn hierarchy of princes, *grands conservateurs*, ministers, counselors, secretaries, and many other distinct grades of the *cour amoureuse*.

This background readily explains the spirit of the *Rhétoriqueurs*, the school which in the fifteenth century dominated French and Burgundian literature. It was a school that prized such traits as ostentatious rhetoric, scorn for the vulgar world below the level of nobility, delight in archaic forms, clinging to the allegories and symbols of medieval poetry, and deep pessimism and melancholy caused by the knowledge that outside the beautiful conventions of the court, knighthood and chivalrous love were everywhere contradicted by the realities of life.[4] There were, it is true, a few great writers who, for various reasons, were able to break loose from the pervasive influence of the school of the *Rhétoriqueurs*; in their works realistic observation and psychology were given more ample scope and produced masterpieces of literature. But since the social structure of the period so strongly favored adherence to the outlook and conventions of the age of chivalry, we find no literary schools determinedly opposing the dominant trend; even masters in the presentation of realistic detail did not de-

---

[4] For the preceding and following characterizations of Burgundian culture, see J. Huizinga's *Der Herbst des Mittelalters*, 6th ed. (Munich, 1952; Engl. version, *The Waning of the Middle Ages* [1924]), passim, and his *Im Bann der Geschichte* (Zurich, 1943), 326–36. For the French parallels, see R. L. Kilgour, *The Decline of Chivalry as Shown in the French Literature of the Late Middle Ages* (Cambridge, Mass., 1937).

velop into conscious rebels against traditional ways or become pioneers of the tendencies of the Renaissance. The great French poet François Villon, known for his blunt self-revelation, was able to free himself from many conformities with his time only because he led the erratic life of a vagabond. His attitude toward life and society made him a late successor to the wandering scholars of the early Middle Ages rather than a precursor of the Renaissance. Another well-known writer, Antoine de la Sale, who has been called one of the pioneers of the modern novel, is an example of how the realism and psychological experience of the period sometimes resulted in a satirical critique of chivalry. His intention, however, was to castigate abuses and human frailties, not to propose new ways. Although La Sale had visited humanistic Italy, his hero's education, of which he gives so masterly an analysis, remains the training of a young knight through tournaments and courtly love.

In historical writing, realism and psychological penetration reached a climax toward the end of the century with Philippe de Commynes, the historiographer of Louis XI. Commynes emphatically condemned chivalry as an antiquated illusion, reflecting in this attitude the spirit of Louis XI's reign (1461–1483), during which a sober concern for the political and economic reconstruction of France briefly overshadowed the royal patronage of traditional culture. To an extent, Commynes' ruthless probing into human motives, his maxim that success alone—not honor—counts in politics, and his pessimistic view of human nature are northern parallels to the thought of his younger Italian contemporary, Machiavelli. Yet there remains an important difference. In Commynes' historiography, these fruits of fifteenth-century realism are not part of a new causal theory for interpreting historical and political life—the ultimate attainment of Machiavelli and the Italian Renaissance. The framework within which Commynes' discerning description of detail is placed remains a naïve attribution of the causes of war and defeat, of all historical change, to a divine intention to punish or educate. It is in the light of observations like these that the era of Louis XI falls into historical place. The realistic tendencies of his reign did not result in any permanent changes in the life of the French court and the direction of royal patronage. Except for the modifications gradually brought about by Italian influence, the French court of the Renaissance was to continue in the chivalrous tradition of the court of the fifteenth century. Even at the time of Louis XI, as we have seen, one of the few broader cultural measures introduced by this usually realistic regime was the foundation of one of the new courtly orders. Moreover, when the history of France was written by Louis' secretaries, these *Grandes Chroniques de France* embodied all the legendary, fantastic medieval traditions which were to give way to a new type of historiography only in the course of the sixteenth century, after the historical criticism of the humanists had done its work.

In the Burgundian area, a unique cultural role devolved upon the bourgeoisie of the Flemish and Brabantine cities. In an account of the art of the fifteenth century, no region north of the Alps would be represented by so many leading names as Flanders and Brabant. Indeed, the story of the growth of sensitivity to nature and the realization of human individuality in fifteenth-century painting is to a large extent the story of the Flemish school, beginning with Hubert and Jan van Eyck. In a chapter on the rise of the new spirit in the plastic arts, the names of the greatest pioneer, Claus Sluter, and of many of his followers would take us again to Flanders-Brabant or to neighboring regions. Yet, in order to determine the historical place of these attainments in art, we must also remember other facts. The new trend did not originate as a genuine creation of the cities of the Low Countries; even the paintings of the "Flemish school" were not strictly products of workshops in Flemish towns, executed in an urban atmosphere to suit the taste of bourgeois patricians. The social background of the art of the Low Countries was different from that of the art of the early Italian Quattrocento which arose in the civic domain of Florence and other Tuscan city-states. In Flemish-Burgundian art, the seeds were sown in an urban milieu but growth took place in the world of the dukes of Burgundy. Jan van Eyck and most of the other leading painters and sculptors lived, and created many of their major works, in the employment of the chivalrous ducal court, surrounded by its princely atmosphere. Their sensitivity to minute detail in portraying man and scenery had largely been anticipated not in any urban art but in the work of the miniaturists of precious manuscripts produced for the libraries of the French kings and princes of the fourteenth century. In many respects the character of these medieval surroundings left its mark on the realism of the Flemish school. As in the historiography of Commynes, the skill achieved in reproducing realistic detail was not matched by the power to organize according to rules and laws derived from nature; the total view of the world and man's place in it remained religious, spiritual, and symbolic in the medieval manner. As a consequence; the still imperfect grasp by Flemish artists of the human organism and perspective did not develop into a systematic, scientific study of anatomy and optics—an indispensable contribution of art to the Renaissance mind—as we find it in Italy.

The influence of the Burgundian court made itself strongly felt even inside the walls of Flemish cities. As a recent historian of Burgundian culture has said, the finely adorned town halls of the time, in Ghent, Bruges, Louvain, and other cities, have an appearance more of jeweller's work than of architecture; they resemble graceful shrines for relics, executed in the ornamental style characteristic of the ducal court.[5] Nothing could be further removed from the organic simplicity that distinguishes the contemporaneous architecture of the early Italian Renaissance. As for literature and poetry, the cities of Artois, Flanders, and Brabant possessed a singular type of institution: the *chambres de rhétorique* (*Rederijkerskamers* in the Germanic-speaking provinces), a secularized sequel to the medieval associations for the performance of religious miracle plays. The *chambres* served two major purposes in the fifteenth

---

[5] J. Huizinga, *Im Bann*, 332.

century: the training of a troupe for the performance of plays—now often moral-allegorical in content—and the constant exercising of all members in the "art of rhetoric." For education in this art, formal meetings were held, with a strict social ceremonial, in which everyone present had to compose and recite, in a prescribed time, compositions in verse on a common theme assigned by the chairman, often a high-ranking member of the Burgundian nobility. With their emphasis on etiquette and the teachable elements of literary expression, the *chambres* were a bourgeois counterpart to the *cours d'amour* of the nobility; in both institutions the preservation of socially accepted forms and traditions far outweighed individual originality in value. A few generations later, during the sixteenth century, the *chambres* were to provide a social forum for the dissemination of new ideas, first of Erasmian humanism, and subsequently, in the northern provinces of the Netherlands, of the Reformation. But to discover the channels through which new intellectual forces gradually spread from the latter half of the fifteenth century onwards, we must turn our attention away from the cities of Flanders and Brabant to cultural centers outside the sphere of Burgundy.

IV

There were three focal points, or areas, in continental western and central Europe that kept aloof from the overpowering influence of the French and Burgundian courts. One was the University of Paris, the old international meeting place of European scholars. There we observe conditions which closely resemble the course of development in the universities of England. In spite of France's proximity to Italy, the Parisian Schoolmen scorned Italian influences and made no major changes in their curriculum until the last decades of the fifteenth century. True, after 1450 a few Italian humanists were admitted by the faculty of arts as teachers of Greek; some humanistic textbooks replaced medieval Latin grammars; and Parisian printing presses, from their inception in 1470, pro-

duced some books of humanistic interest. But these were minor innovations which did not influence the trend of studies in
any of the faculties. The center of university life remained the
bitter controversies between the schools of Aquinas, Scotus,
and Occam and the traditional discussions of logical and metaphysical problems. Students who searched for more nourish-
ing food in their spiritual education found satisfaction in reading the works of the late-medieval mystics. In Paris, as in
Oxford, the reserve toward Italian Humanism did not change
until the latter began to apply the interpretative methods of
classical scholarship to the Scriptures and to explore humanistic avenues for theology by turning attention to the mystical
and religious elements in the legacy of Antiquity. In Paris,
too, the ice was broken about the middle of the last decade of
the fifteenth century. Like Colet in Oxford, Lefèvre d'Étaples
(Faber Stapulensis) in Paris brought home from a journey to
Italy enthusiasm for a new learning that offered at one and the
same time training in the methods of classical scholarship, an
eager interest in Plato and Neoplatonism, a fresh theological
start, and the warmth of a new piety penetrating all studies.
Lefèvre differed from Colet only in that the aspect of Florentine Neoplatonism which chiefly caught his attention was not
the study of the Epistles of St. Paul but Ficino's and Pico della
Mirandola's interest in the ancient works on mysticism, the
occult sciences, astrology, and the symbolism of names—a
late-classical corpus of writings which afforded a glimpse of
pre-Christian piety. The interest in this body of literature was
to become almost as influential as was the humanistic interest
in the Scriptures.

As for the later course of relations between the French humanistic movement and Renaissance Italy, in Paris as in Oxford it was only after these contacts had been made with religious sentiment and theological scholarship that Italian
Humanism was embraced as a new attitude toward contemporary life and the traditions of the past. Even then the change
did not come about suddenly. When, in his early history of
France, written about 1500, Paolo Emilio, an Italian humanist

in the employ of the French king, rejected the legend of the Trojan origin of the knights of France, the results of his scholarship failed to impress French writers. Not until the generation of Jean Bodin, in the second half of the sixteenth century, did the historical criticism of the Renaissance definitely begin to do away with the fantastic world of French knightly legend.

The second focal area outside the sway of French-Burgundian courtly culture was the galaxy of towns on the eastern flank of Brabant-Flanders and Burgundy, reaching from the northern mouths of the vast valley of the Rhine in the lands around the Zuider Zee to Switzerland in the South. Compared with the phenomenal concentration of the cloth industry and international trade in Ghent and Ypres, Brussels and Antwerp, this eastern area was more remote and provincial and more moderate in wealth, and it was the home of some of the greatest of the fourteenth-century mystics. In the fifteenth century it saw the spread of a pietist movement, the *Devotio moderna*, which had originated during the preceding century in the quiet districts between the Rhine and the Zuider Zee. Among the most interesting fruits of this "new devotion" were the "Brethren of the Common Life," associations of men (occasionally also of women) who, though not taking irrevocable monastic vows, gave up their private property and lived a chaste and strictly regulated life in common houses, devoting each waking hour to divine service, labor, reading, and the preaching of sermons in accordance with a prescribed schedule, their common meals being accompanied by readings from the Scriptures. Judging from the ascetic discipline and intention of this life, it had few features which distinguished it from life in a monastery. Members occasionally joined a convent of the Windesheim Congregation of reformed Augustinian canons, another reflection of the "new devotion." Yet even though the Brethren lived in the shadow of the monastery, the existence of associations which laid down their own rules for religious life without seeking guidance from any of the established orders was something new; and the consequences were felt in the Brethren's attitude to-

wards church, theology, and education. Their confidence that
a spiritual discipline similar to that of the monk was possible
without binding vows, combined with their emphasis on conduct, produced a tendency to value character and piety more
highly than strict adherence to rite and doctrine. To a degree,
the brotherhood shared this tendency with the mystics of the
fourteenth century, but unlike them they were no longer seeking essential nourishment for the soul in mystic rapture. In the
regulated life of brotherhood houses, the spirit was fortified
by a persistent and methodical reading of the Scriptures and
devotional works of a practical educational nature. Books and
a common library, therefore, were the center of life in these
houses; and even the manual labor prescribed for certain hours
of the day preferably involved the making of careful and reliable copies of manuscripts, the sale of which would contribute
to the support of the common life as well as help to dissemi-
nate the books in which the Brethren had found their spiritual
guides.

To be sure, the books read and circulated by the Brethren
had little in common with the intellectual interests of Humanism. Nevertheless, the Brethren's dislike of abstruse theological discussion bore some resemblance to the humanists' opposition to the intellectual subtlety of Scholasticism. Their
love of books that give spiritual and moral guidance could
serve as a bridge to the humanists' love of classical poets and
moralists who educate the mind; and their insistence on hon-
esty and faithfulness in manuscript copying could be a preparation for the humanists' philological accuracy in the reconstruction of ancient texts. This is not to say that the Brethren
developed into humanists or produced a new secular culture.
The intellectual independence and experience of life needed
for the growth of humanistic scholarship would have been difficult to find in these brotherhood houses. But the affinity
with essential aspects of Humanism went far enough for the
Brethren to recognize in humanistic pedagogy something of
their own intentions and to readily associate themselves with
schools run by men who had pursued studies in Italy or had

24

elsewhere come in contact with Humanism. In such cases, the Brethren founded and supervised dormitories, connected with their houses, for the pupils of the school; they thus were able to imbue the pupils' lives with their religious earnestness and methodical discipline. Indeed, so widely did they engage in this work of educational assistance that the Netherlands, Brabant, and Flanders, and even large parts of Germany, were eventually strewn with humanistic schools whose unusual size and pedagogical excellence largely derived from their cooperation with a brotherhood house and the availability of dormitories under the Brethren's supervision.

As early as the beginning of the fifteenth century, we find in Nicholas of Cusa a great philosopher whose mind was formed first by an education in the school connected with the Brethren at Deventer near the Zuider Zee, and afterwards by university studies at Heidelberg and in Italy. Out of the marriage of northern and southern elements in Nicholas' thought emerged the first philosophy in which the spirituality of mysticism and of the "new devotion" was fused with the thought of the Italian Renaissance. During the last decades of the fifteenth century, the leading figure bred in the atmosphere of the Netherlands was Erasmus. He did not visit Italy in his formative years, but as a boy in the school at Deventer he had found himself under the twofold influence of the Brethren and of teachers influenced by Italian Humanism. Early in life he met Colet in Oxford. By this meeting the Humanism of the Low Countries, already tinged with the spirituality and the biblical interest of the Brethren, was brought in contact with the new theology and approach to the Epistles of St. Paul which Colet, only a few years earlier, had brought home from Italy and continued in England. Thus, at the crossroads of various northern and southern influences, there emerged a Biblical Humanism, a school of studies which also gained a foothold in Paris, where Lefèvre became a great biblical scholar during his later years. Between 1500 and 1520, under Erasmus' leadership, Biblical Humanism was to be the most significant trend of Humanism outside Italy.

V

Spreading to the Upper Rhine and south Germany, Erasmian and Biblical Humanism entered a region which had been in closer contact with Italy for several generations—the third major area of important cultural development outside the sphere of the French and Burgundian courts. This area, too, had a marked urban character. South Germany, indeed Germany as a whole, had not produced a centralizing monarchy; and the courts—or centers of administration—of the rising territorial states were still too provincial in outlook and composition to exert a decisive influence on German culture. The German lower nobility found little opportunity in princely service during the fifteenth century. It was not until the second half of the sixteenth century that the German noblemen as such began to play a predominant political and cultural role in the greater states; from then on, the glamorous life of the nobility of the western courts became an object for imitation at every princely seat.

In the two centuries from 1350 to 1550 many factors were conspiring in favor of the German cities and urban classes. In industry and commerce the baneful effects of the fourteenth-century epidemics were more than counterbalanced by the advantages of the country's geographic position. From the late fourteenth century on, advances in long-distance inland transportation linked more and more of the east European countries in inter-European commerce. Large eastern resources of food and raw materials supplied a substitute for German agricultural losses caused by the depopulation of the Black Death. The need of industrial goods for exchange resulted in a rapid growth of new handicrafts and industries in the German cities; at the same time new mines were opened, with the consequent establishment of highly skilled metal arts and crafts. In addition, these cities had not yet ceased to be the center of a network of trade stretching from England and the Scandinavian countries in the North to Italy in the South.[6]

[6] For German fifteenth-century economic history, many aspects of which

German life in the fifteenth century, therefore, was characterized by a sharp contrast between the vigor of countless small communities—among them many half-independent imperial towns—and the weakness of all uniting and integrating forces that might have fused these teeming energies on a regional, if not national, level. The political consequences were strife among the cities and territorial states, revolutionary stirrings in many social groups, and a dissatisfaction with the outdated medieval structure of the Empire. In sculpture and painting, no modern school comparable to that of Flanders in singleness of purpose and freedom from provincialism emerged; but a new grasp of the material substance of things, and the growing ability to represent human character realistically, appeared in the art of many German provinces and towns, independently producing counterparts to the Flemish achievements. In literature and intellectual culture, too, the lack of centers with more than merely local influence was fatal to the rise of broad, let alone national, trends. But because there was so little courtly life to uphold medieval conventions and traditions, many German scholars and writers in provincial places had open minds and looked for new discoveries in the humanistic world beyond the Alps, long before western scholars and writers did so.

In the southern parts of Germany, it early became customary for students of jurisprudence and medicine and young patricians of Nürnberg, Augsburg, and Ulm, to attend the universities of Bologna and Padua, whence they might bring home the recent products of humanistic literature. At the same time this literature continuously reached south Germany through Italian visitors. During the earlier part of the fifteenth century, the church councils of Constance and Basle had caused a great number of Italian secretary-humanists to spend years on the Upper Rhine; Aeneas Sylvius Piccolomini (later

---

still defy generalization, I have used the chapter on the preeminence of the city in F. Lütge's *Deutsche Sozial- und Wirtschaftsgeschichte* (Berlin, 1952), 142ff.; on the role of the German nobility, ibid., 149ff.

Pope Pius II), one of the most effective humanist writers of the century and at one time a secretary in the imperial chancery, played a vital role in the dissemination of these new interests. Before the middle of the century, the German public had received from his pen not only a vast Latin correspondence and elaborate programs for the *studia humanitatis* and the humanistic philosophy of life, but also a pioneer psychological novel and exemplary descriptions of Germany's geography and history. Thus educated in their tastes, translators of Latin literature into the German vernacular soon took an interest in the writings in which Italian humanists of the early fifteenth century had first proposed the new ideas of humane studies and civility, of human nature, the role of women, and public and family life; almost none of these pioneering works made available in German by the 1470s became accessible to French, Burgundian, and English readers in fifteenth-century translations. The influence of the new historiography spread with equal swiftness among German writers. As early as 1456, a semi-humanistic chronicle of the city of Augsburg repudiated the customary city legend that the early settlers were descended from Trojan fugitives. Thirty years later, the legendary history of Nürnberg was similarly repudiated, and by about 1500 Germanic origins—based on data in Caesar and Tacitus and the medieval history of Germany—had widely become a critical field of study among German scholars.

The acclimatization of university instruction of a humanistic type was easier in this atmosphere than at the old centers of Scholasticism in Paris and Oxford. New universities were founded whose arts faculties showed a great interest in humanistic studies. The first was at Basle (1460), where the influence of Aeneas Sylvius coincided with the stimulus of other visitors to the council. Humanistic beginnings such as these blended with another new tendency. In the German industrial towns—the area of cross-fertilization between Italian influences and practical experimentation in workshops—the mathematical and astronomical studies which had flowered in the Occamist school of Scholasticism during the fourteenth century were early revitalized. It was at the University of Vienna, during the 1450s and 1460s, that Peuerbach and Regiomontanus initiated the association of humanistic studies with mathematics, astronomy, and mechanics which was to become an essential trait of the later Renaissance, particularly in Germany. The great part Nürnberg was to play in Dürer's day in these fields of Renaissance science was prepared as early as the 1470s, when Regiomontanus received through patrician patronage the observatory and workshop he needed for his astronomical and mechanical researches. By that time Nürnberg had also established its great place in the new art of printing with moveable types, invented on the middle Rhine by 1450, along with its leadership in many other arts and crafts.

Although the road to the Renaissance had been opened earlier in Germany than in the western countries, one must not overlook the fact that, for a long time, those who traveled the new route were chiefly students who had spent some of their formative years in Italy or had made contacts with Italians in south Germany; their influence remained restricted to scattered places and small circles during the fifteenth century. In Germany, as in the West, Humanism did not take root until, toward the end of the century, it became allied to religious tendencies without which no lasting effect on late-medieval lay society was possible. In the time of Erasmus, the expectation that the new studies would bring about a spiritual as well as cultural reform was crucial in giving rise to the optimism with which men faced the great intellectual changes of their time and looked forward to the future. There had been no trace of this optimism in German literature during the fifteenth century, except in the small groups connected with Italy. German didactic poetry of the fifteenth century shows at every turn that even in Germany, where we find no magnificent courts displaying knightly conduct, the new standards had not as yet sufficiently matured to compete with the respect paid to the time-honored virtues of the knight. Since these virtues had all but disappeared in urban society, the critics, burghers themselves, expressed the melancholy conviction that the world had become old and disjointed and was heading toward demoralization and decay—a note sounding through all late-medieval literature. And just as Renaissance optimism and faith in new values had not as yet emerged, so Renaissance pride in originality and unconventionality was still foreign to German urban culture in the fifteenth century. In the associations of the *Meistersinger*—the counterpart among German artisans to the *chambres de rhétorique* of the bourgeoisie of Flanders and Brabant—the traditionalism of late-medieval guild society decreed that no competing member could use a tune when reciting his poems that was not ascribed to one of the "twelve great masters, the legendary authorities of the singers; to try to go beyond the set forms smacked of presumption. It is in the humanistic milieu of Nürnberg at the turn of the fifteenth and sixteenth centuries that the singer's right to individual creation was first recognized; soon a singer was called a master only after he had invented at least one tune of his own. During the early sixteenth century, this principle—proof that growing individualism was at last breaking down traditionalism in all urban classes—became the rule for the German *Meistersinger* in all German towns.

VI

In every European country outside the Italian peninsula, then, we have found a similar situation at the beginning of the last decade of the fifteenth century. Everywhere—Spain, which space does not permit us to include in this survey, would be a less pronounced example, but no exception—minds turned toward Italy. This contact of the North with the South was made at the time when citizens and scholars in the northern countries, having begun to free themselves from the traditions of Scholasticism and chivalric culture, were searching for a type of education which was at once humanistic and religious; hence the key position of Florentine Neoplatonism, the phase of the Italian development in which, more than in any other, humanistic culture seemed capable of providing a religiously motivated approach to Antiquity and a devout philosophy of life. The European recourse to Italian civilization coincided with the invasion of Italy by French armies; from then on, the northern portion of the peninsula was to be an annex alternately of the French and Habsburg monarchies. Thus, from the 1490s onward, Italy became an object of incessant attention, not only for traveling clerics and scholars but also for diplomats and courtiers from all the European countries, and it was soon realized that religious philosophy and the critical study of the Bible, brought home from Italy by Christian humanists like Colet and Lefèvre, had been but one phase of a much more diversified political, social, and cultural innovation.

A major cause of the peculiar evolution of Italy was the history of her nobility. From the early Middle Ages on, in large parts of the peninsula, there had been no lasting feudal separation of the burgher class from a knighthood that monopolized political, military, and cultural leadership. At least in northern and central Italy, where the emperor and the pope were the sole, but weak, overlords, most cities had developed into city-states at an early date, practically, if not legally, independent—the only republics in the western world before the seventeenth century, except for a few rural and city-state cantons of Switzerland. The landed nobility had been forced to move into adjacent cities, whose ruling commercial classes, especially in Florence, were usually engaged by the thirteenth century in long-distance trade and the manufacture of woolen cloth, Europe's earliest major export industry. Through this congregation within a single city wall of important segments of the Italian nobility and leading commercial and industrial groups, a relatively integrated civil society was formed, earlier than anywhere else in Europe, in which the balance gradually swung away from the knightly element and the chivalric tradition.

When the love poetry of the Provençal troubadours was taken over and adapted by this Italian town patriciate, it began to lose its conventional form and assumed a simpler, more personal, and more natural note; this was the trend in Italian literature at the time of Dante, about 1300. By the middle of the fourteenth century, in the humanistic movement led by Petrarch, we find a conscious reaction in Italy against the style and content of chivalrous poetry as well as of Scholastic learning—a change in taste and judgment which gave aggressive power to the classicism of that period. The cultural ideals of the ancient Roman patriciate, as handed down in Cicero's writings, began to furnish a new standard; Ciceronian *humanitas* became the watchword for an education which claimed to free man from social conventions and professional narrowness by making conduct, speech, and writing a genuine expression of moral and intellectual individuality. Virgil's epic, it was thought, provided a model of poetry echoing simple human loyalties and passions and love of country; it was a national epic free from the bizarreness of the knightly code that dominated medieval poetry. Livy seemed to fulfill a similar function for historical literature, providing a standard for the dramatic portrayal of the growth of a nation and teaching, by contrast, the barbarity of delight in pomp and irrelevant detail.

Enjoyment and considerable knowledge of the ancient poets, orators, historians, and moral philosophers had not been lacking in the Middle Ages; they had been widely studied by French and English clergymen before the rise of Scholasticism, especially during the twelfth century. The novel element in Petrarch's humanism was his singleness of mind in using the Ciceronian idea of *humanitas* as a guide in the interpretation of Antiquity. In spending the larger part of his life at the courts of tyrants, who by the middle of the fourteenth century had replaced republican government in many cities of northern Italy, Petrarch did not become unfaithful to his ideals. The political dictator of the city-state, the *signore*, was essentially a strong, self-made personality capable of attracting an entourage of unusual men in politics and culture, whom he befriended and with whom he could have informal intercourse;

hardly ever was he the center of a ceremonial built on courtly customs and differences of caste. The intellectual climate in the tyrant state was, indeed, initially almost as congenial as that of the city republic to a type of culture based both on humane contact between man and man and on a liberal education; and the triumph of Petrarch's humanism greatly helped to retard until late in the fifteenth century the slow, though finally inevitable, transformation of the Italian tyrants' seats into new centers of courtly culture. During the greater part of the period stretching from 1400 to 1500, and especially at its beginning, Renaissance humanists, building on the foundations laid by Dante, Petrarch, and Boccaccio, were busy creating a culture and literature intended to be the common property of educated men of all social classes—laymen as well as clergy. In the famed boarding schools of humanistic early Quattrocento educators like Guarino da Verona in Ferrara and Vittorino da Feltre in Mantua, the same curriculum of classical studies and physical exercise was required for every pupil, even for the sons of princes.

A corollary to the belief that a new and more valuable culture had replaced the medieval pattern was the changed perspective in Quattrocento works of the historical past and of the relationship of the past to the present. Through Dante and Petrarch, it was argued, genuine poetry and ancient wisdom had been "reborn" after a deathlike sleep of a thousand years, just as true art had arisen again as if from the grave; the subsequent resurgence of the *studia humanitatis*, the recovery of major Latin works, among them Tacitus' historical works and Cicero's letters, and the new access to authentic texts of Greek literature facilitated by refugee scholars from Byzantium, seemed to introduce an age which, if it did not equal Antiquity, at least marked the beginning of similar achievements in all fields of culture. It should be noted that this confidence grew in Renaissance Italy at the very time when we find a widespread melancholy feeling of decay in the countries which still accepted the code of chivalry.

To be sure, if the freedom of the city-state had been re-

33

placed everywhere in northern and central Italy by autocratic governments and if all of Italy had become an area of monarchic or despotic rule, the strongly urban and civic strain in Italian culture could hardly have survived far into the Renaissance. But during the two generations from 1390 to 1450, the bourgeois element in the Italian republics—although the time of the greatest industrial power and predominance in European trade had already passed—gained buoyancy and prestige by the defense of city-state independence in a crucial struggle with tyranny. At the close of the fourteenth century, the strongest dictatorship, that of the Visconti of Milan, as is often stressed in this book, had by incessant expansion reached the point where it was threatening to transform northern and central Italy into one absolute monarchy. If this had happened, Quattrocento Italy would not have become an area of great, stimulating variety within a small compass, a civilization with a city-state basis in some respects akin to the pattern of ancient Greece; and the Italian Renaissance would not have been uniquely prepared for rediscovering the ancient world. Owing to a determined Florentine-Venetian resistance, however, Milan was restricted to the region of Lombardy by the middle of the century; and meanwhile the republics of Florence and Venice had built up regional states of their own, and due to the establishment of a balance of power, a number of minor free cities and tyrannies had also managed to survive. Upon these foundations there emerged in the second half of the fifteenth century a system of five major states differing greatly from each other in their histories and institutions (the republics of Venice and Florence, the duchy of Milan, the kingdom of Naples, and the Papal State): the first modern example of an interrelated family of states guided by the idea of equilibrium through continual readjustment of the balance of power.[7]

[7] For this estimate of the political situation, cf. N. Valeri, *L'Italia nell'età dei principati dal 1343 al 1516* (Verona, 1950), esp. 189ff., 260ff., and H. Baron, *Crisis*, esp. vol. 1, pp. 7ff., 315ff., vol. 2, pp. 379ff. L. Simeoni, *Le signorie*

The political struggle of the early Quattrocento and the resultant preservation of republican freedom side by side with tyranny left lasting marks on humanistic thought. By studying the constitutional life of the ancient city-states in Livy and Greek sources, now read in their original texts, and by appraising the history of the modern Italian city-states against this background, the humanists of the early Quattrocento paved the way for the political science and historiography of the Renaissance. In their endeavor to understand the natural causes of the emergence of the Italian system of states out of the dying body of the Empire, they came to question the basic assumptions of medieval historiography—faith in the divine ordainment of a universal empire, heir of Rome, and the haphazard tracing of noble family and city pedigrees to Troy or Rome, Aeneas or Caesar. In Italy these legends were replaced in the early Quattrocento by a realistic reconstruction of the historical roles of the republic and the monarchy in ancient Rome; the genesis of Florence, Venice, and Milan was conceived in the framework of the pre-Roman civilizations, Rome's colonization of Italy, the later decay of the Roman Empire, and the cataclysms of the Germanic migrations. Thus the histories of the regional states of Quattrocento Italy became the early models of the new historiography which, in most cases not until a whole century later, superseded the medieval myths of the past in all European nations.

(Milan, 1950), attempts to make a stronger case for the Visconti, and the tyrant state in general.

Interpretations of the Quattrocento emphasizing socioeconomic rather than sociopolitical factors are numerous but so far have resulted in a confusing variety of views. Besides the older theories of W. Sombart (*Der Bourgeois*; Engl. trans., *The Quintessence of Capitalism*) and A. v. Martin (*The Sociology of the Renaissance*), cf. F. Antal's *Florentine Painting and Its Social Background* (London, 1947), together with the criticisms by T. E. Mommsen, *Journal of the History of Ideas* 11 (1950): 369ff., and M. Meiss, *Art Bulletin* 31 (1949): 143ff. For the divergence of viewpoints see also C. M. Cipolla, *Economic History Review* (1949): 181ff.; A. Sapori, *Atti del III. convegno internazionale del Rinascimento* (1952), 107ff.; R. S. Lopez and H. Baron, *American Historical Review* 61 (1956): 1087ff.

Another mark left by the early Quattrocento on the humanistic mind was made by the values which determined the citizen's outlook on life. Petrarch and his contemporaries had read the classical writings on moral conduct with the eyes of devout late-medieval laymen; both ancient wisdom and Christian persuasion appeared to give preference to the contemplative life and to teach renunciation of material goods and the need to free the mind from passion. It was because of this interpretation that Petrarch's treatises on moral questions immediately became so popular all over Europe. In Italy after 1400, however, the citizen's pride in his way of life and the increasing knowledge of Antiquity combined to bring about a revolt against such concessions to ascetic and contemplative views. Nature, it was now argued, had equipped man for action and usefulness to his family and fellow men; the culture of the humanist should not lead man into seclusion. Material possessions must not be viewed merely with suspicion; for they provide the means for virtuous deeds, and the history of man has been his progress in becoming lord of the earth and its resources. Passion, ambition, and striving for glory are springs of action for a noble mind; these must be encouraged in a humanistic education. There was no branch of humanistic literature in early fifteenth-century Italy in which some of these ideas did not play a part, and even in the later phases of the Renaissance, when movements different in spirit had arisen in philosophy and literature, the early humanistic philosophy of life remained a spreading and transforming influence. The views of human nature, history, and politics found in the generation of Machiavelli and Guicciardini were still substantially molded by this influence.[8]

[8] For these interpretations of Quattrocento humanistic culture and its relations to the society and the politico-historical ideas of the Renaissance, see E. Garin, *Der italienische Humanismus* (1947; Ital. version, *L'umanesimo italiano: filosofia e vita civile nel Rinascimento* [1952]); H. Baron, *Crisis*; and R. v. Albertini, *Das florentinische Staatsbewusstsein im Übergang von der Republik zum Prinzipat* (Bern, 1955). Cf. also A. Renaudet, "Le problème historique de la Renaissance italienne," *Bibliothèque d'Hum. et Renaiss.* 9 (1947): 21ff.; R. Spongano, "L'umanesimo e le sue origini," *Giorn. stor. della lett. ital.* 130

By the time of Machiavelli, however, Italy had gradually reverted to some of the social conditions and cultural trends from which Renaissance civilization had turned during the first hundred years after Petrarch. But, though certain medieval traditions were resumed from the second half of the Quattrocento onwards, they reappeared transformed by the spirit of the Renaissance. One of these regressions was a marked change in the character of the Italian courts. During the period of a stabilized states-system after 1450, a new courtly society and nobility developed in some of the monarchical states, particularly in Milan where the influence of France was strong, but also in the Ferrara of the Este family and the Mantua of the Gonzaga, both of whom had risen as vassals of the Empire and had preserved a certain air of feudal lordship even in the early Renaissance. It was especially in these courtly circles that the knightly themes of the medieval epic and the ideals of chivalry were revived. Until about 1450, the legends of Charlemagne's and King Arthur's knights had been used by wandering singers in Italy for popular entertainment; during the second half of the century they were admitted to literature as an alluring subject for romantic poetry—even in the circle of Lorenzo de' Medici in Florence. Before the invading French armies appeared on the peninsula, Matteo Boiardo wrote his *Orlando Innamorato* at the court of Ferrara, the work which introduced a new phase in the history of medieval epic tradition. Yet this revival of long-discarded themes took place only on the level of artistic imagination; neither the medieval faith in the historicity of the glorious knightly feats nor the medieval mingling of legend with historical truth were really renewed. A measure of irony pervaded the resurgent admiration for chivalrous bravery, loyalty, and love, revealing

---

(1953): 289ff.; and the chapter "The Early Humanist Tradition" in Wallace K. Ferguson's *The Renaissance in Historical Thought* (Boston, 1948). A different appraisal of early Italian Humanism—seen basically not as a new philosophy of life and history but as continuation, on a higher level, of the work of "medieval rhetoricians" in grammar, poetry, and eloquence—has been given by Paul O. Kristeller, "Humanism and Scholasticism in the Italian Renaissance," in his *Studies in Renaissance Thought and Letters* (Rome, 1956).

a state of mind no longer medieval. It is in a similar light that we must view the late Renaissance recasting of the ideal of the perfect courtier, which was to find its ripest expression in Baldassare Castiglione's *Il Cortegiano*, published in 1528 but begun as early as about 1510. In contrast to the civic character of early humanistic education, the new idea of the "courtier" appears to be a throwback to the standards of a noble class. Yet, as conceived by Castiglione, the *cortegiano* was also the *uomo universale* of the Renaissance. Essentially, this notion of the courtier had not grown from the soil of medieval knighthood but was a transformation of the humanistic program for the culture of a rounded personality, based on the training of body and mind as well as on encouragement of ambition and all noble passions befitting human nature.

In late Quattrocento philosophy, the secularism of the early Renaissance was thrust into the background both through the reemergence of Neoplatonism and a religious reinterpretation of Aristotle's thought. The Englishmen and Frenchmen who sensed a kindred spirit in Ficino were correct in thinking that Italy, after long concentration on the problems of the temporal life, had returned in many respects to spiritual interests and a devout attitude of mind. From the beginning of his career as a philosopher, Ficino had rejected some of the basic tenets of the early humanists: their insistence on the inseparable unity of soul and body, their high esteem for material goods, and their preference for the active life and disregard for the values of contemplation. The basic ideas of Ficino's and Pico della Mirandola's metaphysical speculation, their abstract logical arguments, and the very structure of their writings did, indeed, testify to a reversion to medieval and partly even to Scholastic thinking. Yet within this framework, Ficino as well as Pico conceived the position of man in the universe, his dignity and creative powers, in Renaissance terms. Ficino's Neoplatonism, despite its ascetic and Scholastic elements, was more profoundly molded by the humanistic spirit of Plato's dialogues than any medieval philosophy had been. And if Ficino's view of life reflected a waning of the early Quattrocento civic spirit—a waning ultimately caused by the rise in Ficino's day of a disguised principate in Florence under Lorenzo de' Medici—the relationship of Lorenzo, the first Florentine citizen, to artists and men of letters still bore little resemblance to the patronage at late-medieval princely courts. Social intercourse in Lorenzo's circle fulfilled the ideal of human companionship that had guided Italian humanists since Petrarch: a conscious attempt to revive the ancient forms of cultivated association as they were found in Cicero's and Plato's dialogues and letters. Some of Ficino's northern visitors during Lorenzo's last years could still attend informal meetings of friends in the "Platonic Academy," whose members, emulating Plato and his disciples, gathered in Lorenzo's villa at Careggi for philosophical discussion and a social life in which art and music played a prominent role. It was in these gatherings, and through the work of Ficino, that the Platonic philosophy of love obtained the central position in Renaissance thought that it continued to occupy in European literature, philosophy, and art during the sixteenth century.

The encounter between northern scholarship and the Italian humanistic Renaissance in the 1490s was thus fraught with potentialities for the future of European culture. Although the "new learning," which arose at Oxford, London, Paris, in the Low Countries, the Rhinelands, and in Spain, was meant to give direction to religious studies, its actual effect was to open a window on the wide new world which had emerged in Italy in the course of two centuries. Thenceforth the assimilation and adaptation of the Italian achievements in education and politico-historical thought, in literature and art, social intercourse and the Weltanschauung of the age, became a basic task of all cultural life. The performance of this task was mainly the work of the period from 1490 to 1520, when the Renaissance issued forth as a movement of European scope; but the process was to continue until the seventeenth century—throughout the long years in which the Reformation, the overseas discoveries, and the beginnings of modern natural science gradually reversed the cultural balance between Italy and the rest of Europe.

TWELVE

A Sociological Interpretation of
the Early Florentine Renaissance★

I

EACH generation of historians has a preferred road into the past which affords easier access to it than other avenues of approach. This road in present-day historical discussion is one that leads to sociological interpretation. Intellectual life, we have learned, cannot be understood as an isolated process. Its full scope can be conceived only if an attempt is made to recall the impressions that social and economic conditions in a given age were bound to make on the human mind.

The sociological focus of historical research has not left untouched the interest of contemporary students of Humanism and the Renaissance. Once Humanism is no longer regarded simply as a movement of reform in scholarship and education, new aspects of humanistic thought come to the fore. If light is thrown on the socioeconomic factors from which humanists drew much of their experience, new features are bound to become visible.

Socioeconomic facts speak for themselves, one might think, and may be used as background just as they stand. Yet many long-accepted concepts regarding the socioeconomic nature of the Renaissance have proved inadequate. The appearance of great merchants and bankers—the patrons of Humanism and the arts—was long regarded as the primary factor distinguish-

★ A lecture delivered on several occasions in 1938–1939 and published in *The South Atlantic Quarterly* 38 (1939) under the title "A Sociological Interpretation of the Early Renaissance in Florence." Only the first half has been reproduced here, because the second half overlaps with other essays published in this book. The text has undergone stylistic changes and some significant material has been added both in the text and in the notes.

ing the society of the Renaissance from that of the Middle Ages. But gradually we have been shown that large-scale trade and an international banking system were already fully operative in the feudal age. Merchant trading at the height of the Middle Ages was not limited to a few luxuries, but involved a much larger volume of economic goods than was realized even a short time ago. For centuries merchant traders and bankers, by charging high interest and aiming at unlimited acquisition, had contributed to the disintegration of the medieval world. In this respect, humanists of the fifteenth century were not confronted with conditions essentially new and different from those of the preceding generations.

Moreover, Florentine commerce had begun to decline after the middle of the fourteenth century; there was no steady expansion of the merchant's range in Renaissance Florence. The attention paid to economic activity by Florentine humanists by no means centered on the praise of commerce or even of the banker's profession. The theoretical justification of money interest, as is well known, never made much headway in the Italian Renaissance.

In many respects, therefore, the economic background of humanistic thought is open to discussion. The vital question is, were old traditions simply carried on or were new sectors of economic life developed in the Renaissance and added to the earlier medieval base? Only a look at conditions in the thirteenth and fourteenth centuries can lead to an answer.

Recent research in medieval economic history has led to fresh discoveries concerning not only the volume but also the unique structure of medieval merchant trade and finance. The great Italian traders of the thirteenth century, who at first sight appear to be the direct ancestors of modern merchants and bankers, were in fact a typical product of the feudal age. Commerce and trade were merely the starting-point of the great medieval fortunes. The activities that raised the merchant trader to a dizzy height and gave him power and enormous wealth were financial transactions carried on with the help of original commercial capital. One could not call these dealings banking activities in the modern sense. They were usury on the largest scale—usury of the type stigmatized by the theory of the medieval Schoolmen.

This usury arose from the chronic incongruity between income and expenditure that characterized the later feudal centuries and threatened small knights and clerics as well as kings and the pope. Whereas the money economy advanced and financial demands increased, the revenues of feudal landowners remained essentially at their fixed traditional levels. The merchant trader, who could lend cash in an hour of need, was therefore in a unique position. Neither a mere merchant nor a mere banker in the modern sense, he might be described as a feudal financier. He could make exorbitant demands, and if the feudal mortgagor could not pay his debts on time (and it was in the nature of the matter that he often could not), part of his land was seized by his financier. If the debtor was a prince or king, he was forced to mortgage customs duties and taxes or else grant monopolies from which his lenders could repay themselves. In this way the most successful of the medieval financiers practically dominated kingdoms, attaining to positions which might best be compared to those held by European trading companies in backward countries during the first colonial period.

The most typical and successful among them were the Florentines, who laid the foundations for the prosperity of Florence in the Renaissance at this early date. About 1200 they began to lend out their still modest commercial capital to the secular and clerical feudal lords of their region. By imposing penalties if money could not be repaid on time, they exacted interest reaching as high at times as 33.3 percent. In the end Florentine merchants took over a considerable portion of the feudal estates. With these landed estates as the basis for an increased credit, the Florentines, like traders in other Italian towns, became bankers to the papacy. In its service they went to all parts of Europe, and particularly to England, which in medieval Europe was the unrivaled producer of first-class wool and still an agricultural country struggling to pay large subsidies to the popes in Italy for their long fight against the Hohenstaufen emperors.

The loan of Florentine merchant capital to feudal lords, who could not be expected to repay their debts in the normal way, through cash payments, was then repeated on a vast scale. We hear of "penal interest" up to 60 percent which the king of England had to pay. The mortgage given to the foreign lenders was, above all, control of the export of English wool. Since the workshops in Florence were not yet able to make full use of this precious material, it was sent for manufacture chiefly to Flanders, Florence limiting itself to high-quality finishing.

The leading social group of medieval Florence, the Arte di Calimala, was established entirely on this basis. It is difficult to classify economically the one hundred great firms that composed this guild. They combined the importation and exportation of cloth with wool manufacture and banking. But the main source of their dominant position was neither their industrial activity (restricted as it was to the refinement of imported cloth) nor the cloth trade itself. The main source of Calimala influence was the enormous financial business carried on with capital initially derived from trade. It was a business that flourished wherever foreign money was able to exploit backward conditions in Europe. In England, as in Naples, Sicily, and in part France, the Florentine Calimala firms, in compensation for their loans, were given added privileges: the right to collect public and feudal revenues, which promised high profits in financially strong hands; to exploit salt mines; to administer the royal mint; and to control taxes and seaport customs duties. Italian merchants even held high positions at many courts and acted abroad as ambassadors of foreign kings.

The lesson to be learned from this structure of medieval merchant trade seems clear. Despite its importance for the stimulation of large-scale commerce, the financial capitalism of the thirteenth century was an anomaly and not a factor capable of transforming the thinking of the period in a lasting way.

Socially, indeed, the great financiers of the thirteenth century remained a separate group, between bourgeois society and the feudal circles. At a time when the general standard of living in towns was still modest, the Florentine Calimala merchants possessed castles taken from feudal lords. They were familiar with princes and dwelt in townhouses of a splendor surpassing that of the town hall and other public buildings. These merchant princes adapted themselves without much difficulty to the manners and customs of the old urban nobility, with whom they shared power in the state. Forming as they did a foreign body in the feudal world of the nobility and yet living at its expense, they were not the potential bearers of a new outlook on economic life.

Moreover, the transitoriness of this medieval plutocracy eventually became obvious. The first half of the fourteenth century witnessed the financial downfall of nearly all the great Calimala firms. In the forty years between 1307 and 1346, an uninterrupted series of popular revolts took place in England, Flanders, France, and Naples against the foreign profiteers, leading to the destruction of their houses, the expulsion of their agents by the government, and the suspension of payments on the part of the authorities concerned. The royal exchequers proclaimed their insolvency, whether real or pretended, and in the end the Florentine firms went bankrupt. Their monopoly of economic resources and political positions was resented everywhere as soon as the home economy and national feeling were sufficiently developed. In all the western countries, national economic history began with the termination of the ephemeral episode of medieval haute finance.

II

The downfall of Florence's international finance did not spell the end of the city's economy. On the contrary, the catastrophe spurred a new economic and social evolution—the very evolution that created the society of the Florentine Renaissance.

Florence, in fact, had never been content with the small volume of manufacture allotted to it in the finishing industries of the Calimala. An independent wool industry had grown up in the shadow of the Calimala firms which not only finished foreign-made goods but dealt with all aspects of cloth making, from the raw wool to the finished cloth. Whereas the trade of the Calimala supported a comparatively small number of citizens and many of their commercial agents lived permanently abroad, the activities of the wool guild gave work to many throughout the population.

The differences in the social influence of the two Florentine guilds are evident in statistics drawn up at a time when the firms of the Calimala had not yet suffered their severest shock. In 1338, we hear, the Arte di Calimala imported more than 10,000 lengths of precious cloth from countries north of the Alps for finishing and sale at home, as well as a quantity of cloth to be resold abroad. But at the same time the Arte della Lana, the wool guild, manufactured no less than 70,000 or even 80,000 lengths of less expensive material, so that their workshops, numbering about two hundred, provided occupation for at least one-third of the inhabitants of the city.[1]

These figures, however approximate they may be, give an idea of the deep-rooted sociological changes that preceded the Florentine Renaissance. Beneath the surface of medieval finance a prelude to industrial labor had developed, an economic transformation that affected the whole view of social life on the threshold of the Renaissance.

A violent reaction against this economic and social revolution can be observed in Dante's *Divina Commedia*. As the son of an old and noble Florentine family, the poet complains against a new spirit of acquisitiveness in Florence in a manner typical of this time of transition. When he wrote his poem

[1] These are the statistics given by the chronicler Giovanni Villani.

shortly after 1300, a whole century had elapsed during which Florentine money changers, bankers, and Calimala merchants had been filled with the commercial spirit of economic acquisition. But the nobility had put up with them as long as only the comparatively small group of Calimala merchants was involved. Members of the old families had taken part in commercial enterprises and the merchants had adapted themselves to the mode of life of the nobility. The industrial merchant class of the wool guild, whose material interests were bound up with those of the majority of the population, was socially more enduring than the Calimala group, with an outlook on life more independent of the traditions of the feudal world. Dante despised the new economic spirit, yet it was at the root of all later developments in Renaissance Florence.

Wool had, of course, been manufactured in Florence before the first half of the fourteenth century, and banking and large-scale commerce continued to play their part, as is sufficiently shown by the rise of the banking house of the Medici. The predominance of the Medici family in the fifteenth century was due, however, to the very fact that their economic position in the city was unique. Except for the Alberti, the Medici were the only old banking and merchant family to survive the catastrophes of the fourteenth century. Before Cosimo de' Medici attained to political leadership after 1434, the family kept in the background and left the guidance of the state to an oligarchy centered around the leaders of the wool guild. Raised to power, the new rulers in the Medici party encouraged a new industry, the manufacture of silk, which in part replaced the wool manufacture from the middle of the fifteenth century onward. Thus they maintained the industrial base that was indispensable for Renaissance Florence, without strengthening the branch of industry which had been the nerve center of economic activity and civic sentiment for the generations around 1400.

Medicean ascendancy, we see, does not belie the assertion that the center of gravity in economic life and outlook had shifted. Until Dante's time nobles and feudal financiers had

46

been at the helm of the state. After the middle of the four-teenth century, the influence of the wool guild—and later of the silk industry—rivaled that of the bankers and Calimala merchants, ruling the state according to the view of the textile industries until the time of the Medici principality. In a nut-shell, in the thirteenth century merchants and bankers had lived on the edge of the feudal world; in fifteenth-century Florence they lived on the edge of an industrial society. This growth of industrial forces was to have an unmistakable influence on the outlook on life and work in the Florentine Renaissance.

An industrial society, in contrast to a relatively static feudal age, is apt to regard economic progress, productive work, and ceaseless labor as values in themselves—as moral values, be-cause they promote human energies. In fifteenth-century Florence, this tendency was accelerated by political conditions.

The growth of industrialism in textile manufacture did not remain restricted to a single town. Wool manufacture was spreading throughout all western European countries and many parts of Italy. The rise of nationalism in economic life, which caused the downfall of Florentine world finance in England, France, and Naples, also forced Florence into keen and ceaseless competition in the field of industry. After the four-teenth century only a well-considered state policy and system-atized economy were able to maintain healthy conditions in Florentine manufacture. Whenever exports into one country were lost, public measures on a large scale had to provide for an outlet in other lands or even on other continents. As the obvious concern of the whole community, industrial labor gained in the eyes of Florentine citizens and humanists a dig-nity previously unknown.

Now, all these factors—the rise of industrial society, the protection of manufacture, and the growing attention paid to the provision of labor—were among the potent forces which in the sixteenth and seventeenth centuries, the period of mer-cantilism, gave the final blow to the decaying economic world of the Middle Ages. All these forces, though to a lesser degree, were already at work in the Florence of the fifteenth century. Thus the economic outlook of the Florentine Renaissance became what one might call the first approach to a mercantilist attitude.

Only a concentrated effort of the community, we have said, could make amends for the grave losses of Florentine trade in western Europe. An inland city until 1400, Florence procured an outlet to the Mediterranean by conquering Pisa in 1406 and purchasing the port of Livorno in 1421. As Pisa's successor it developed a surprising and extensive naval policy. A naval office (the board of the *Consoli del mare*), a commercial navy, and a regular boat service were instituted under state control to bring home the vitally necessary English wool in Florentine vessels and to build up new commercial positions in the eastern part of the Mediterranean.[2]

[2] Armando Sapori (in vol. 3 of his *Studi di storia economica* [Florence, 1967], 3–19) has succeeded in showing that the climax of this new economic policy of early Renaissance Florence came in the first half of the 1420s; that is, we should add, at the very time when the new values of civic Humanism were also at their zenith. Sapori judges that the new economic policy was accompanied at that time by an "enthusiasmo dei cittadini" and "vere manifestazioni di esultanza di tutto un popolo" and that "lo stato di euforia generale del governo e del popolo risulta anche dal testo delle istruzioni agli ambasciatori mandati presso i vari principi . . . ," an example of which is the proud comment in a request of 1422 for trading privileges in the eastern Mediterranean: "et se per lo passato non s'è fatto, è stato per non avere avuta la marina spedita come al presente . . . et mostragli [to a signore of Athens and Corinth] che a lui e alla sua Signoria ne sequirà honore et utile che' nostri legni et nostri mercatanti vi usino, mostrando che siamo adatti a farvi gran cose" (ibid., 11–12). Sapori, it is true, emphasizes that the Florentines were deceiving themselves and that these great hopes were mostly not realized. But the continuing edicts and plans put out by the Florentine authorities in the second half of the century, to which attention is drawn in the text above, prove that the consequences of the new energy infused into Florence during the 1420s remained perceptible for decades.

For the examples that follow in the text, see Robert von Pöhlmann, *Die Wirtschaftspolitik der Florentiner Renaissance und das Princip der Verkehrsfreiheit* (Leipzig, 1878), passim, esp. 102, 106f., and Alfred Doren, *Studien aus der Florentiner Wirtschaftsgeschichte*, vol. 1 (Stuttgart, 1901), 417 and 425.

The methods hitherto employed by the older maritime powers in Italy were now applied to the needs of a thoroughly industrialized city. When a naval department was founded after 1421, the new authorities were commissioned to investigate whether other branches of industry and craftsmanship should be introduced into Florence. As a result of this inquiry, the *Consoli del mare* made proposals in 1426 of an entirely mercantilist nature, stating that it would benefit Florence to manufacture at home all the articles which were being imported at great expense from abroad. If the stimulation of prohibitive customs duties should induce the Florentine population to engage in these new arts, many poor people in the Florentine territory would find work. In the second half of the century, when the manufacture of Perpignan cloth, a more practical brand of textile which had formerly been imported extensively, was so far advanced that all further imports could be prohibited, it became a point of honor for the city to have Florentine artisans fully master its industrial technique. "It would damage the honor and reputation of Florentine industry," read an official proclamation of 1472, "if it should become known that in Florence there was not sufficient enterprise" to compete with other industrial centers in this field.

One can see from these examples how easily such practical aims developed into something like moral maxims. Provision of work for as many hands as possible and the training of the population in crafts were regarded as increased "honor" for the city and at the same time recommended as a cure for poverty and idleness. When a new state fleet was outfitted for the eastern Mediterranean in 1458, the reason given was that the government could do nothing better for the "exaltation" of Florence than to give its merchants and young citizens an outlet for their abilities and its poor a chance to live on their own skills rather than on charity. "For alms may give relief for a certain time," reads the government decree, "but in the end they cause men to deteriorate by making them lazy and disinclined to work."

An episode related in a source from the second half of the

century shows how deeply such persuasions were already rooted. A Florentine citizen who had been sent as governor to a small backward mountain town (Borgo S. Sepolcro), full of strife, gambling, and idleness, concluded that he could make its people useful local citizens and loyal subjects of Florence only by inducing them to take up regular work. He drew up a list of inhabitants and told everyone without occupation of the dangers of idleness to body, soul, and possessions and of the advantages resulting from regular employment. Thus he induced idlers to give up gambling and do useful work—in the wool manufacture or in some other branch of production. In the end, the former seat of unrest devoted itself to strenuous labor and its Florentine adviser was revered as a benefactor.[3]

III

The story of events in Borgo S. Sepolcro has been handed down to us by a humanistic source, the *Vite di Uomini Illustri*

---

[3] For the economic philosophy behind this praise of industrial activity one should also compare the answer given by Giannozzo Alberti in the third book of Leon Battista's *Della Famiglia*, when he was asked whether he would not agree that trade was the best choice for an economic career: "Yes—yet to increase my tranquillity, I would like to have something safe, something I could see improving under my hands from day to day. Perhaps I would have men working in wool or silk or something similar. This kind of business is less trouble and much less nerve-racking than trade. I would gladly take on such an enterprise, which requires many hands; for there the money goes to a large number of persons. It helps many poor people." The concept that provision of work is superior to distribution of alms is important in other writings of Alberti's, especially in the fifth book of *De Re Aedificatoria*, where work, if possible, is recommended in place of alms even for blind people and for prisoners; and in the Latin essay *Pontifex* we read: "I cannot fail to praise [the bishops] when they feed the poor, although I cannot stand to look upon most of the vagabonds, whom I would prefer to have gain a living by some labor instead of seeking it by idleness."

To complete this background one must also mention Bernardino of Siena, the prominent Tuscan saint of this period (see Essay Eight, note 55). "When the cities of Siena and Perugia requested Bernardino to reform their statutes, this scholastic advised the towns to require all persons under the age of fifty, regardless of rank, to engage in some occupation—the greatest evils spring

del Secolo XV, composed by the Florentine book manufacturer Vespasiano da Bisticci. This leads us to ask whether any characteristics in the humanistic background were particularly congenial to the described tendencies.

It was certainly not the learned lore of classical scholarship that pointed Humanism in this direction. As they were reproduced in humanistic writings, the economic teachings of Antiquity suggested little of this kind of thinking. There was, however, an inclination in Humanism that contradicted the traditional psychology. Medieval writers had held a static view of economic life. They believed that men were destined to occupy a particular station and should not desire more or disturb the ordained order of things. This static view of economic activity was closely bound up with the medieval ideas of culture and the limits placed upon human earthly aspirations. The very dignity of philosophy, Dante had thought, derived from the fact that intellectual activity "comes to an end at a fixed point," allowing the human mind to rest in the possession of full wisdom and the peaceful contemplation of the divine.

The humanist Petrarch expressed a different point of view half a century later. For him, in opposition to medieval teaching, the nature of true learning was unlimited progress of mind—a boundless thirst for knowledge. Acquisition should have its fixed limits, he said in one of his letters, recalling a saying of his admired Seneca. But with respect to culture and learning, a man who thinks he has reached his goal "becomes inactive, and inaction means retrogression; a scholar can never put an end to reading and thinking or seal up his memory as if it were a treasure—like a rich merchant who at the end of his voyage keeps his wealth at home." For it is in the nature of man's memory, Petrarch insisted, that "if he does not always add to it, he will one day find it hollow and empty." Study,

---

from idleness, he believed" (John McGovern [note 6, below], 232, who was following Iris Origo, *The World of San Bernardino* [New York, 1962], 153). Thus the story about Borgo S. Sepolcro is only an application of Bernardino's utopian scheme to the actual life of Florence.

therefore, must have no limits and "learning must not cease till the last day of life."

Methodical use of one's time, the smallest particle of which must not be lost—this, then, became the pedagogical maxim which Petrarch recommended to his followers. The reader of his intimate letters sometimes sees the old man awakening with a start and remembering the enormity of his intellectual tasks and the brevity of life. He then rushes to his study in the dark of night, for he claims that he has long accustomed himself to this arrangement of his time: six hours have proved sufficient for sleep, two for the other exigencies of life; all the rest should be devoted to work and the activity of the mind.

A few decades after Petrarch's death, Humanism became dominant in the civic world of Florence. The same businessmen, manufacturers, and merchants who laid a new foundation for Florentine strength in the effort to promote industrial activity, grew up in close contact with the humanistic ideas of Petrarch's circle. In this milieu, economic attitudes and humanistic culture met halfway—much as economic life would combine with religion after the Reformation. That man should strive to rise above his traditional station, that he should budget his time and direct his life toward continuous progress and ceaseless activity, this seemed to the men of the Quattrocento a cultural as well as an economic necessity. In the first generation after Petrarch, a Florentine humanist remarked that even if man has no absolute power over anything else in life, he safely possesses time. Another recommended that clocks be placed in libraries to remind scholars of the passing of precious time. A generation later, when members of merchant families began to contribute actively to literature, this humanistic trend began blending with the new economic outlook on life. Leon Battista Alberti, in his dialogues *On the Family*, describes the fine spectacle of a man who has made his fortune and become independent, yet has not renounced economic activity or his desire to continue productive work.

Among Alberti's contemporaries, the citizen and humanist Gianozzo Manetti is depicted by Vespasiano da Bisticci as the model of one who knows how to make the right use of his time.[4] In his youth Manetti had obeyed the humanistic doctrine that the student should continuously improve his mind, indeed that he should grudge himself time to eat and sleep. Later, we are told, when he was busy both in the service of the republic and with his own commercial affairs, "he always esteemed time highly and never lost an hour." He knew how to adapt the humanistic warning against wasting time to a merchant's mode of thought. Paraphrasing the parable from the Gospels, he compared God, who gave man the gift of time, with the manager of a business ("uno maestro d'uno trafico"), who entrusts his cashier with a fixed sum of money and expects him to give an exact accounting of every penny. "In the same way Almighty God, when man departs from this life, will ask him how the time He gave him has been spent, down to the smallest fraction of a minute. Making allowances for the time man needs to sleep and eat, God will examine the use he has made of his life, the years, months, days, hours, nay every second."

IV

Perhaps one should not conclude these sociologically oriented observations without citing the sixteenth-century view of the civic world on the Arno presented by Benedetto Varchi in his *Storia Fiorentina*, written in 1527–1538, soon after Florence had lost its final struggle for republican liberty. "The food of the Florentines is simple and frugal," we read in this late portrait of the Florentines, "but it is prepared with striking and incredible cleanliness; and one may say that the workmen and other common people who make their living by manual labor generally live less parsimoniously in Florence than its citizens. For, while the former visit now one tavern and now another if they think good wine can be gotten there, without any thought but of having fun and a good day, the latter stay at

[4] Such a description even appears twice, in Vespasiano's *Vite* and in his more detailed memoire on Manetti, which I will use along with the *Vite* in the lines that follow.

home showing the parsimony becoming to merchants, who ordinarily make things but do not enjoy them, and to the modesty of bourgeois people, who maintain custom and measure and do not go beyond the golden mean."

After admitting that Florence also has a group of families that lay a rich table at home "e vivono splendidamente da gentiluomini," Varchi goes on to relate how "everybody in Florence is called by his first name or nickname, and generally, unless there are distinctions in social class or substantial differences in age, a single person is addressed as *tu*, not *voi*," except that knights, doctors, and canons are addressed with the title of *messere*, medical practitioners with that of *maestro*, and a friar as *padre*. Varchi finishes his analysis by saying: "I entirely disagree with those who pronounce the Florentines incapable of nobility and generosity and vile and plebeian because they are merchants. Quite the contrary, I have often marveled how it could happen that these people, who are accustomed . . . from childhood to carry bales of wool like porters or baskets of silk like silkworkers, and who, when all is considered, spend their days and a good part of their nights in textile making, little better than slaves, that these very people, in the right place and at the right time, . . . so often show such greatness of mind and noble thought, both in their actions and their way of speech."[5]

These attitudes and ideas help to round out the picture of the Florentine Quattrocento and its after-effects. They should not be omitted from an analysis of the world of civic Humanism.[6]

---

[5] Benedetto Varchi, toward the end of Liber IX of his *Storia Fiorentina*.

[6] There are now several synthetic publications in this formerly neglected area, of which I will name only Christian Bec, *Les marchands écrivains: Affaires et humanisme à Florence, 1375–1434* (Paris, 1967), and John F. McGovern, "The Rise of New Economic Attitudes—Economic Humanism, Economic Nationalism—During the Later Middle Ages and the Renaissance, A.D. 1200–1550," *Traditio* 26 (1970): 217–53. But neither of these authors has drawn attention to the material offered above or tried to work out the profile of the trend of thought that is the focus of the present essay.

THIRTEEN

The Humanistic Revaluation of the *Vita Activa* in Italy and North of the Alps★

I

IN A keenly argued and well-written study called *The Renaissance Idea of Wisdom*, Eugene Rice explores the definition and conception of *sapientia* in about a score of authors from Petrarch in the fourteenth century to the Frenchman Pierre Charron in the sixteenth. He proposes "first to give a detailed analysis of what a selected number of fifteenth- and sixteenth-century theorists thought wisdom was; second, to relate these individual conceptions to each other in an intelligible pattern of historical change" (*RIW*, vii).

The result is a new and original profile of Renaissance thought. Starting with the fourteenth century, Rice observes that Petrarch did not yet clearly distinguish between wisdom sought through piety and secular wisdom, but that his ideal of a *humilitas operosa* marked a new advance, "the humble beginning of wisdom's transformation from an intellectual to a moral virtue, from a type of knowledge to an ethical category" (*RIW*, 31). For several generations after Petrarch, we are told, the alternative between "active and contemplative ideals" remained a problem, especially in Florentine Humanism. Coluccio Salutati became the first decided advocate of the active life, propounding the superiority of the will over the intellect. Even though few humanists of the Quattrocento accepted this extreme doctrine, many, utilizing Aristotelian

★ Apropos of Eugene F. Rice, Jr., *The Renaissance Idea of Wisdom* (Cambridge, Mass., 1958). This review essay was first published in the *Journal of the History of Ideas* 21 (1960). It has been augmented in many places, abridged in others, and generally revised, especially at the beginning and end.

ideas, tried to balance philosophical speculation with virtue acquired during a life of civic action. On this basis there began to develop in early Quattrocento Florence from the time of Leonardo Bruni onward, as Rice puts it, "an ethic distinct from the chivalric code of the nobility and the monastic virtues of the clergy which the ruling class of republican Florence could make their own. . . . The quest for wisdom no longer defines a separate spiritual estate" (*RIW*, 49). Religious motivation waned. Whereas Salutati did not yet really view human virtue as autonomous, strongly insisting that all wisdom is a gift of God, Bruni and the generation after 1400 separated the treatment of human wisdom de facto from religious transcendence.

Except occasionally in Venice, however, the ideal which "ties a speculative wisdom indissolubly to civic action" did not gain a secure footing outside Florence. Rice illustrates this by two characteristic examples. One is Francesco Filelfo, itinerant man of letters, whose doctrine of wisdom is said to be hardly more than a continuation of contemplative attitudes and a fusion of wisdom with religious motivation. The other is Gioviano Pontano of Naples. This Neapolitan official and humanist esteemed the "prudent" man of the world, regardless of whether he was engaged in the *vita activa politica* or was a "solitary *sapiens*, . . . lonely in his pursuit of truth"; he deemed both types necessary, but irreconcilable in one person. By the last quarter of the fifteenth century, the emergence of religious and metaphysical Neoplatonism had brought about the disintegration of the early Quattrocento civic ideal even in Florence.

In general, Rice's presentation of these phases supports the view of the Quattrocento best described in Eugenio Garin's *L'umanesimo italiano: filosofia e vita civile nel Rinascimento* (Bari, 1952). But Rice adds to the picture by including some post-Quattrocento developments, especially outside Italy. After discussing the ambivalent position of the Renaissance Neoplatonists and Platonists, and later the Reformers, he notes that a few of the salient features of Salutati's and Bruni's humanism reemerged not only in Erasmus' and Vives' preference for moral action over speculation, but even more markedly in the outlook of French Humanism. He undertakes to show that in four successive stages humanists in France marched on—or marched again—in the direction initiated by the Italians of the Quattrocento, especially the Florentines.

To characterize these four stages briefly: As early as about 1530, the Florentine aversion to withdrawn erudition reappears in Guillaume Budé's *De philologia*, where we read that great knowledge may make the sage useless to himself and society if it is dissociated from prudent practicality and apt social behavior. Who does not know pedants among the learned "wise," marked by vulgarity and a rude lack of humanity, scoffs Budé. About twenty-five years later, the new values of the active life are made more explicit in a rarely remembered work by Louis Le Caron, *Les dialogues*, from which Rice quotes: "Who could . . . know and judge things truly without a commitment to human experience? The world is the true theater in which the man who wishes to be called noble and virtuous should exercise himself. Wisdom must be sought in the world." The man of action who has been successful in his career is worthier, therefore, than an improvident and frivolous philosopher (*RIW*, 152–54). In the third stage, during the 1570s, the influential Pierre de Ronsard reads a *Discours des vertus intellectuelles et moralles* before the Académie du Palais. It is virtually impossible, he says, adequately to combine action and contemplation; everyone must make a choice. As Rice tells us, Ronsard is "renewing Salutati's criticism of intellectual, contemplative conceptions of wisdom" when he proclaims the intellectual virtues to be good only for the lazy, for "hermits and other such fantastical and contemplative people." In Ronsard's view, "God has put such curiosities in man's mind only to torment him" (*RIW*, 154–55). In the final stage, Pierre Charron's *De la sagesse* of 1601 "successfully concludes the transformation of *sapientia* from contemplation to action and from knowledge to virtue." Knowledge of any kind is no longer considered wisdom; in fact, it is sometimes regarded as its very opposite. At least, knowledge and wisdom "are almost never found together," writes the skeptical Charron. "They are usually mutually exclusive—the learned man is rarely wise, the wise man is generally unlearned." Knowledge and learning do not make men happier or more virtuous; they only make them arrogant and opinionated. Wisdom depends on the will, and the will is the only thing which is free and really under man's control. Memory, imagination, and every other intellectual faculty may be taken from him by a thousand accidents. Rice concludes that for Charron, "just as Salutati and Bruni, Le Caron, and Ronsard had insisted," wisdom "is active." It is also for Charron "an autonomous and naturally acquired moral virtue," distinct from "religion [which] is a gift of grace." This makes the treatise *De la sagesse*, in Rice's eyes, "an extraordinarily representative work" that draws together most of the threads of "secularization" in the Renaissance. "The result was a conception of wisdom which remained a European ideal until the collapse of the humanistic tradition in the later nineteenth century" (*RIW*, 178–83, 205, 215).

From a restricted beginning Rice has thus arrived at an "intelligible pattern of historical change." The strength and merit of this pattern is that in interpreting some of the trends of Renaissance thought in the countries north of the Alps, it makes use of an approach which in the past had been applied only to Italian conditions. This gives Rice's delineation of philosophical developments in the fifteenth and sixteenth centuries a broad potential. Such a bold expansion beyond a local area of Italy is of course liable initially to miss some of its intended targets, despite Rice's excellent historical research. In particular, it seems to me that two of his propositions could be misleading if accepted as they stand.

II

The first of these propositions concerns the extent of the lead taken by France in the sixteenth century. The close parallel between developments in Florence and England observed in our study of the controversy over Franciscan poverty and the new values of the Renaissance[1] suggests that France and England were not as dissimilar as Rice's readers are led to expect. French and English thought regarding the *vita activa* developed in basic conformity to each other during the sixteenth century, as we shall see later in this discussion.[2]

Some of the characteristic features of the philosophy of the *vita activa politica* were not entirely lacking even in sixteenth-century Germany, although they are hardly ever encountered where one would expect them most—in the German imperial cities, which in so many respects paralleled the Italian cities. However, Rice's inquiries can be extended by the observation that some of the arguments for the superiority of the *vita activa*—arguments ultimately traceable to the Florence of the early Quattrocento—recur in the circle of Reformers at Wittenberg. In his *Table-Talks*, Luther criticized Aristotle for having been "lazier" than Cicero, who combined concern for his commonwealth with extensive literary work. Almost like a humanist engaged in the active political life, Luther remarked that only someone "who has lived a score of years in an important republic can really understand Cicero's letters."[3] Even more to the point is Melanchthon's discussion of the relative value of the two *vitae* in his commentary on Aristotle's *Ethics*, which unifies humanistic and Reformation thought in a characteristic manner. The so-called *vita contemplativa*, Melanchthon says, is almost identical with the *vita studiosa*. If the controversy over *vita contemplativa* or *vita activa* merely involved the question whether a life of *otium in studiis* is more valuable than life in public office (in *gubernatio*), it would be "ridiculous." "For though *otium* is sweeter, activity [*actiones*] must be preferred." Moreover (and again one recalls the humanists of the early Quattrocento), engagement in the active,

---

[1] See Volume I, Essay Nine, pp. 254ff.
[2] See pp. 69–71 below.
[3] Martin Luther, "Kritische Gesamtausgabe," *Tischreden*, II 2412b, V 5468.

public life need not prevent the pursuit of studies; in fact, the two must be combined ("qui in actionibus, hoc est, in gubernatione versantur, hoc necesse est adiungere studia"). Christ's preference for Mary over Martha in the Gospels means that the kind of contemplation for which Mary stands is not the same as *otium* for the sake of letters; for the inclusion of *discere* and *docere* makes the contemplative life represented by Mary a life of action. It is not, to be sure, an existence like Martha's, spent in "negotia vitae corporalis," but it is nevertheless devoted to *negotia*. As we learn from the prophet Isaiah, who "cum docet, habet suas actiones," it serves a "business" of a higher sort, that of contributing to the common good and fulfilling the obligations of an upright citizen, good counselor, and judge.[4] Thus the schools founded during the Lutheran Reformation clearly reflect the effects of what we may call the humanistic emphasis on the *vita activa*. Even before looking at England, therefore, we may say that France did not stand alone in its defense of this philosophy north of the Alps.

III

My second reservation concerns Rice's evaluation of the preference for the ethical over the intellectual virtues. It may be asked why the ascendancy of such a doctrine should have been so important that it can form the basis of our reconstruction of the Renaissance conception of wisdom. For although it is a welcome addition to our knowledge to learn that moralism and activism were embraced even more widely during the Renaissance and Reformation than had been realized, it is not made sufficiently clear why a preference for action and the moral virtues should have been so decisive a factor in the replacement of medievalism by a new Weltanschauung. After reading Rice's account of the history of the *vita activa* controversy, one may wonder whether the type of Humanism that

---

[4] See vol. 16 of *Corpus Reformatorum*, 289–90.

first appeared in early Quattrocento Italy may not have been overemphasized in recent scholarship.

Our rating of humanists according to their estimation of the active life does not, indeed, become fully persuasive until some other implications of the *vita activa* philosophy are added to those considered in Rice's analysis. In comparing early Quattrocento Humanism with kindred phenomena of the later Renaissance, the vital issues are not sufficiently grasped so long as humanists are regarded as having been engaged chiefly in an abstract effort to work out a theory of the value of the human will or of the moral virtues. Salutati's theses on this score were no longer followed at the time when civic Humanism came to maturity; Bruni and his school were less concerned with opposing action to intellectual pursuits than with achieving a culture in which, as Rice himself says, "the happy, mature man combines contemplation and action, political and literary activity, wisdom and prudence" (*RIW*, 49).

The decisive objective of Florentine civic Humanism was thus to create a range of intellectual interests that could be pursued by members of an active political citizenry: professionals, officials, and merchants. But even this definition misses the crucial point: The newly emerging culture was meant to educate the humanist to be a good citizen and member of his society and *respublica*. In preceding centuries, political training, apart from that of legal and administrative specialists, had been available only for knights; late-medieval city life had not basically changed this fact. Among the Trecento patriciate, education had continued to lean toward a chivalrous way of life. The only counterinfluence had come from the widespread religious lay movements of the late Middle Ages. Under their impact the humanistic culture of the Trecento had fused introspective piety with the Stoic notion of ataraxy and the self-sufficiency of the sage—quite the opposite of the idea that the right kind of education will produce a more aware and active member of society. The ultimate historical significance of the humanistic city-state culture that emerged about 1400, especially in the remaining city republics in Italy, is that it prevented Humanism from becoming a mere heir to chivalry and late medieval lay religiosity. Instead, it produced an alternative framework, one necessary for the education of public-minded citizens.

A mainstay of the contemplative ideal had always been the conviction that true wisdom demands freedom from passion. In the early Quattrocento it was felt that without ambition citizens would not make the sacrifices necessary for the *patria*; without a keen sense of indignation they would not work adequately for justice, and without fierce passion they would not be brave on the battlefield. Accordingly, the new emphasis on the active virtues not only was inseparably bound with the vigorous patriotism of the Italian communes but was closely conjoined with a new psychology: an increasing observation and acceptance of the emotional forces in human nature. In the fourteenth century, even Petrarch's standard had been that the sage should subdue or at least diminish his *affectus*. In the Quattrocento, instead, the "wise man" recognized the danger of becoming a "senseless block"; he acknowledged that in the active life ambition and other strong passions were a necessary stimulus. One root of this train of thought had existed in Humanism from the start. Petrarch and other humanists of the Trecento had vehemently defended the "thirst for glory" against the Stoic ideal of ataraxy for the sage and the ascetic hermit. But the new psychology did not become firmly established until man's ability to live up to his social obligations became the primary issue.

Rice's choice of *sapientia* as a point of departure does not permit emphasis on this new psychology. But there is a second, related development of which he does take note, though only superficially: a growing interest in history as the source of a concrete knowledge of life. After 1400, we should add to Rice's argument, history was considered to be one of the disciplines that could stimulate the new appreciation of the *vita activa*. In an environment in which the ultimate aim was a humanistic education for good citizenship, it was indispensable to explore the past of one's own *patria* in the light of the greatness achieved by ancient cities and nations. Wherever we find humanists proclaiming the value of training for the *vita activa politica*, we can therefore also expect them to leave their mark on historical observation and thought.

The closeness of this interrelationship in Florence as early as the first decades of the Quattrocento can best be illustrated by some contemporary statements about the significance of historical studies which, in their way, are as revealing as discussions of the nature of *sapientia*. In the preface to his *Historiae Florentini Populi*, Bruni expressly calls a knowledge of history the best access to *sapientia*. If seeing much of life can make old men wise, he says, "how much more can history . . . give us this wisdom" (*quanto magis historia nobis . . . hanc praestare poterit sapientiam*).[5] Other Florentine humanists also throw light on the ties between the *vita activa* ideology and the new attitude toward history and, therefore, a changed conception of wisdom. Shortly after Bruni, Naldo Naldi argued in his *vita* of the citizen-humanist Giannozzo Manetti that as philosophers we "perceive only mentally and spiritually" (*mente atque animo ea solum capiamus*), whereas in the study of history, just as in looking at a painting, we grasp the world "through both cogitation and the senses" (*cogitatione ipsa simul atque sensibus corporeis*) and form our conceptions from what we apprehend through sensory experience and participation in events.[6] Philosophy, therefore, is not enough. It would be "much more useful" studying history "than spending all our time on those studies [that is, from philosophy] in which, after all, our thoughts do not extend beyond ourselves and in which we contemplate what ought to be done instead of learning from experience [that is, from history] how to translate them into action."[7]

Another contemporary example is Matteo Palmieri's pref-

---

[5] Muratori, *Rerum Italicarum Scriptores*, new ed., vol. 19, pt. 3, p. 3.

[6] ". . . ad ea facienda, quae meliora esse intra nos statuerimus non solum, verum etiam sensu et actione in nos admiserimus" (Muratori, *Rer. Ital. Script.*, new ed., vol. 20, pp. 527–28).

[7] ". . . multo magis profuturos, quam si versarentur semper in iis studiis, quibus intra nos cogitamus quidem, contemplamurque potius quae sint facienda, quam quonam pacto in actionem traducantur, experiamur" (ibid.).

ace to his *De Captivitate Pisarum*. The best life, he writes, is one devoted to our *respublica*, which requires an education in a *civilis disciplina*. But the latter, in turn, is based on knowledge rarely acquired before a citizen is advanced in age. The alternative is to acquire a "rerum et temporum cognitio" through historical studies. "It is the epochs of history that make men cognizant of the truth."[8] This statement, which may be an adaptation of the formula *veritas temporis filia* (from Gellius' *Noctes Atticae* XII 11.7) to the new emphasis on history, anticipates a much later period, when *veritas temporis filia* was quoted everywhere,[9] and Giordano Bruno and Francis Bacon concluded that modern people, with the knowledge of the ages behind them, have a better right to be called "the ancients" than men who lived at a time when there were still so many centuries of human experience to come.[10] That this "modern" idea had indeed been foreshadowed by Florentine humanists about 1400 is demonstrated by a letter written in 1396 by Bruni's friend Pier Paolo Vergerio, following a visit to Salutati's Florence. After discoursing on the wonderful power of historical studies to bring home the experience of centuries—"vivere mihi videor aetatem illam cuius historiam legimus"—Vergerio concludes that "a man who has stored the record of ages in his memory appears to have lived in every age." If he had the choice, he said, he "would rather be born as near as possible to the end of time, provided that full testimony of past events remained available." He concludes that "according to nature, then, the older [person] is he who is born earlier; according to this study [the study of history], it is he who is born later."[11]

[8] "Veritatis profecto cognitionem dant tempora . . ." (*Rer. Ital. Script.*, new ed., vol. 19, pt. 2, pp. 3f.).

[9] See G. Gentile, "Veritas Filia Temporis," in his *Il pensiero italiano del Rinascimento*, 3d ed. (Florence, 1940), 331ff.

[10] See my note in *Journal of the History of Ideas* 20 (1959): 15.

[11] "Secundum naturam enim, is est senior qui prior est natus; secundum hoc studium, qui posterior" (P. P. Vergerio, *Epistolario*, ed. L. Smith [Rome, 1934], 172–73). To what extent this argument was not original but, rather, the first modern revival of some of Seneca's ideas is a tangential question. It is important, however, to note that like the new psychology the new relation-

One major reason for emphasizing the Florentine revaluation of the *vita activa* is that much of the later transformation of thought was anticipated by the changes in historical thinking of that early period. The full importance of Rice's analysis of the vicissitudes of the conception of wisdom becomes evident only when it is viewed against this broader background.

IV

Having thus observed the intimate connection between the *vita activa* philosophy and a new sense of history in early civic Humanism, we can attempt to fill in the map of political Humanism for the later phases of the Renaissance.

On the Italian peninsula, the isolated cases when the *vita activa* was still discussed after 1500 are rarely connected with the courts. In Castiglione's *Cortegiano*, the *vita activa politica* ideal of the humanistic citizen has given way to the nobleman's role in courtly society and as a courtier in the service of his prince.[12] Reflections of the humanistic *vita activa* ideology are encountered, rather, in the Florentine republic of Machiavelli's and Guicciardini's day and in the Venetian patrician world of a generation or two later. About 1540 the old humanistic debates were revived by such champions of the active life as Sperone Speroni in his *Dialoghi* and Alessandro Piccolomini in his *Della institutione dell'uomo nato nobile e in città libera*[13]—both teachers at Padua, the university of Venice's ter-

---

ship to history was a lasting gain for Renaissance thought. It did not disappear in the period of Neoplatonism, even though the connection with the *vita activa* ideology receded into the background, and *experientia* gained from history was now said to provide *prudentia* rather than *sapientia*. Cf. Marsilio Ficino's letter, *Opera Omnia* (Basel, 1561), 658: by the study of history "juvenis cito maturitatem senis adaequat. Ac si senex septuaginta annorum ob ipsarum rerum experientiam prudens habetur, quanto prudentior, qui annorum mille, et trium millium implet aetatem. Tot vero annorum millia vixisse quisque videtur quot annorum acta didicit ab historia."

[12] Cf. A. Loos, *Baldassare Castiglione's 'Libro del Cortigiano'* (Frankfurt, 1955), 85ff.

[13] See Eugenio Garin, *L'umanesimo italiano: filosofia e vita civile nel Rinascimento* (Bari, 1952), 215ff. and 222ff.

ritorial state—and later by Lorenzo Grimalio (Grimaldus Gos-
licius) in his *De optimo senatore* (1568)[14] and Paolo Paruta in his
Della perfettione della vita politica (1572–1579). A fervid patriotism and concern for the community reappear in this group,
especially in the writings of the active Venetian statesman Paruta. We also find here one of the last Italian chapters in the
new secularized historiography, which had originated in early
Quattrocento civic Humanism and still flourished in the Florentine republic after 1500. In Speroni we encounter the connection of this train of thought with the struggle for the emancipation of the modern vernaculars.[15]

The Venetian school of the mid-sixteenth century was perhaps the only sustained Italian succession to the Florentine humanists of the Quattrocento.[16] Outside Italy, however, a kind

[14] Rodolfo De Mattei, in "Sapienza e Prudenza nel pensiero politico italiano
dall' umanesimo al sec. XVII," read before the Congresso Internazionale di
Studi Umanistici (Rome and Florence, 1949), *Umanesimo e Scienza Politica.
Atti del Congresso Internazionale di Studi Umanistici . . . 1949* (Milan, 1951),
134f.

[15] A. Pompeati, "Le dottrine politiche di P. Paruta," *Giornale Stor. della Lett.
Ital.* 46 (1905): esp. 288ff. On Speroni as an advocate of the *vita activa*, see
Garin, *Italian Humanism*, trans. P. Munz (New York, 1966), 180f.

[16] The sixteenth-century Venetian development was, to be sure, a phenomenon that had minor parallels in other parts of Italy, wherever remainders of
the old urban pattern survived to play a modest role beside the new courtly
culture. For example, as late as 1617 in Genoa, Ansaldo Ceba surveyed the
(aristocratic) citizen's duties and public activities, elective offices, military
prowess, diplomacy in dealing with ambassadors of foreign countries, and so
forth, in his *Il cittadino di republica*. And in Siena, which lost its independence
in the 1550s, Alessandro Piccolomini, scion of a patrician family, had in his
youth been influenced by the civic sentiments in his native city. His *Della
institutione dell' uomo nato nobile e in città libera* in turn kindled similar reactions
in Paolo Caggio, patrician chancellor of Palermo, a city that enjoyed some
degree of municipal autonomy under the Spanish crown. In Caggio's *Ragio-
namenti . . . in veder se la vita cittadinesca sia più felice del viver solitario fuor le città
e nelle ville* (Venice, 1551) we have a little-known example of a vigorous defense of the superiority of the active over the contemplative life. But these
were byways, along which mere fragments of the original humanistic pattern
were carried. Piccolomini's "uomo nato nobile e in città libera" has already
lost nearly all active political interest and shows himself contemptuous of
commercial pursuits, as a characterization of the *Della institutione* by August
Buck has pointed out ("Das humanistische Lebensideal in Alessandro Picco-

of politically oriented Humanism developed in various nations in the sixteenth century, particularly during certain stages of the growth of the western monarchies, where Humanism for a while became the culture of the high bourgeoisie and at least of an elite among the nobility. Although a systematic comparative history of the successive phases of Humanism in Italy and the countries north of the Alps does not yet exist, a number of studies (in addition to Rice's) have established sufficiently characteristic profiles of some of the crucial developments in England and France.

The story begins very early in England with the London circle of citizen officials and humanistic intellectuals around Thomas More, to which Erasmus and Vives belonged. More's *Utopia*, as is well known, opens with a debate on the need for both the *vita activa* and the *vita politica*: Raphael Hyslodaye admonishes the wise to flee political life in view of the hypocrisy and corruption found in the service of contemporary princes. More, on the other hand, or at least the More of this dialogue, stoutly upholds the duty of the true philosopher to make the best possible use of his influence by serving as a counselor of kings.[17] By the 1530s, when the ascendancy of the Tudor monarchy under Henry VIII had generated a new spirit and patriotism among the cultured classes of England, the old humanistic alternatives were again debated under the direct influence of Italian Quattrocento writings. According to Elyot's *Governour*, man cannot long remain lost in contemplation of the divine; he should return to the world and perfect it through virtuous action. And Starkey's *Dialogue Between*

---

lominis . . . *Della instituzione* . . . ," in *Im Dienste der Sprache—Festschrift Victor Klemperer* [Halle/Salle, 1958], 118–34, esp. 122, 127ff.). Something similar to this attitude holds true for Guazzo's *La civil conversatione* of 1574. Everything considered, it appears that only in the Venetian circle was there still room in Italy for a full epilogue in which the basic features of Quattrocento civic Humanism could continue to play a part. For Venice, we now have William Bouwsma's path-breaking book, *Venice and the Defense of Republican Liberty: Renaissance Values in the Age of the Counter Reformation* (Berkeley, 1968).

[17] Cf. F. Caspari, *Humanism and the Social Order in Tudor England* (Chicago, 1954), 52f.; and the discussion of More's problem by J. H. Hexter, *More's 'Utopia,' the Biography of an Idea* (Princeton, 1952), 126ff.

Reginald Pole and Thomas Lupset (1535) runs the gamut of issues in the Italian Quattrocento controversy, reformulating
each in a fresh manner. It asks how the author "coude in some
parte helpe" the king in "the restitutyon of the true commyn-
wele." He is trying by his writing to persuade Pole, a relative
of the king, to return to England and cooperate in the
strengthening of the monarchy. "You see your country . . .
require your help," Pole is admonished in the dialogue, "and
you—as drowned in the pleasure of letters and private studies—give no ear thereto." When Pole insists that the great philosophers of Antiquity "forsook the meddling with matters of
common weals" and preferred to investigate God and nature,
the rejoinder is that Aristotle had asked for a combination of
the active and contemplative life, that man is indeed "born to
common civility," and that human perfection "standeth not in
bare knowledge and learning without application of it to any
use or profit of other."[18]

To complete this brief outline of the English chapter in the
history of the *vita activa* controversy, one must also say that
under the influence of "growing nationalism" and an "exalted
conception of the monarchy" during the same 1530s, England, which until then had continued to produce chronicles of
the medieval kind, saw the appearance of "a new and radically
different" historiography;[19] that under the impact of this advance, the English reading public experienced the beginnings
of a struggle for the right of the mother tongue to stand beside
Latin as an equal; and finally, that the humanistic controversy
between studious contemplation and civic responsibility ap-

[18] See the analyses in Caspari, *Humanism and the Social Order*, 97f., 117ff.,
and Albert J. Schmidt, "Thomas Wilson and the Tudor Commonwealth: An
Essay in Civic Humanism," *Huntington Library Quarterly* 23 (1959): 49–60. On
the similarities between "the citizen-counselors of Tudor England," especially
during the 1530s and 1540s, and "the 'civic humanists' of the preceding century in Italy," we now have the synthetic work of Arthur B. Ferguson, *The
Articulate Citizen and the English Renaissance* (Durham, N.C., 1965); see in particular chs. 6 and 7 and p. 405 of the conclusion.

[19] In the words of W. R. Trimble, in *Journal of the History of Ideas* 11 (1950):
40f. See now the excellent analysis of Fred J. Levy, *Tudor Historical Thought*
(San Marino, Calif., 1967).

parently ceased in the second half of the century.[20] Just as the
ideal of Castiglione's *Cortegiano* had superseded the issues of
Quattrocento Humanism in Italy, English life became largely
dominated during the following generations by a courtier
ideal on which Castiglione's code had as profound an influence as the literary works of the Italian Quattrocento had had
in the first third of the sixteenth century.

Against this profile of the English *vita activa* controversy, it
becomes easier to put in true perspective the controversy that
developed in France between the generation of Budé (climax-
ing in the 1520s and 1530s) and the end of the century. In that
long period, the high officials and jurists of the *noblesse de robe*
in the French monarchy played a social and cultural role comparable to that played by the chancery officials, professionals,
and patricians who had upheld civic Humanism in Florence
and Venice. Because the courtly ideal did not penetrate the
culture of the French high bourgeoisie until the era of Louis
XIII and Louis XIV after 1600, politically oriented Humanism
lasted considerably longer in France than it did in England,
and its creative effects were correspondingly greater. Herein
lies the inherent truth and justification of a genetic scheme
such as Rice's, which for important aspects of the humanistic
development begins with Quattrocento Florence and culminates—or culminates again—in late sixteenth-century France.

---

[20] Not until Francis Bacon, as far as I am aware, did the *vita activa* debate
reemerge, in a vastly changed world but nevertheless again with the emphasis
on the *bonum communionis* characteristic of the active life and on the citizen's
responsibility for his state; see Napoleone Orsini, *Bacone e Machiavelli* (Genoa,
1936), 118ff., 137ff.

Even under the changed conditions of the advancing seventeenth century,
these literary controversies would not entirely disappear in England. I am
thinking of the treatise by the diarist John Evelyn, *Publick Employment and an
Active Life* (London, 1667), which was an answer to an essay titled *Preferring
Solitude to Publick Employment* and urged active public participation by citizens
in state and economic affairs. For the second half of the century one should
have in mind Obadiah Walker's *Of Education, especially of Young Gentlemen* (1st
ed., Oxford, 1673; 5th ed., 1687), which states in the preface that the book
will vindicate the *vita activa* and that much of its argument is based on Italian
authors, who have been too much neglected.

Nowhere, indeed, did the philosophy of history that arose in the Florentine republic during the two periods of Bruni and Machiavelli more conclusively undermine the medieval notion of the divinely appointed Four Monarchies than in the France of Bodin and Le Roy. Nowhere did the struggle for the equality of modern languages and literatures that had been initiated in Quattrocento Florence and carried on in sixteenth-century Venice and Padua achieve greater results than in the France of Ronsard and Joachim Du Bellay. Moreover, as in Quattrocento Florence, the preeminence given to the moral virtues and the active political life in sixteenth-century France demonstrates that Humanism fostered a culture and education befitting the social responsibilities of a politically minded patrician class.

This underlying motivation of French sixteenth-century Humanism is less clearly suggested by Rice's selection of personalities and texts than one might wish. But the political and patriotic component in the outlook of the French group can be illustrated by other known examples. We should, perhaps, not take Ronsard's preference in his oration for the *vertus moralles* over the *vertus intellectuelles* as representative, considering that of five speeches delivered before the Palace Academy his was the only one to prefer the active to the contemplative life.[21] However, we have persuasive information on the reaction of another of the royal humanist statesmen of the period, Guillaume Du Vair. After a humanistic journey to Italy in his youth and some initial experience in princely service, Du Vair confined himself to his studies during the 1580s and became the author of neo-Stoic works with a strongly spiritual cast. His *Sainte philosophie*, written in this period, celebrated the bliss of contemplation. But after the murder of Henri III in 1589, when France threatened to disintegrate in civil war, Du Vair began actively to exercise his civic responsibilities. In his *De la constance et consolation ès calamités publiques*, a new tone of

---

[21] Cf. Frances A. Yates, *The French Academies of the Sixteenth Century* (London, 1947), 109. Rice should also have mentioned that, in his formal philosophy, even Bodin was among the upholders of the *vita contemplativa*.

political concern appeared, and on the eve of his distinguished administrative career in the service of Henri IV, the former contemplative philosopher wrote an *Exhortation à la vie civile* on the following theme: When our country is in danger and needs our help, we must make every sacrifice, even that of Stoic tranquillity of mind and the sweetness of an introspective life. Du Vair pointed out that the great solitaries among the Church Fathers did not hesitate to give up their beloved solitude in an hour of need. Indeed, they viewed their *vita contemplativa* as a reward for labors performed in the *vita activa.* "We are not born into this world for ourselves; we are but a tiny particle of the universe, bound to a great and principal sector of it by firm ties which do not permit us to retire at such a moment without violating charity and love."[22]

These are echoes of the kind of Humanism that made itself heard for the first time in the Florence of the early Quattrocento. When we consider that by 1557, the Florentine *Vita Civile* of Matteo Palmieri had been translated into French and repeatedly revised in Paris, it should come as no surprise to hear those echoes in France.[23]

[22] Cf. L. Zanta, *La renaissance du stoicisme au XVIᵉ siècle* (Paris, 1914), 241ff., esp. 260f., 306f.

[23] See the entry in the Bibliothèque Nationale catalogue of printed books: "La vie civile de maistre Matthieu Palmier, traduit par Claude Des Rosiers et . . . reveu et corrigé par C. Gruget. Paris 1557" (vol. 129, col. 607).

There are now counterparts, in neighboring areas, to the above picture of the rise of the new humanistic attitude toward history in Quattrocento Italy and the spread of this intellectual pattern to France and England during the sixteenth and seventeenth centuries: Peter Burke's "The Sense of Historical Perspective in Renaissance Italy," *Journal of World History* 11 (1969): 615–31; and the chapters "The Humanist Historian in Fifteenth-Century Italy" and "The Sixteenth Century" in Denys Hay's profile of the development from medieval to modern historiography, *Annalists and Historians: Western Historiography from the VIIIth to the XVIIIth Century* (London, 1977). Cf. also the chapters "The Florentine Renaissance" and "The Reception of Humanist Political Thought" (i.e., in the countries north of the Alps, especially in England) in Quentin Skinner's *The Foundations of Modern Political Thought*, vol. 1, *The Renaissance* (Cambridge, England, 1978). All of these recent British works follow the same kind of schema used in the present essay.

FOURTEEN

The *Querelle* of the Ancients and the Moderns as a Problem for Present Renaissance Scholarship★

I

THE USE of the phrase "the quarrel of the ancients and the moderns" for one of the intellectual struggles of the seventeenth century is roughly as old as the use of the concept "the Renaissance" for the preceding period. Ever since Hippolyte Rigault's pioneer work, the *Histoire de la Querelle des Anciens et des Modernes*, was published in 1856—almost simultaneously with Michelet's and Burckhardt's books on the Renaissance—the "Querelle" of the seventeenth century has been a household word to scholars.

For a long time, however, the word rarely served as a label for a new phase in the history of thought; rather, it signified only a revolt against the traditional acceptance of Antiquity as a superior model in literature and art.[1] Students were well aware, of course, that when Charles Perrault and Bernard de Fontenelle, in 1687 and 1688 respectively, proclaimed the superiority of the age of Louis XIV over that of Augustus, they proposed some general ideas that reflected the philosophy of the epoch in which the rationalism of Descartes and the new natural science emerged triumphant. Nature, Perrault and

★ First given as a lecture and published in the *Journal of the History of Ideas* 20 (1959); republished in a slightly revised form in *Renaissance Essays*, ed. P. O. Kristeller and P. P. Wiener (New York, 1968). The revised form of the essay is reprinted here with additional, mostly stylistic changes and some additions to the notes.

[1] A notable exception, H. Gillot's *La querelle des anciens et des modernes en France* (Paris, 1914), has failed to exert a large influence.

Fontenelle argued, always remains the same, inexhaustible and constant in her effects; there was no reason to think that fewer great intellects were being born in the France of Louis XIV than had been born in any past period. But strictures upon the belief that the world could never again produce the equal of the ancients were mere accessories in a contest which chiefly concerned *belles lettres* and the arts and centered on the assertion that various recent authors, whose names are largely forgotten today, were greater than the greatest poets and writers of Antiquity; and that even Homer would have become a better poet had he lived in the enlightened age of Louis XIV. The controversy, in spite of these extravagances, had an enduring historical effect in that it substantially helped to demolish faith in the rigid rules, supposedly of ancient origin, characteristic of French classicism. Still, there seemed to be no reason for modern scholars to consider the debate as more consequential than a literary feud. As for the repercussions that reached England, beginning with the dispute between Sir William Temple and William Wotton during the 1690s, students of English literature were for a long time even less prepared than students of the French development to view these clashes as milestones in the growth of modern ideas.

In 1920, however, two works appeared simultaneously which placed the *Querelle* in a different light. In England, John B. Bury published his history of *The Idea of Progress*, while in America there appeared Richard F. Jones' monograph on "The Background of *The Battle of the Books*" (that is, of Swift's satire), followed in 1936 by Jones' *Ancients and Moderns*, the first coherent history of the *Querelle* as far as it concerned England.[2] Both authors pointed out that in the intellectual climate of Baconian England, attacks upon the authority of the ancients had started early in the seventeenth century, long before

---

[2] Richard F. Jones, *Ancients and Moderns: A Study of the Background of the 'Battle of the Books'* (St. Louis, 1936). A second edition (St. Louis, 1961) appeared with a changed subtitle, *A Study of the Rise of the Scientific Movement in Seventeenth-Century England*, but with the text "almost entirely in its original form" (p. vii).

the literary and artistic debates approached their climax in France, and that in England the battle for recognition of the equality of the moderns had from the first been intimately related to the struggle against the time-honored opinion that the earth and its inhabitants, if not the universe itself, was growing old and decaying with the passage of the centuries. Only after liberation from this burdensome belief (so Bury and Jones argued, and so their successors have argued ever since) could the spirit of modern science and the faith in progress unfold—a liberation which began with Francis Bacon and with a book first published in 1627, little known today but influential throughout the seventeenth century: George Hakewill's *Apology . . . of the Power and Providence of God, . . . and Censure of the Common Errour Touching Nature's Perpetuall and Universal Decay.*

Liberation of the modern scientific spirit from what? The answer, since the 1920s, has invariably been: from the oppressive ideas of the humanistic Renaissance. "The quarrel of the Ancients and Moderns," said Bury, "was part of the rebellion against the intellectual yoke of the Renaissance." In the crucial matter of intellectual freedom, Humanism had merely replaced the authority of Scholasticism with a new authority, that of "the ancient writers." Whereas the Renaissance had worshipped and imitated "what was old," the true revolt signifying the rise of the modern mind was the revolt "against the tyranny of antiquity" during the seventeenth century.[3]

It would be unjust to assert that Richard F. Jones also clearly equated the trends opposed by seventeenth-century science with "the Renaissance" or with "Humanism." In characterizing the adversary, Jones often speaks of the "neo-classical dogma." Although he writes of the "despotic sway" of Aristotle and Ptolemy over the "science of the Renaissance," he notes repeatedly that revolts against their authority had taken place long before in the continental countries, and that Giordano Bruno during his sojourn in Elizabethan England felt

---

[3] John B. Bury, *The Idea of Progress* (London, 1920), 30ff., 78.

74

that he had entered a different environment, one where he found himself unable to "dent . . . conservative thought." But for all these modifications, Jones did not change his central thesis. This thesis was that so long as the theory of the aging and decaying of man and nature had not been finally refuted, there was no escape from "enervating," "blind reliance upon antiquity." "How else," Jones asked, "could a critical theory like that of close imitation secure such a strong hold upon intelligent people, or how could there have been such extravagant and servile worship of men who had lived many ages before?" All such conceptions and attitudes "had to go" before science and "the ideal of liberty of thought and discussion could find a place in the sun." Since, furthermore, the ideas fought by the "Moderns" in early seventeenth-century England are often called "Renaissance" by Jones, while the partial survival of neoclassicism during the eighteenth century is termed a victory of "Humanism" which "retarded" the growth of science, the sum total appears to be a war of the scientific spirit against the authoritarianism of the humanistic Renaissance.[4]

It is from this angle that the history of the *Querelle* in England has been interpreted by an ever-widening circle of scholars. For instance, since Bacon reckoned among the obstacles to the steady progress of science the belief that human history moves in cycles of rise and decay, the "cyclical idea of history" is also often considered to have been one of the "unfavorable concepts" that had to be "offset" by a new mode of thought before it was "possible to carry on progressive studies."[5] Again, although nobody denies that some of the ideas championed by Hakewill and his followers were foreshadowed on the Continent before 1600, it is taken more or less for granted that any resistance against submission to ancient authority must have come from forces adverse to the humanistic Ren-

[4] Jones, *Ancients and Moderns*, 4f., 11f., 23f., 42, 279, 282f.

[5] E. A. Strathmann, *Renaissance News* 2 (1949): 24; see also H. Weisinger, *Journal of the History of Ideas* 6 (1945): 416f.

aissance. As a consequence, the new idea of the *Querelle* has been complemented by a view of the Renaissance in which the humanistic scholarship of the fifteenth and sixteenth centuries no longer appears as one of the roots of modern thought but rather as the converse of the attitude which came to the fore with the *Querelle*. Thus, in a recent reexamination of the cultural situation in seventeenth-century England, Herschel Baker's *The Wars of Truth* (1955), we find the argument that since any program of "imitation" presupposes a model superior to the imitator, the natural consequences of the Renaissance idea of imitation were the rise of literary authoritarianism and the doctrine of the deterioration of the world. Consequently, the Renaissance failed to develop a basic concept indispensable for the future: "in spite of its high evaluation of human reason, it lacked the necessary view of nature as everywhere and always the same." Perhaps the classic formulation of this view is to be found in John H. Randall's *The Making of the Modern Mind*: "The Renaissance, which actually accomplished so much, could not imagine that man could ever rise again to the level of glorious antiquity; its thoughts were all on the past. Only with the growth of science in the seventeenth century could men dare to cherish such an overweening ambition."[6]

These contentions and conclusions cut deep into traditional conceptions of the Renaissance. For we must not forget that our customary concepts of epochs are interdependent; if one is changed, the others, too, must be adjusted. If it is true that the modern attitudes emerging from the seventeenth-century *Querelle* were basically different from the outlook that preceded Galileo and Bacon, our estimate of the role of the Renaissance in the growth of modern thought will have to be modified. But we should also remember a striking parallel from the history of the opinions about the relationship of the Renaissance to the Middle Ages. Everyone today is aware of the snares into which we fall if we accept at face value the

[6] Herschel Baker, *The Wars of Truth* (Cambridge, Mass., 1952), 69, 78; John H. Randall, *The Making of the Modern Mind*, rev. ed. (Boston, 1940), 381.

statements on the Middle Ages made by the early humanists. We all take into account that the humanistic reaction to Scholasticism was conditioned by a knowledge of the Middle Ages which was very limited in comparison with what we know today. Can we be certain that complaints by English writers of the seventeenth century about deficiencies in their past— the material on which the recent views of the *Querelle* rely— are applicable to as long a period as the two or three preceding centuries? Or do these complaints merely reflect the distorted view of the generation immediately following, comparable in their myopia to the view that many early humanists had held of the Middle Ages?

II

One of the merits of Jones' presentation of the early seventeenth century is that, in introducing the important figure of Hakewill into the scene of Baconian England, he clearly noted a difference between the first two protagonists of the English *Querelle*. Hakewill, whose use of Bacon's works can be traced only occasionally, remained so much a stranger to the new science that one of his major arguments against belief in the world's decay was the alleged correctness of the old Ptolemaic assumption that the stars and heavens were immutable; this proved, he thought, that the whole idea of a deteriorating universe was impossible.[7] Another of Hakewill's chief objections to the theory of a progressive "corruption of nature" was grounded in his belief in historical cycles alternating between decay and new ascendency—the very idea which Bacon reckoned among the obstacles to the growth of a progressive scientific spirit. Hakewill, Jones concluded, in many respects does not yet "look forward in proving his points. He stands in the afterglow of the Renaissance."[8] But then the situation is

[7] Cf. also R. Hepburn, "George Hakewill: The Virility of Nature," *Journal of the History of Ideas* 16 (1955): 135–50, esp. 137, 141, 145f.

[8] Jones, *Ancients and Moderns*, 36.

much more complicated than is assumed by those who would like to trace the key ideas of the *Querelle* to the new science alone. Before we can establish the final balance of ideas in the controversy, we must identify the forces which, through the agency of Hakewill, cooperated with the Baconian revolt.

Where Bacon's and Hakewill's views are farthest apart and least adaptable to a common pattern of thought is precisely in their attitude toward the Renaissance idea of cyclical rotation—the belief in an alternating rise and fall of states and civilizations. For Bacon, the assumption of periodic destruction seemed to undermine the confidence that the moderns could gradually progress beyond Antiquity. Adherence to the cyclical idea was, in his eyes, one of the reasons why undue submission to ancient authority had not disappeared and why reliance on the continued progress of human knowledge had not yet dissipated the old fears that man and the world were aging and deteriorating. For Hakewill, on the other hand, there was no better remedy against these fears than the knowledge that every decline is temporary and will be followed by a new cycle. Hakewill himself mentions those who convinced him that history, in the arts and sciences as well as in the realm of "manners," was constant "vicissitude, alteration, and revolution," and consequently not continual decay. Among them he names such writers of the Italian Renaissance as Gasparo Contarini and (from the second edition of the *Apology*, 1630, on) Machiavelli, who, however objectionable many of his teachings might be, was in this "matter of civic wisdom and observation" an unparalleled witness.[9] Was Hakewill, then, carrying on a tradition of Renaissance thought at the very center of his work, or had he essentially changed the meaning of his sources by giving an optimistic interpretation to the cyclical theory?

As Machiavelli's absence from the first edition of the *Apology* suggests, the legacy of the preceding era must originally

---

[9] *Apology* (ed. 1630), 38, 289, 298, Z z 3 (1a); (ed. 1635), 40, 331, 340f. (Here, as in most subsequent quotations from the original sources, the orthography and sometimes the punctuation have been modernized.)

have reached Hakewill through other sources. From his own quotations there can be no doubt that French humanistic literature of the late sixteenth century was the primary medium; we find references especially to Bodin and Le Roy. Bodin's *Methodus ad Facilem Historiarum Cognitionem*, first printed in 1566, was indeed read by every serious English student of history, and in 1594 the English translation had appeared of a French work, published in 1575, that supplied an even broader background to some of Bodin's views: Loys Le Roy's *De La Vicissitude ou Variété des Choses* (*Of the Interchangeable Course or Variety of Things*, in the English translation). In his younger years, Le Roy had been a close friend of Du Bellay, and we may regard him in many respects as a representative or heir of the *Pléiade*. He was a humanist whose foremost wish was that the example of Antiquity should inspire modern France to develop its own genius, and that contemporary men should react to the teachings of Antiquity "not by . . . resting on that which men had formerly done, said, or written . . . but by the adding of somewhat of their own, . . . considering that there remain more things to be sought out, than are already invented and found." Le Roy was already among those who believed that knowledge and the arts gradually improved through observation and experience and who took courage from the argument that the sun, planets, and elements were still what they were in Antiquity and that, consequently, it was a prejudice to assume that man had changed. Countless new discoveries and methods unknown to Antiquity had emerged "in this age" of ours; still others would be made by posterity. "That which is now hidden, with time will come to light; and our successors will wonder that we were ignorant of them."

These passages have often been praised as having been inspired by the new inventions—as harbingers of the modern ideas of progress and perfectibility. But they appear in the concluding pages of a work whose preceding eleven books present a comprehensive analysis of the "cyclical" view of history. The bulk of Le Roy's work is a comparative study of the growth, flowering, and decline of successive empires and cultures from the Egyptians, Assyrians, Persians, Greeks, Romans, and Saracens, to "this age," which for him, in humanistic fashion, began about 1400 with the revival of letters and languages in the western countries. His study, as far as I know, is the most developed example of a philosophy of history based on the concept of successive cycles and on the typical Renaissance view that in any given culture, competition and the thirst for glory raise man higher and higher, until perfection has been reached—"where it is hard to remain, since everything that cannot go forward or upward does naturally descend and retire." The conclusions for the future of our own cycle are honestly drawn: "If the . . . knowledge of that which is past be the instruction . . . for that which is to come: it is to be feared lest the power, wisdom, sciences, books, industry, workmanships, and knowledges of the world, being come to so great excellency, do fall again, as they have done in times past. . . . I foresee already in my mind many strange Nations, differing in fashions, colours, and habits, rushing into Europe as did in old times the Goths, Huns, Lombards, Vandals, and Saracens; which will destroy our towns, cities, castles, palaces, and temples: will change the manners, laws, languages, and religion; burn the libraries, spoiling whatsoever good things they shall find in these countries. . . ."[10]

What we learn from Le Roy's work is that the consciousness, derived from the cyclical theory, of the temporary character of every advance did not necessarily thwart optimism and a progressive outlook on life. For Le Roy, the simple consolation that although decay is inescapable its date is not known and may long be postponed by human endeavor or divine providence, was strong enough to minimize its adverse psychological effects. On the other hand, the cyclical view of history could act as a weapon against classicistic dogmatism. Why did leadership in politics and culture continually change from one land to another? My interpretation, says Le Roy, is

[10] Loys Le Roy, *De la vicissitude*, used in its English translation, *Of the Interchangeable Course or Variety of Things* (London, 1594), 32v, 126r–127v.

that God wants to grant "the excellency of arms and of learning" to all parts of the earth, "to the end that every one in his turn might have part of good hap and ill; and that none should wax proud by overlong prosperity." This historical relativism provides the basis for one of the most energetic expressions of anticlassicism in the epilogue of Le Roy's book: his protest against the opinion that every important subject has already been dealt with by ancient writers and merely requires modification and commentary. For people thus disheartened, Le Roy avers, the knowledge that all civilizations periodically flower and wane offers some comforting and invigorating thoughts. Not only must the greater part of literature be written anew time and again, since very few books and libraries are saved from the destruction that occurs between cycles, but constant re-creation is needed for a more profound reason: except for the work of a few towering minds, such as Plato, Aristotle, Hippocrates, and Ptolemy, says Le Roy, "there are not any writings which please and satisfy all people, or which are received in all places." He observed that "books are different according to the disposition of the times and inclination of the countries wherein they are made: even as wines are divers according to the territory . . . and disposition of the years. . . . Every age has its peculiar kind of speech; every nation and age its phrase: the Greeks and Latins write with one sort, the Hebrews, Chaldees, and Arabians with another. . . . Works which are respected here as holy, are burned elsewhere as abomination." Works of poetry lose their "grace," and consequently their appeal, in translation. Like the rest of things mortal, therefore, the arts and sciences can be perpetuated only through constant re-creation. "For as other things, being subject to mutation, have need of continual generation, to renew themselves and to maintain each of them his kind: so must learning also be provided for by seeking of new inventions instead of those that are lost, by changing that which is not well, and by supplying that which is wanting." This insight into the nature of history must determine our attitude toward Antiquity. "Plato says that the Greeks have bettered that which they received from the Barbarians. Cicero is of [the] opinion that the Italians have of themselves better invented than the Grecians, or made that better which they borrowed of them. And why should not we endeavor to do the like; amending that which the Barbarians, Greeks, and Romans have left unto us?"[11]

The length of the discussion we have allotted to Le Roy's late-humanistic philosophy of history is justified, because the mere existence of this work and its use by Hakewill raises grave doubts about the assumption that a "progressive view" of culture and the disavowal of passive imitation could not have arisen before the idea of scientific progress that characterizes the Baconian school. Less than a decade before Le Roy's *De La Vicissitude*, Jean Bodin's *Methodus* had used the cyclical movement of history as the basis for an outright criticism of the assumption of progressive degeneration; Le Roy agreed so completely with this criticism that he came near to plagiarizing Bodin, who had pointed out that the belief in man's perennial decay was closely linked with the idea of a golden age at the dawn of mankind, which implied that history could only run downhill. This myth is criticized by Bodin along with another interpretation of history linked to the idea of a golden age. In his chapter entitled "A Refutation of those who postulate Four Monarchies and the Golden Age," he argues that these two postulates logically belong together because they are both related to the traditional conception of decadence. If the history of mankind comprises four monarchies, the last of which, the Roman, will in some form endure to the world's end, the present and future are no more than the declining phases of the history of Rome; the moderns can claim neither originality nor a new beginning. Similarly, if the history of man began with a golden age, its end can never hope to rival its beginning. After repudiating both of these theories, Bodin compares ancient with modern manners, to the advantage of the latter, and concludes with glow-

[11] Ibid., 32v, 129r–130v.

ing praise for modern inventions and discoveries which had been unknown to the ancients.

The fact that Bodin found it necessary to relate the belief in an aging and degenerating world to the historical theory of the Four Monarchies gives us a clue to the sources of the ideas which the champions of the *Querelle* opposed. The doctrine that the Roman monarchy, recognized by Christ, would endure until the end of the world had been a characteristic part of medieval thought, and so had the lack of an historical understanding of the differences between the ancient and the medieval empires. The Humanism of the Renaissance, it is true, did not destroy the medieval outlook everywhere. The concept of the Four Monarchies remained strong in sixteenth-century literature; otherwise there would have been no need for Bodin to attack it so earnestly as late as 1566. But when Bodin and Le Roy substituted the new dynamic philosophy of cycles and perpetual rotation for the static notion of four predestined empires, they consummated ideas which had evolved in the course of the humanistic Renaissance.

From the very beginning, as we know, Florentine Humanism, in spite of its veneration of Antiquity, had leveled an historically minded criticism against the idea of perennial Rome—an outmoded notion, it was felt, that endangered the inherent autonomy of the city-state republics and principalities which were the *patriae* of the Italian humanists. From the early Quattrocento, Italian humanistic historiography had learned to see in the *Imperium Romanum*, as in all other products of human life, a natural phenomenon which had to give way, when its life span was over, to new creations of later epochs. As Leonardo Bruni put it in his *History of the Florentine People*: When the gigantic ancient Roman Empire, which had shut out so many competitors and condemned them to obscurity, disintegrated after several centuries, its death meant the generation, or regeneration, of many other states and nations, which, freed from suppression, now found a place in the sun.[12] Incorporated in such works as Flavio Biondo's *Histories*

[12] See Volume I, Essay Three, pp. 60ff.

from the Decline of the Roman Empire and Machiavelli's *Discourses*, this concept became familiar to the French humanists of the sixteenth century in various ways; and in the work of Machiavelli its implications were joined to the theory of historical cycles.

There can be no question that in Machiavelli's formulation of the idea of cyclical movement, a faith in the regenerative power of history overshadows the enervating effects of the cycles. All states, says Machiavelli, "pass from order to disorder and from disorder back to order. For, as the affairs of this world cannot remain stationary, when they have reached a perfection beyond which they cannot ascend they must decline. And when they have descended to their lowest point, they must rise again. So they always decline from good to bad, and from bad they rise again to good."[13] No less strong is the note of confidence in Vasari's *Lives of the Most Eminent Painters, Sculptors, and Architects*, as first published in 1550. Here the logical consequence of the cyclical view, that different cycles may be equal at their peaks, is drawn without hesitation. With Raphael, Vasari affirms, painters in modern Italy became the equals, and perhaps the superiors, of Apelles and Zeuxis, masters in the analogous phase of the ancient cycle; finally Michelangelo appeared, who in all three arts surpassed "the most famous of the ancients." As for Vasari's forecast of the future, he admitted that in his time art had reached its acme and could be followed only by decline. But still he hoped that after its renascence and so much progress God would not allow it to fall again into decay. A definite feeling that he was witnessing the beginning of a time of decadence did not creep into Vasari's work until its second edition, of 1568, when a description of the most recent phase of Italian art, that of Mannerism, was added. But then, what discouraged him more was the recognition that Michelangelo had been greater

---

[13] *Istorie Fiorentine*, Lib. v. Machiavelli's belief that only few states will run through the cycle repeatedly before being destroyed does not detract from the optimism of his statements on the dynamic nature and cyclical rotation of history as a whole.

than his successors, rather than any implication of the idea of cycles.[14]

Let us return from the history of the belief in historical cycles to Hakewill's *Apology*. His attack on the idea of ancient superiority is climaxed by a criticism of the saying, widely used in Scholastic times, that the relationship of the moderns to the ancients is comparable to the situation of dwarfs who stand on the shoulders of giants and consequently see further than the colossi who have lifted them up. As Hakewill objects: "It is not so, neither are we *Dwarfs*, nor they *Giants*, but all of equal stature, or rather we somewhat higher, being lifted up by their means, conditionally there be in us an equal intention of spirit, watchfulness of mind, and love of truth: for if these be wanting, then are we not so much dwarfs, as men of a perfect growth lying on the ground."

Here again we sense an attitude that is reminiscent of Humanism. The Scholastic simile of the dwarfs who have a wider vision than the giants on whose shoulders they stand was often repeated in scientific circles during the seventeenth century (even by Isaac Newton) without giving offense; the thought that each new age, having advanced a little further in knowledge, must of necessity have a broader horizon than its predecessors appealed to the generations which began to experience the steady growth of science. Hakewill, on the other hand, as Jones comments, "sounds a rallying call for man to use the powers given him." "The spirit of Bacon" and his school "is splendid, but the sight of this courageous man standing at the close of the Renaissance and delivering a message that will suit all ages is indeed inspiring."[15]

[14] Giorgio Vasari, *Le vite de' più eccellenti architetti, pittori, e scultori italiani*, ed. Milanesi (Florence, 1878), vol. I, pp. 13, 96, 244; cf. J. v. Schlosser, *Die Kunstliteratur* (Vienna, 1924), 277–80. Vice versa, Fontenelle's pride in the superiority of the age of Louis XIV over Antiquity was not irreconcilable with a feeling that the apex had passed, "for one must honestly confess that the good time came to an end some years ago" (*Digression* of 1688; quoted by A. Tilley, *The Decline of the Age of Louis XIV* [Cambridge, 1929], 331).

[15] Jones, *Ancients and Moderns*, p. 33. Hakewill's passage against the simile of the "dwarfs" is found in *Apology* (ed. 1630), 229.

What Jones failed to mention is that Hakewill was not delivering a message of his own, but was translating a humanistic passage written a hundred years earlier by a member of Erasmus' and More's circle, the Spaniard Juan Luis Vives. And Vives had accompanied his criticism with further arguments that illustrate to what extent the motifs considered typical of the seventeenth-century *Querelle* had been present among humanistic writers of the Renaissance. The authors of Antiquity were truly great, Vives had said, "yet they were men as we are and were liable to be deceived and to err." "The good men amongst them undoubtedly stretched forth their hands in friendship to those [of later ages] who, as they knew, would mount higher in knowledge than they themselves had done. For they judged it the very essence of the human race that it should daily progress in arts, discipline, virtue, and goodness. We ought not think ourselves [mere] men, or even less, whilst we regard them as more than men."

This is not all that Vives had to offer when the work from which we have been quoting (his *De Disciplinis*) was reprinted by an Oxford scholar in 1612, fifteen years before Hakewill's *Apology*. In the preface Vives calls it his scholarly duty to proceed in a spirit of criticism, notwithstanding his gratitude to the ancient authors, rather "than to merely acquiesce in their authority." In Vives' view, "Nature is not yet so effete and exhausted as to be unable to bring forth results in our time that are comparable to those of earlier ages. She always remains equal to herself, and it is not rare for her to advance more strongly and more powerfully than in the past, as if she were mustering her forces. So in this present age we must regard her as reinforced by the confirmed strength which has gradually developed over so many centuries." Having set forth this opinion, worthy of any true participant in the *Querelle* of the seventeenth century, Vives rejects the dogma of the superior wisdom of the ancients. "Truth is not yet possessed," he says. "Much truth has been left for future generations to discover. I do not profess myself the equal of the ancients, but I compare my views to theirs. . . . You who seek truth, take your stand wherever you expect to find her."[16]

Not only were these passages accessible to Hakewill's generation, but we have at least one other piece of evidence which suggests that they were thoroughly appreciated. All of the quoted passages are reproduced almost verbatim in *Timber, or, Discoveries*, the well-known work (first published in 1640) of Hakewill's great contemporary, Ben Jonson—although Jonson does not acknowledge his indebtedness. As in the case of Hakewill, Ben Jonson's source has long been known to students of Vives,[17] but it is not sufficiently familiar to all students of the post-1600 *Querelle*. Only recently the editor of a critical edition of *Timber* aptly called attention to the passages in question in his preface, but showed himself unaware of their humanistic origin.[18]

III

Several conclusions may be drawn from our observations so far. In the first place, if, having given Hakewill his due place in the English seventeenth-century *Querelle*, we perceive that his contribution continued some of the central convictions of Renaissance humanists, does this not amount to a warning that not everything should be attributed—as has been done in recent years—to the new science? It would be foolish, of course, to minimize the magnitude of the change which occurred in the modern attitude toward Antiquity with the coming of Galileo, Bacon, and Descartes. Still, there is a world of difference between the alternatives presented: an historical

[16] *De Disciplinis*, Engl. trans. in F. Watson's *Vives: On Education* (Cambridge, 1913), pp. cvf., 8f. Hakewill's use of Vives' "dwarfs" passage is noted by Watson, ibid., p. cvi.

[17] Watson, *Vives*, p. xxxiff.; also noted by J.W.H. Atkins, *English Literary Criticism: The Renascence* (London, 1947), 313ff., and D. Bush, *English Literature . . . 1600–1660* (Oxford, 1945), 279.

[18] Ralph S. Walker, ed., *Ben Jonson's 'Timber or Discoveries'* (Syracuse, N.Y., 1953), 14.

picture in which a time of new philosophy and science are opposed to a preceding Renaissance identified with slavish classicistic submission to the tyrannical yoke of the ancient
models; and one in which the Renaissance appears as a struggle between a veneration of Antiquity, leading to classicism,
and a defense of the innate powers and equality of modern
man, leading to the *Querelle*—a struggle which continued
long enough to prepare the ground for some of the most vital
arguments of the seventeenth-century *Querelle*. For, most of
the observations we have made with regard to Hakewill
could, if space permitted, also be made, with certain varia-
tions, about other seventeenth-century figures, including Bacon. As has long been known, even Bacon's dictum that the
moderns were the true ancients, because they had the experience of several thousand years behind them, was influenced by
that other heir of the humanistic Renaissance, Giordano
Bruno.[19]

Second, we may note that if historians of the post-1600
Querelle have sometimes lacked an adequate vision of the immediately preceding centuries, it was ultimately due to the
failure of students of the earlier period to emphasize sufficiently that the humanists of the Renaissance waged a constant
battle against the dangers of classicism. On this score, however, the situation has perceptibly changed since the days
when Bury and Jones composed their pioneering works.
More recently, conclusive studies have shown how seriously,
beginning in the fifteenth century, humanists wrestled with
the problems inherent in their program of "imitation." The
fact that *aemulatio*, instead of *imitatio*, became the battle cry of
the best humanists, from Poliziano in Lorenzo de' Medici's
Florence to Erasmus and subsequently throughout the sixteenth century, is today a commonplace; all the great documents of this battle have found their commentators and have

[19] See esp. G. Gentile, *Studi sul Rinascimento* (Florence, 1923), 123ff. I have
already mentioned the fact that the ancestry of this dictum takes us to Florentine Humanism in the Quattrocento. Cf. Essay Thirteen, notes 9–11.

received critical editions. Again, we are today clearly aware that, notwithstanding their love for the values of Greek and Roman life, numerous humanists paved the way to historical relativism by their efforts to defend the vital rights and peculiar merits of their own states, nations, and cultures; they thus opened another road for the assault of the *Querelle* on the classicistic dogma. Finally, Eugenio Garin, in his fundamental *L'Educazione in Europa, 1400–1600* (Bari, 1957), pointed out a similar pattern in the history of education: the same persistent struggle against the danger, which always loomed large, that humanistic admiration of Antiquity might be corrupted into pedantry and mere repetition without originality. Here, too, the answers given in the Quattro- and Cinquecento were the direct forerunners of those which under the impact of the *Querelle* were to predominate after 1600.

The only point in this synoptic picture about which we might still be skeptical is the extent to which the overseas discoveries, the new inventions, or the successes of modern science were indispensable for building up the confidence and self-esteem of the moderns. In the circles of Vives and Sir Thomas More, we already find a considerable interest in mathematics and the inventiveness of contemporary artisans.[20] Rabelais, who more than anyone else inherited Vives' tendencies, was not only a humanist but also a medical student; in him and many others in the sixteenth century, pride in modern attainments and a critical attitude toward Antiquity were indubitably encouraged by scientific pursuits. One might, therefore, venture upon the hypothesis that classicism and pessimism gradually lost their hold only where Humanism was joined by the rise of science. Thus, the theory that Humanism had to be replaced or basically transformed before the modern spirit could unfold would be readmitted through the back door. Something like this, indeed, has been the inter-

---

[20] Francis R. Johnson, *Astronomical Thought in Renaissance England* (Baltimore, 1937), 82–87, 290.

pretation of a number of recent students,[21] but their conclusion may turn out to be hasty. For it can be shown that the
humanistic Renaissance had wrestled with the problems of
classicism in its own fashion, and that the modern spirit had
already triumphed over submission to Antiquity, not necessarily in science, but in other vital fields.

It has already been noted that much recent research into the
origins of the *Querelle* has traced the beginnings of the battle
against classicism to Quattrocento Italy. At that time, modern
science had not yet emerged; humanists were still nearly de-
void of interest in scientific studies, and nothing would have
been further from the minds of most writers of the Quattrocento than to base a claim of modern superiority on the advance of scientific knowledge. What then, one wonders, made
Italian Quattrocento humanists bold enough to feel that their
world equalled, or would soon equal, that of the ancients? A
few examples may suggest an answer.

Space does not permit consideration of the complicated
problem of the extent to which Petrarch and the fourteenth
century prepared the way for later humanistic claims regarding Antiquity. Suffice it to say that by the early Quattrocento
the situation had developed which was to remain characteristic
of Renaissance Humanism: while humanists worked with
dedication toward the revival of the classical past through
scholarship and imagination, they also felt themselves, and
were proud, to be Florentines, Venetians, and Milanese, and
later French, German, Spanish, and English nationals. They
were bound, therefore, to look at the fruits of their labors as
results achieved in imitation of ancient attitudes and forms but
executed in different materials and for fresh needs—in the
service of new political loyalties and new national literatures.

In Florence, the tension between unmitigated classicistic
convictions and contemporary tasks came into the open from

---

[21] Cf. esp. A. C. Keller in *Renaissance News* 2 (1949): 21ff., and *Publications of the Modern Language Association* 66 (1951): 236ff.

the moment that humanistic circles began to form in civic society. During the first Quattrocento generation, which also
experienced the first full influence of classical Antiquity on art,
radical classicism became so predominant for a while that self-
confidence and even productivity were weakened. Niccolò
Niccoli, the arch-classicist of the period, was so firmly convinced of the futility of any attempt to equal the perfection of
the classical models he admired that he never published a single line. And when his friend and intimate, Leonardo Bruni,
planned during his early years to write the biography of their
humanist teacher, the chancellor Coluccio Salutati, he, too,
was frustrated by the feeling that—with the possible exception
of the humanistic *studia et litterae*—nothing in his time could
compare to the subject matter at the disposal of the ancient
biographical writers. "In what are we similar or equal? . . .
We are today plainly dwarfs [*homunculi*], and even if we were
not dwarfs in spirit our lives would not have the stuff needed
for lasting glory."[22] Bruni's biography of Salutati was never
finished—an irreparable loss for our knowledge of the early
Renaissance and a prime example of classicistic discouragement. Overwhelmingly impressed at the time by the greatness
of the ancients, with whom his translation of Plutarch had
brought him into close contact, Bruni wrote: "If we want to
judge correctly, without self-deception, we shall have to acknowledge that our times are unable to compete with the ancients either in the conduct of war, in the *gubernatio rerum pu-
blicarum*, in eloquence, or in the study of the *bonae artes*."

But from the standpoint of the history of Humanism, the
more important observation is that this discouragement did
not last long. During the generation of Niccoli and Bruni, the
Florentine republic emerged from the wars for survival between the Italian states in a position which, in the eyes of con-

---

[22] Cf. Leonardo Bruni, *Epistolarum Libri VIII*, ed. L. Mehus, vol. 1, pp. 28–
30 (letter of 1408). For the quotations which follow and for fuller evidence,
see *Leonardo Bruni Aretino: Humanistisch-philosophische Schriften*, ed. H. Baron
(Leipzig, 1928), 124–25, and *Crisis*, 2d ed., 282–85.

temporaries, appeared comparable to that of Athens in ancient Greece and Rome in ancient Italy. Less than a decade after the contemporary world had seemed to Bruni so inferior to Antiquity that he found himself unable to compose the biography of a Florentine chancellor in the style of the ancients, he was at work on the *History of the Florentine People*. It was then that he discovered that Florence's past greatness was commensurate with her present position as an Italian power capable of withstanding the challenges of both the Milan of Giangaleazzo Visconti and the Neapolitan monarchy of King Ladislaus. The greatness of Florence, he wrote in the preface of his *History* (written between 1415 and 1419), was evident in every phase of her growth, and her attainments could be described in such a way "that they will not appear inferior in any part [*nulla ex parte inferiores*] to those great deeds and events of Antiquity which we are wont to admire whenever we read of them."

About twenty years later, the young Florentine citizen-humanist Matteo Palmieri, in his *Vita Civile*, wondered why the accomplishments of previous generations had suddenly been surpassed in his time. The answer throws an interesting light on early Renaissance ideas of originality and progress. The only reason for the lack of advance among our ancestors, says Palmieri, was that they were content to carry on the ways of their predecessors without trying to improve upon them. When this attitude changed, painting suddenly revived in the hands of Giotto; and later, humanistic letters were revived by Bruni. After such achievements, one could expect a period of flowering like that of Greece and Rome. "Whoever, therefore, has been born into this time and been given a talent should thank God." The same perspective of recent progress, but seen against a religious background, reappears in the well-known *De Dignitate Hominis* by the Florentine, Giannozzo Manetti. There, it is argued that through the ages man has improved his surroundings far beyond the state in which Earth was given to him by God, and that the present epoch, in many respects, has brought those labors to their culmination. Man, who once conceived that wonderful invention, the ship, has recently navigated "ultra terminos antea navigabiles," where some inhabited but previously unknown islands (the Canaries and Azores, no doubt) have been discovered. Meanwhile, Giotto's paintings compare with the most famous works of ancient art, and Brunelleschi's dome for the Florentine cathedral has risen to rival the pyramids.[23]

It is important to recognize that although the very first experience of Portuguese overseas discoveries at once added to modern pride, it did not do so in combination with modern science but with those two other achievements which awed the early Renaissance: the boldly original new art and the productiveness and vigor of life in the Florentine republic. How these two springs of Quattrocento optimism combined and gradually brought forth the motifs of the later *Querelle* is evident in Leon Battista Alberti's dedication of the Volgare version of his treatise *De Pictura* to Brunelleschi. During his youth in exile, Alberti confesses there, he had always assumed and deplored that in today's world the great ancient leaders of the arts and sciences had few, if any, equivalents. "So I believed what I had heard many people affirm; namely, that nature had grown old and tired and was no longer producing giants in body or mind."[24] And, indeed, in one of his earliest writings, *De Commodis Litterum atque Incommodis*, which was composed just after his student years in Padua and Bologna, Alberti had shared the pessimistic view of the moderns characteristic of humanistic classicists on the threshold of the

[23] Palmieri, *Vita Civile*, ed. G. Belloni (1982), 43f.; for Manetti, see G. Gentile, *Il pensiero italiano del Rinascimento*, 3rd ed. (Florence, 1940), 106f., 110f. For the problem of the impact of the discovery of new islands, see also G. Padoan, "Petrarca, Boccaccio e la scoperta delle Canarie," *Italia Medievale ed Umanistica* 7 (1964).

[24] See the quotations from *De Commodis* in Cecil Grayson, "The Humanism of Alberti," *Italian Studies* 12 (1957): 41. For Alberti's initial belief, according to his own testimony, in the doctrine of the aging of nature, see also *Crisis*, 2d ed., 348.

Quattrocento. At that time he believed that the example set by the ancients could never again be realized; although a man should try to win fame by helping to fill the relatively small lacunae left by the creative minds of Antiquity, there was ultimately nothing left for the moderns to do "but look up admiringly" to the ancients and accept the fact that nature had grown old and was no longer producing such human greatness. But in his dedication to *De Pictura* he goes on to say: "When I returned from exile to our beautiful native city, however, I realized that talents sufficient for any worthy task are still alive in many people, in the first place in thee, Filippo [Brunelleschi], but also in our dear friend Donato [Donatello], the sculptor, and in others . . ., [among them] . . . Masaccio—talents that cannot be valued less in these arts than those of the famous ancients [*non posporli aqual si sia stato antiquo e famoso in queste arti*]." He now realized, said Alberti, that industry and *virtù* can be more powerful than the gifts of time and nature; for here in Florence we find *arti e scienze* that had never been seen or heard of before, among them those employed in the erection of Brunelleschi's dome—a skill which "may not have been understood or known at all by the ancients."[25]

[25] See the Prologus of the Volgare version of *De Pictura*, addressed to Filippo Brunelleschi, in Leon Battista Alberti's *Opere volgari*, ed. Cecil Grayson, vol. 3 (Bari, 1973), 7–8.

This is not the place to decide how widespread the tradition of the defense of the moderns was in the world of Florentine civic Humanism, but the fact should be mentioned that about a decade after Alberti (in the early 1460s) there originated in Florence the most comprehensive glorification of the moderns to appear in Italy before the seventeenth century: the *Dialogus [de praestantia virorum sui aevi]*, written by the third successor to Bruni in the Florentine chancery, Benedetto Accolti. This work was briefly mentioned in *Crisis*, 2d ed., 347, 396, 435f. Since then, however, the first biography of Accolti, by Robert Black, has appeared (*Benedetto Accolti and the Florentine Renaissance* [Cambridge, 1985])—an excellent monograph, which doubts that Accolti's eulogy of the moderns is a sincere expression of his opinion rather than being primarily the audacious statement of a rhetorician who "wished to show that he was capable of defending the indefensible" (pp. 199–201). Clearly, the answer to the question whether Accolti's apology for the moderns was more

IV

Behind the scattered utterances of this kind there loomed the problem of historical relativity. If the Venetian and Florentine republics were not to be considered merely less perfect counterparts of ancient Sparta, Athens, and Rome, and if the language of Dante, Petrarch, and Boccaccio was not second to the languages of ancient Greece and Rome, one had to face the conclusion that every state, culture, and language has its historical life span and must eventually give way to those of later ages. This, in fact, was the foundation on which the humanistic contribution to the *Querelle* was finally to rest; but the beginnings lay in the early Quattrocento. We have already discussed how in historiography the fall of the *Imperium Ro-*

---

than mere rhetoric must take into consideration the fact that the period in which Accolti wrote—not very many years after Bruni and Alberti—came to the very recognition which Black calls into doubt in the case of Accolti; namely, that "a progression occurred in which the first stage was characterized by deference to antiquity, the second by self-confident equality with the ancients." Yet this is what happened in the lives of Bruni and Alberti, as we have seen. That Accolti was indeed under the direct influence of the ideals of civic humanists is also indicated by the observation that he "listed among the reasons for modern Italy's equal claims the emergence of city-republics that were the peers of ancient Athens, Sparta, and Rome—and especially the fact that Florence, Venice, and Siena had preserved their independence to the present day" (*Crisis*, 2d ed., 396). Finally, Alamanno Rinuccini, one of the last Florentine citizens under the full spell of the Bruni-Palmieri tradition, "[in the 1470s] praises moderns in comparison with ancients for their achievements in the visual arts, grammar, philosophy, eloquence, statesmanship and warfare," to use Black's own characterization. All this is more than rhetoric lacking personal conviction. Add to this that, conversely, in the early 1490s, when the civic tradition was already greatly weakened, Bartolomeo Scala, the chancellor of those later years, wrote the following to Politian: Compared with Antiquity we are but little men. "And what happens when I consider our military affairs, literature, philosophy, painting, our sculpture and the other adornments of our age and compare them with the ancients? My spirits fall and I begin to be ashamed of our studies" (Alison Brown, *Bartolomeo Scala, 1430–1497, Chancellor of Florence: The Humanist as Bureaucrat* [Princeton, 1979], 277). Quite evidently, there was an organic development of the quarrel of the ancients and the moderns in early Renaissance Florence under the impact of the growth and decline of civic Humanism.

manum was viewed after 1400, for the first time, in the light of the dawning history of the various states and nations that rose after Rome's dominance had come to an end. A pendant to this historiographical tendency was the gradual recognition of the historical right of the post-Roman languages and literatures.[26]

Bruni, in his *Vita di Dante*, already wrote in defense of the Italian vernacular: "Whether the writing is done in Latin or the Volgare does not matter; the distinction is no different from that between writing in Greek or Latin. Every language has its own perfection, its own sound, its own refinement and *parlare scientifico*." The next major step came with Lorenzo de' Medici, who was both a statesman and an Italian poet. Latin, like any other tongue, Lorenzo argued, was originally the language of a single city or region. Its rise to the position of a universal language was not due to any inherent superiority. It occurred because "the expansion of the Roman Empire made the adoption of its language almost inevitable." All the languages of the past, Hebrew as well as Greek and Latin, were "spoken languages and vernaculars" before their rise as media of great literatures. Against this background a Florentine might be permitted to hope that his own tongue was embarked upon such a course since the days of Dante, Petrarch, and Boccaccio. As Lorenzo saw it, ancient and modern languages were on the same historical footing.

From late-Quattrocento Florence we can trace a road map, as it were, that eventually leads to the various contenders in the *Querelle* of the sixteenth and seventeenth centuries. On this map the crossroads still lie in Italy, where, about the middle of the sixteenth century, in the shadow of the north Italian universities, leading representatives of philosophy and science joined ranks with those who called for the equality of the Volgare. Sperone Speroni of Padua, who had come from the Peripatetic school of Pomponazzi, was a student of philosophy

[26] For what follows, see also *Crisis*, vol. 1, pp. 300–312, vol. 2, pp. 422–29, and *Crisis*, 2d ed., 335–53.

and medicine, as well as a highly educated heir to the humanistic tradition. When we read in his *Dialogo delle Lingue* (1547) that "the languages of all countries, Arabic as well as Indian, Roman as well as Athenian, are of one and the same value, created by human beings for one and the same purpose, with equal power of reasoning," we should perhaps not try to turn a conversational utterance in a dialogue into a maxim. But the conclusion to be drawn from the *Dialogo delle Lingue* (the plural is notable) is that through contact with scientific philosophy the historical relativism of Humanism has become complete. The fact that the Volgare has been the spoken language of Italy for four or five centuries, Speroni argues, means that it is deeply rooted in Italian history and culture, and that its organic growth is assured. In our own time, Speroni continues, Latin and Greek are no longer living languages; they have long completed their natural cycles and have been artificially preserved only as media for learned thought. Although still indispensable for many purposes, they have laid upon the moderns the heavy burden of spending the best years of youth, which in Antiquity could be used for creative thinking, on the mastery of languages unsuited for our present needs. It is for this reason that the moderns have remained inferior to the ancients. But if some day they should succeed in making even philosophy and science speak a language that reaches everyone, perhaps "the modern age would give birth to those Platos and Aristotles which were produced by Antiquity."[27]

If this remarkable text were to be slightly changed by an adaptor less sentimentally attached to the Roman past than Speroni, as an Italian of the Renaissance, still was, would it not sound as if it had been directly taken from a manifesto of the seventeenth century? Only two years later (1549), Joachim

---

[27] *Dialogo*, ed. P. Villey (in the work quoted in note 28, below), 120, 128f., 137f. About the same time, Benedetto Varchi of Florence wrote that the Italian vernacular is a language which, when compared to Latin, "ought not to be considered a corruption but a new birth." See Eugenio Garin, *Italian Humanism: Philosophy and Civic Life in the Renaissance*, trans. P. Munz (New York, 1965), 163.

Du Bellay, without saying so, used a portion of Speroni's dialogue, slightly retouched, for his *Deffence et illustration de la langue françoyse*, the literary program of the French *Pléiade*. The bold claim of one of the speakers in Speroni's Italian dialogue—namely, that all languages are potentially of equal worth—is not only reiterated in the French work but used in it as the first link in the chain of reasoning. There is no use in extolling or depreciating any language, says Du Bellay in his introductory chapter, because all have the same origin in human nature and are developed by the same kind of human intellect; if we find some languages richer than others, it is because greater effort has been spent on them in the course of history. With the dictum "étant la fin et corruption de l'un le commencement et génération de l'autre," a new positive note—which heightens the already optimistic tone of the cycle image—has been added to Speroni's argument that, like other mortal things, languages must complete their cycles and die in order to make room for the new. And concerning the prophecy that the day will come when the attainments of the moderns will equal those of the ancients, the mid-sixteenth-century Frenchman makes the following observation: We may indeed be confident that we shall reach this goal, because great things have already been achieved by the French monarchy as well as in the "ars mécaniques," where the modern age has brought forth "printing, the tenth sister of the Muses, and gunpowder, . . . along with so many other inventions not made by the ancients—clear evidence that over the long course of centuries the human mind has by no means become as degenerate as some would have it." It is thus Du Bellay's conviction that "nature has certainly not become so sterile as to be unable to procreate men like Plato and Aristotle in our time."[28]

---

[28] "La Nature certes n'est point devenue si brehaigne, qu'elle n'enfentast de nostre tens des Platons et des Aristotes" (*La deffence et illustration de la langue francoyse*, ed. H. Chamard [Paris, 1904], 133f.). Du Bellay's dependence on Speroni was first proved by P. Villey, *Les sources italiennes de la 'Deffence . . .'* *. . . de Du Bellay* (Paris, 1908). This is not to underrate the native roots of the

Such was the state of the *Querelle* halfway between the Quattrocento and the seventeenth-century debate. Evidently, it was the triumph of modern inventions and discoveries—and before long it would also be the triumph of modern science—that provided the final leaven; but this leaven acted upon a concept of historical change created by Quattrocento Humanism that would remain vital far into the seventeenth century. The situation is clearly reflected in the work and educational programs of many French humanists who were connected with the *Pléiade* or carried the banner of that circle. They teach us that the new philosophy and science were eventually necessary for the final change in climate, but that the national vernacular literature and the newly established humanistic relationship to history and past culture were fundamental to it. Through the instrumentality of such "progressive" works as that of Le Roy, this outlook directly influenced the England of about 1600 and thus prepared the atmosphere in which so many books and ideas of the anticlassicistic wing of the humanistic Renaissance gained their relevance.

While this was happening in Bacon's England, a similar crucial development was taking place in Galileo's Italy. It must suffice here to mention those literary contests with Antiquity, presented in an objective fashion and decided largely in favor of the moderns, in such works as Tassoni's *Miscellaneous Thoughts* (1620) and Lancilotti's characteristically titled *The Present* [*L'hoggidi*], *or That the World Has not Become Worse nor More Wretched than in the Past* (1623). In these southern counterparts to books like Hakewill's, the new science joined

---

development of the French ideas; whoever reads the most recent studies on Budé (by Donald Kelley, Samuel Kinser, and August Buck) will be surprised how much of Du Bellay's basic outlook had already been growing in France two generations before him. But the fact remains, and is of basic significance, that the new program for the French language and poetry by Du Bellay was decisively influenced by Sperone Speroni of Padua, whose attitude in the *Dialogo delle Lingue* would in turn not be imaginable without the precursorship of the Italian Quattrocento, especially in Florence.

forces with many elements of the still highly respected legacy of the Italian Renaissance.[29]

Within this broader framework, seen as a phase of the protracted development of European Humanism as a whole, does not the prevailing view of the *Querelle* in England seem in need of considerable change?[30]

[29] Cf. esp. Benedetto Croce, *Storia dell'età barocca in Italia*, 2d ed. (Bari, 1946), 64ff., and Giacinto Margiotta, *Le origini italiane de la querelle des anciens et des modernes* (Rome, 1953), 151ff.

[30] A simultaneous historical perspective in welcome accord with some features of the present essay, and containing interesting complementary material, may be found in an article by August Buck, "Aus der Vorgeschichte der *Querelle des anciens et des modernes* in Mittelalter und Renaissance," published in *Bibliothèque d'Human. et Renaiss.* (September 1958) and reprinted in Buck's *Die humanistische Tradition in der Romania* (Bad Homburg v. d. H., 1968).

FIFTEEN

Machiavelli the Republican Citizen
and Author of *The Prince**

EW subjects humble and caution the student of history so much as the history of the interpretation of Machiavelli's works. It would be complacent to assume that our understanding has steadily been increasing. The fact is that there have been losses as well as gains; as some facets have caught the light, others have passed into shadow. To Florentines still close to Machiavelli, his life and work seemed to have two faces. According to Giovanni Battista Busini, an anti-Medici republican, writing about the middle of the sixteenth century, Machiavelli "was a most extraordinary lover of liberty," but he wrote *The Prince* to teach Duke Lorenzo de' Medici how to rob the rich of their wealth and ordinary citizens of their freedom, and later in his life he accepted a pension from the head of the Medici family, Pope Clement VII, for writing his *Florentine History*. So here, in the language of the partisan passions of Machiavelli's time, we already find the puzzle confronting his later readers: how could the faithful secretary of the Florentine republic, the author of the *Discourses on the First Ten Books of Titus Livy*, also be the author of *The Prince*? In the history of Machiavelli's influence, this question has not yet been definitively answered.[1]

---

* First published in 1961 in the *English Historical Review* 76, and now considerably revised. The text of this essay and the extensive commentary in the notes are two distinct entities. I have aimed at making the essay fully understandable without requiring readers to consult the documentary annotations.

[1] Some of the inquiries on which the answer proposed in the present essay relies were first formulated in 1956 in an article entitled "The *Principe* and the Puzzle of the Date of the *Discorsi*," *Bibliothèque d'Human. et Renaiss.* 18 (1956): 405–28. A number of objections were raised by G. Sasso in *Giornale Storico della Letteratura Italiana* 134 (1957): esp. 500ff., and 135 (1958): 251f., and by J. H. Whitfield, in *Italian Studies* 13 (1958): esp. 38ff. Whitfield, in the journal

I

Until the end of the seventeenth century, the view that Machiavelli had two faces was unfamiliar to most readers, overshadowed as it was by the overwhelming impression made by the teachings of *The Prince*—for the sixteenth and seventeenth centuries a diabolical guide for princes, prescribing lies, treachery, and cruelty. That a few great intellects like Bacon and Bodin made use of the *Discourses* did not change the fact that Machiavelli was usually known only as the author of *The Prince*. The awareness that he had also been a Florentine republican citizen became general, however, with the Enlightenment. This was a realization of lasting significance, even though the arguments on which the eighteenth century relied are to us unacceptable. It was now reasoned that since Machiavelli showed himself in the *Discourses* to be an adherent and great teacher of political freedom, and since he lost his position and was punished when the Medici rose to power, he cannot have wanted to help the selfsame Medici with the advice given in *The Prince*. The pamphlet must have been misunderstood by its readers. Either Machiavelli wished to expose the

---

Le Parole e le Idee I (1959): 81ff., subsequently indicated strong disagreement with Sasso's arguments, while seemingly assenting to the chronology proposed in my paper of 1956. The reader who consults those controversies will find that none of the doubts of my critics, even if accepted, would destroy the substance of the proposed theory. In restating it here on a much enlarged basis and adding a glimpse of its consequences for the appraisal of Machiavelli and his time, I have considered Sasso's and Whitfield's objections implicitly, making few direct or polemical references. I have avoided reliance on the studies of the genesis of the *Discourses* by Felix Gilbert ("The Composition and Structure of Machiavelli's *Discorsi*," *Journal of the History of Ideas* 14 [1953]: 136–56) and J. H. Hexter ("Seyssel, Machiavelli, and Polybius VI: The Mystery of the Missing Translation," *Studies in the Renaissance* 3 [1956]: 75–96), which were used in my article of 1956 as a starting point. Since Gilbert's and Hexter's theories have been shown by critics to be not fully demonstrable and partly incorrect, and since my own thesis is independent of the validity of their conclusions and can stand on its own, I will use Gilbert's discussion only to draw one inference from his observations (see below, p. 129), and will remain entirely aloof from Hexter's argument (see below, note 66).

striving for ruthlessness on the part of absolute princes, in order to warn the people against tyrants, or he wanted to tempt the Medici on to a career of crime, foreseeing that it would eventually recoil on the malefactors.

We encounter these arguments among the first heralds of the Enlightenment (Spinoza, for instance) in Rousseau, and into the late eighteenth century, when the first edition of Machiavelli's complete works, published in Florence in 1782, asserted that reinterpretations of the author of *The Prince* from the perspective of the republican *Discourses* had dislodged the notion of a diabolical counselor of despots.[2] Indeed, the author of the *Discourses* had for the first time come into his own. Not only was he celebrated as a virtuous republican by political doctrinaires, but one notes that in Montesquieu the politico-historical ideas of the *Discourses* were exerting a genuine influence. Its key ideas could be reconstructed from their echo in Montesquieu's *Considérations sur les causes de la grandeur des Romains*. There one finds all the tenets dear to the politico-historical philosopher of the *Discourses*, little modified by the eighteenth-century Frenchman. Montesquieu maintains, for example, that while states must be founded by great individuals, it is the energy of the people, demonstrated by their civic and military devotion to their commonwealth, that sustains them; that this energy is best generated in small states and only where no feudal inequality exists between a few great lords and a dependent mass; and that the Roman Republic flourished only so long as both patricians and plebeians maintained their status in the community, even at the cost of occasional civil strife, and so long as the expanse of the Empire did not become oppressive.[3]

---

[2] The passage quoted from Busini at the beginning of this essay is in his *Lettere a Benedetto Varchi* (Florence, 1861), 84–85. For eighteenth-century interpretations of Machiavelli, see A. Sorrentino, *Storia dell' antimachiavellismo europeo* (Naples, 1936), and Ernst Cassirer, *The Myth of the State* (New Haven, Conn., 1946), 119ff.

[3] E. Levi-Malvano, *Montesquieu et Machiavelli* (Paris, 1912), esp. 46, 51ff.,

It is strange to think that after so much study and absorption of the ideas developed in the *Discourses*, the historical conception of Machiavelli could once again be reduced primarily to that of the author of *The Prince*. But this is what happened at the end of the eighteenth century. Whereas to Montesquieu the "Machiavellian" teachings of *The Prince* had been offensive, opinion was reversed about 1800, when a more relativistic historical attitude developed which was prepared to base judgment on the specific circumstances of the past. Now *The Prince* began to seem the most intelligible, and even the most precious, part of Machiavelli's works. This happened first in Germany, where from Herder to Hegel, Fichte, and Ranke, it was argued that *The Prince* was written at a moment when only power and cool "reason of state" could save Italy from foreign domination; that the key to the work was the impassioned appeal in the last chapter for national liberation through a "new prince"; and that the pamphlet was not intended to lay down rules valid for all ages, but rather to prescribe a bitter medicine for the invigoration of a desperately sick body. *The Prince* was seen as an example for the Germany of the early nineteenth century, similarly divided into small states, invaded by foreigners, and waiting for a strong unifier. At least in Germany, then, Machiavelli again became the author of principally one book, *The Prince*, although now he was praised instead of cursed for the ruthless advice he offered to a savior prince.[4] In Italy, the other country still waiting for national unification after 1800, the same shift of perspective and emphasis occurred; only there it took a considerably longer time—until the triumph of the Risorgimento in the mid-nineteenth century—before the eighteenth-century incli-

63f., 74ff.; F. Meinecke, *Die Entstehung des Historismus* (Munich, 1936), esp. vol. 1, pp. 130ff., 148, 155f.

[4] A. Elkan, "Die Entdeckung Machiavellis in Deutschland zu Beginn des 19. Jahrhunderts," *Historische Zeitschrift* 119 (1919): 427–58; F. Meinecke, *Die Idee der Staatsräson* (Munich, 1924), 445ff., 460ff.; in the Engl. trans. by D. Scott, *Machiavellism: The Doctrine of Raison d'État* (New Haven, Conn., 1957), 357ff., 369ff.

nation to look upon the author of the *Discourses* as a protagonist of freedom began to dim.[5]

In England, Macaulay protested as early as 1827 against concentration of interest on *The Prince*. Yet his more balanced view of Machiavelli was almost as far removed from that of the eighteenth century as was the narrowing of focus to *The Prince* in contemporary Germany and Italy. Macaulay, too, no longer saw a secret meaning in the pamphlet. With the historical relativism of the new century he concluded that the "Machiavellian" traits of *The Prince* stemmed from the conditions of Machiavelli's age. The same traits, he pointed out, are present in the *Discourses*, with the one difference that there they are applied not merely to the ambitions of an individual ruler but also to the complex interests of a society. In neither work, says Macaulay, do the Machiavellian maxims, though serious flaws, prevent their author from revealing "so pure and warm a zeal for the public good" as is rarely found in political writings. That the goals changed—republican liberty in the *Discourses* and independence from foreigners in *The Prince*—need not astonish us, given the political situation in Machiavelli's time. "The fact seems to have been that Machiavelli, despairing of liberty for Florence, was inclined to support any government which might preserve her independence."[6]

The vindication of the national passion at the end of *The Prince* was the first great reinterpretation of Machiavelli after the Enlightenment, but Macaulay's penetrating essay also pointed to other major changes that were to take place in the remembrance of Machiavelli during the nineteenth and early twentieth centuries. In this period, the "Machiavellianism" of his teachings came to be better understood historically; it was soon to be traced in all his works, and his conception of politics and of the conflict between politics and ethical values was to be scrutinized without bias. But at the same

---

[5] C. Curcio, *Machiavelli nel Risorgimento* (Milan, 1953).

[6] Macaulay, *Machiavelli*, in vol. 5 of his *Works* (London, 1879), esp. 48, 75f.

time, memory of what had most strongly impressed eighteenth-century readers would almost fade: that the *Discourses* were profoundly different in spirit from *The Prince* and, as an epitome of the political ideals and experiences of the Italian city-state republics, represented a precious Renaissance legacy in their own right. As the nineteenth century advanced, the serious differences in political outlook between *The Prince* and the *Discourses* were increasingly denied. Given the nineteenth-century ideal of the nation-state, it seemed natural that Machiavelli, though brought up as, and remaining in sentiment, a Florentine republican, should see national independence and monarchical unification of Italy as the needs of the hour. Like the Italian republicans of the early nineteenth century, who accepted the final triumph of a unified Italian monarchy, or the *Nationalliberalen* in Germany, who submitted to Bismarck's solution for the German question, he was thought to have held that republican nostalgia had to give way to princely Realpolitik. Machiavelli thus appeared to be the father of a cool scientific relativism, and in this seemed to lie his greatness and modernity.

The final definition of Machiavelli's presumed relativism came from Friedrich Meinecke, who during the 1920s recast the historical appraisal of the Machiavellian method from the viewpoint of *Staatsräson*. According to Machiavelli, Meinecke argued, all states are founded by the *virtù* of some great lonely individual, whereas the *virtù* of citizens develops within the framework of institutions created by the original lawgiver and after him slowly degenerates until a new lawgiver begins a fresh cycle. Machiavelli, therefore, must have looked upon the principate as a recurrent and indispensable phase in the life of states, and his descriptions of the cycle of forms of government in the *Discourses* and of the task of the *principe nuovo* in the pamphlet neatly interlock. "Though a republican by ideal and inclination," Machiavelli was "an adherent of monarchy by reason and resignation," and "consequently the contrast between the monarchical attitude of *The Prince* and the republican inclination of the *Discourses* is specious [*ist nur scheinbar*]."

Meinecke remarked that "only later centuries have evaluated the differences between forms of government as a quarrel between basic truths, almost between Weltanschauungen."[7] In Gerhard Ritter's continuation and modification of Meinecke's views, we are told still more pointedly that the once fashionable confrontation "between the [republican] *Discourses* and the 'absolutistic' *Prince* was due to a wrong question." Ritter maintains that "it is the universally accepted result of all modern Machiavelli research that the *Discourses* and *The Prince* derive from a single, uniform conception." So little did Machiavelli's crucial ideas change during his lifetime, Ritter claims, "that one need not hesitate to elucidate the meaning of the *Discourses* through *The Prince* and vice versa."[8]

The sincerity of Machiavelli's call in the epilogue of *The Prince* for someone to deliver Italy from foreign domination has remained a matter of debate until today. But most of those who have questioned the genuineness of his national passion, placed as it is in his guidebook for princes among the odd company of the coldest, most "Machiavellian" of his teachings, have been all the more inclined to believe in his personal disengagement and relativism. They have increasingly aimed to fuse the teachings in his works into a harmonious, static system. As interpreted in the best available, internationally known, synthesis of Machiavelli's ideas in the mid-twentieth century, the French *Machiavel* by A. Renaudet, Machiavelli worked alternately as *un théoricien de la République* and *un théoricien de la Monarchie*, advancing easily from his work on the

[7] Meinecke, *Idee*, 40f., 54 (Engl. trans., 32f., 43); and his "Einführung" to *Machiavelli: Der Fürst und kleinere Schriften. Übersetzt von E. Merian-Genast*, Klassiker der Politik, vol. 8 (Berlin, 1923), 14f., 31f.

[8] G. Ritter, *Die Dämonie der Macht*, 6th ed. (Munich, 1948), 186 (not in the Engl. trans., *The Corrupting Influence of Power* [Hadleigh, 1952]); "Machiavelli und der Ursprung des modernen Nationalismus," in Ritter's *Vom sittlichen Problem der Macht* (Bern, 1948), 40ff., esp., 44, 55f. ("Machiavelli's basic ideas," Ritter says on p. 44, "hardly changed after they were first penned in 1512/13.") An authoritative, widely consulted summary, composed, like a mosaic, of pieces taken indiscriminately from all of Machiavelli's writings, is Francesco Ercole's *La politica di Machiavelli* (Rome, 1926).

Discourses to that on *The Prince* and back again to the *Discourses*; for the essential feature of his work was the creation of a *méthode strictement positive*, one equally applicable to both parts of his *science de la politique*.[9] In a word, ever since the middle of the nineteenth century it has been the consensus of the majority of students that the choice between republican liberty and principate, the fierce struggle which was at the center of Florentine and Italian history in Machiavelli's lifetime, was not a fundamental inspiration for—a shaping force of—Machiavelli's thought and must remain of secondary importance in its interpretation. Indeed, with few exceptions, for a century and more, the study of Machiavelli's works has been rather narrowly directed to his views on the nature of political action, on the autonomy of politics, and on its conflicts with morality. As late as the middle of the twentieth century, a leading Italian literary historian, Luigi Russo, could still aver, in one of the most influential accounts of Machiavelli's ideas, that "Machiavelli was interested not in monarchy or republic, in liberty or authority, but merely in the technique of politics; he wants to be and is always the scientist . . . of the art of government [*lo scienziato . . . dell' arte di governo*]. . . . Liberty or authority, republic or principate are the *subject*, but not, in the Kantian sense, the *form* of Machiavelli's thinking."[10]

---

[9] A. Renaudet, *Machiavel* (1942; rev. ed. Paris, 1955), 117f.; cf. also 119ff., 218f., 289ff. A number of other writers have also tried to give a more proportionate share to the *Discourses*; but, with the exception of the Swiss group referred to in note 21 below, and G. Sasso (see note 25, below), this has in practice only meant—as it did for Renaudet—that Machiavelli's "Machiavellianism" should be studied in the *Discourses* as well as in *The Prince*. A striking English example is Harold J. Laski, "Machiavelli and the Present Time," in *The Danger of Obedience and Other Essays* (New York, 1930), 238–63.

[10] L. Russo, *Machiavelli*, 3d ed. (Bari, 1949), 214. In the background of all Italian interpretations of this type is Benedetto Croce's influential thesis, propounded since the 1920s, that Machiavelli had discovered "the necessity and autonomy of politics, of politics which are beyond good and evil." Cf. A. P. D'Entrèves' introduction (pp. xiif.) to Chabod's *Machiavelli and the Renaissance*, quoted below, note 22.

At this point the impression becomes overwhelming that modern efforts to overcome eighteenth-century republican partisanship by cool, objective appraisal have in some respects exchanged one blind spot for another. When, after so many attempts to reconstruct the allegedly harmonious relationship between Machiavelli's two major political works, we return to a reading of the *Discourses*, we still find ourselves facing the undisguised values of a republican citizen, who is just as far from indifferent to the political and historical role of freedom as eighteenth-century readers had believed him to be. Although it is true that the extension of the rules and maxims of *The Prince* to the life of republics is one of the features of the *Discourses*, it is a different world of values to which the teaching of "Machiavellianism" is here applied—a world that often looks as if it had been conceived by another author.

One could point to many examples of this profound disparity, and although this is not the place for a systematic comparison, a number of observations may easily be made. For instance, in the third book of the *Discourses*, we find in chapters 41–42 a direct reference to the eighteenth chapter of *The Prince*, where the *principe nuovo*, who must know human nature and not expect anyone to keep faith, is himself taught to be unfaithful, to disguise his true character, and to master feigning and dissembling. But in the third book of the *Discourses* (chapter 42) the subject discussed under the chapter heading "Promises exacted by force should not be kept" is the behavior of the Roman consul Spurius Posthumius, who when his troops were defeated at the Caudine Forks showed himself ready to accept any condition in order to save the Roman army, but afterwards persuaded the senate to break faith and send him, as the one responsible for the repudiation of the treaty, back to the enemy in chains. The author of the *Discourses* notes that this is a model case worthy of remembrance by every citizen, because when the commonweal is at stake "no consideration of justice or injustice, of humanity or cruelty, of what brings praise or infamy should be allowed to prevail, but putting every other thought aside, that action should

be taken which might save the *patria* and maintain her liberty."
Nothing could be more different in the two works than the
motivation for breaking promises.

As for the non-"Machiavellian" context, the author of the
Discourses boldly upholds the claim, in opposition to some of
his favorite ancient writers, that a multitude of citizens, disci-
plined by good laws, has better judgment than a prince.[11] He
thinks that republics are more reliable and grateful than
princes and that the major forward strides of nations have been
made in republics, as in Athens and Rome after the expulsion
of their kings. Princes, in the long run, can only prolong the
lives of stagnant societies.[12] Even when decadence has become
advanced, as it has in his own time, the principate will not
bring salvation, because heredity on the throne does not make
available the variety of talents required in different emergen-
cies, nor does it produce the long succession of outstanding
men needed to reform a degenerate people.[13] Garrett Mattingly once suggested, not without reason, that instead of
closing our eyes to the profound difference between such convictions and the counsel for a despotic ruler in *The Prince*, it
would be better to return to the eighteenth-century suspicion

[11] *Disc.* I 58. Here, and throughout this essay, quotations in English from
the *Discourses* follow as far as possible the translation by Leslie J. Walker, *The
Discourses of Niccolò Machiavelli*, with an introduction and notes by the trans-
lator, 2 vols. (London and New Haven, 1950). I have changed Walker's translation wherever it seemed necessary for an exact understanding of Machiavelli's thought or terminology. I am indebted also to Walker's immensely
helpful commentary.

[12] *Disc.* I 29, I 58, I 59, II 2. Cf. also III 9: "A republic has more vitality and
enjoys good fortune for a longer time than a principate because, owing to the
diversity found amongst its citizens, it is better able than a prince to adapt
itself to varying circumstances."

[13] *Disc.* I 11, I 20, III 9. As early as 150 years ago, a well-known German
historian assembled such a list of Machiavelli's instinctive republican reactions, different from my list in details but quite convincing in its results:
G. G. Gervinus in his *Geschichte der Florentinischen Historiographie bis zum 16.
Jahrhundert, mit Erläuterungen über den sittlichen, bürgerlichen und schriftsteller-
ischen Charakter des Machiavell* (Heidelberg, 1833), 133ff.

that some of the prescriptions in *The Prince* were not meant seriously but were intended to satirize the life of princes.[14]

It seems to me that clearly definable differences can be found in the very area which is most basic to the thesis that a harmony exists between *The Prince* and the *Discourses*. The latter is a complex work, but since the history of early republican Rome serves as its central ideal, in accordance with Livy, it has one major, unifying theme and standard: the moral health and political vigor of a free nation as the ultimate sources of power. This standard is so basic to the work that the perspective on the period of the Roman kings as well as that on Caesar and the emperors is determined at all crucial points by the needs of republican freedom. Yet the practical goal of the book—resuscitation of the wisdom of ancient politics for use in the present—is so broadly defined in the preface that (according to the author) everyone, kings as well as republican leaders, generals as well as individual citizens, should be able to find ancient examples in it. The wisdom thus gained from Antiquity stimulates Machiavelli to offer special advice to all types of political leaders, occasionally in evident conflict with the republican foundation of his work. In the famous chapter on conspiracies (*Discourses* III 6), for example, we are told how conspirators must behave in order to succeed, as well as how princes and other rulers must behave in order to suppress them. At several points the author says that if the reformer of a state, in spite of all he has just read about the enduring need in both monarchies and republics for loyal obedience to institutions and laws, nevertheless wishes to establish autocratic and tyrannical rule, he must act in ways which, as here described, are largely identical with those of the pamphlet on the prince. In the *Discourses*, however, these are digressions, sometimes characterized as such, sometimes splitting up a continuous discussion.[15]

---

[14] G. Mattingly, "Machiavelli's *Prince*: Political Science or Political Satire?" *The American Scholar* 27 (1958): 489ff.

[15] This is usually not sufficiently realized but can be illustrated by the fol-

We can call them digressions because the thrust of the argument is that the founder or restorer of a state will become a political savior only if he invigorates the institutions and laws that are the matrix of a people's political health and ethos. Thus the *Discourses* shows constant concern to prevent the rule

---

lowing two examples, which will be useful later on in our inquiry into other aspects of the *Discourses*.

Disc. I 16 and I 17 deal with the difficulties that must be overcome wherever a republican regime has replaced a former monarchy; this theme runs through both chapters, starting with a reference to the regicide Brutus, who condemned his own sons to death when they became traitors to the young republic. Within this discussion on "the sons of Brutus," we find an excursus (from the words "E chi prende a governare una moltitudine o per via di libertà or per via di principato") which tells us that neither a new republic nor a new *principato* can endure unless all political foes are destroyed at the beginning. Or rather, this ruthless precept, most similar to those given in the eighth chapter of *The Prince*, is actually applied (after the initial statement that every new state ought to heed it, regardless whether it is a *principato* or a republic) only to the policy of a new prince, and it has nothing whatever to do with the theme with which chapter I 16 begins: the founding of a *republic*. This is noted by the author himself, who remarks: "and although this argument does not fit the one discussed before, because we are now going to talk about a prince, whereas we had been talking about a republic [*e benché questo discorso sia disforme dal soprascritto, parlando qui d'uno principe e quivi d'una republica*], nevertheless I will say a few words about it, so as not to be compelled to return once more to this matter." After the end of the "Machiavellian" intermezzo, the subject of "the sons of Brutus" is taken up again (from the words "Sendo pertanto il popolo romano ancora . . .") and carried to completion.

As for the origin of this excursus, one might recall a somewhat obscure note in the eighth chapter of *The Prince* that bears a great similarity to chapter 16 of *Disc.* I. In *The Prince*, Machiavelli says that the rise of a private citizen to the position of a prince could be discussed with more particulars "in a context where one dealt with republics" (*dove si trattassi delle republiche*). This seems to suggest that Machiavelli had in his desk at that time materials or notes which did not fit the framework of *The Prince* and were put aside for possible later use in connection with republics. They were eventually used in the sixteenth (perhaps also in the twenty-sixth) chapter of *Disc.* I, even though the treatment of the problem in the *Discourses* was so profoundly different that the integration did not succeed very well.

In *Disc.* I 25–27—our second example—there is a related discussion, based on the following argument: Whoever wishes in a republic (*in uno vivere politico*) to introduce *uno vivere nuovo e libero*, whether in a republican or monar-

of a reformer or "new prince" from developing into absolutism and tyranny. Whereas the founders of states with good
institutions are praiseworthy (we read in *Discourses* I, chapters
9 and 10), those of tyrannies are reprehensible: this applies in
Roman history to Caesar, because he strove, and paved the
way, for absolute power. The unique greatness of Romulus,
on the other hand, rests on the fact that in founding the Roman state he reserved for himself only the command of the
army and the right to convoke the senate. As a consequence,
since Rome's constitution (*ordini*) under her kings was to all
intents and purposes a *vivere civile e libero* and in no respect an
assoluto e tirannico regime, there was no need after the expulsion of her hereditary kings for any change but the replacement of the kings by annual consuls. By the same criterion,
the author of the *Discourses* sees in the French monarchy the
happiest hereditary kingdom of his time, because its kings (he
believes) have absolute power only in military and financial
matters and are otherwise pledged to observe the laws of the
state. The great ability of the French monarchy to regenerate
its internal strength is attributed to the right of the Parle-
ments, especially the Parlement of Paris, not only to take action against princes but even to condemn the king. In principates as well as in republics it is "equally essential to be
regulated by laws. For a prince who knows no other control
than his own will is like a madman. . . ." Machiavelli warns:
"Princes should learn that they begin to lose their state the

---

chical form (*o per via di republica o di regno*; for the terminology used here, cf.
note 16, below), should preserve as many of the former institutions and traditions as possible. In chapter 26, this discussion is for a while followed by
one which considers the exact opposite; namely, that a "new prince" who
does not want to keep within the legal limits of a republic or monarchy, "but
wants to set up an absolute power, also called tyranny by writers" (*vuole fare
una potestà assoluta, la quale dagli autori è chiamata tirannide*), should act to the
contrary. That is, he should change everything in the state, should tolerate
only new creatures dependent on himself, and should shrink from no cruelty,
only from indecision and compromise. This alternative discussion is entirely
out of tune with the often-repeated condemnation in the *Discourses* of *potestà
assoluta*; cf. the examples in notes 16 and 17, below.

moment they begin to break the law." According to the *Art of War*, written soon after the completion of the *Discourses*, well-constituted monarchies "do not grant absolute rule to their kings except in the command of the army."[16]

One way to take the measure of *The Prince* is to determine whether a similar concern appears in the advice given to the *principe nuovo*. Some students have contended that it does; after all, *The Prince*, too, refers to Romulus as a noble example, considers the establishment of *nuovi ordini* as a principal task of the new ruler, and praises the role of the Parlement in the French monarchy.[17] But, although *The Prince* does all of

[16] *Disc.* I 16, I 58, III 1, III 5; *Art of War*, in *Tutte le Opere*, ed. Mazzoni e Casella, 272. Machiavelli's constitutional terminology, to which little attention is usually paid, still awaits integral examination. H. De Vries' "Essai sur la terminologie constitutionelle chez Machiavel ('Il Principe')" (diss., University of Amsterdam, 1957), is a mere beginning, and only for *The Prince*; but one may consider it certain that, as a rule (Machiavelli is never wholly consistent), *il vivere politico*—almost identical with *una republica*—is what we call a republic, while *il vivere libero, il vivere civile*, and *la vita civile* may be found in monarchies as well as republics. If these terms apply to *un regno*, they mean that laws and institutions exist which prevent the ruler from arrogating *una potestà assoluta or tirannide*. Cf. the passages from *Disc.* I 25, quoted in the preceding note, as well as *Disc.* I 26 (if a *principe* in *una città* "non si volga o per via di regno o di republica alla vita civile"); I 18 (". . . E perché il riordinare una città al vivere politico presuppone uno uomo buono"); I 2 ("Perché Romolo e tutti gli altri Re fecero molte e buone leggi, conformi ancora al vivere libero; ma perché il fine loro fu fondare un regno e non una republica, quando quella città rimase libera vi mancavano molte cose che era necessario ordinare in favore della libertà . . ."); I 9 (under the kings, on the other hand, "gli ordini" of Rome—as distinct from single laws—had been "più conformi a uno vivere civile e libero che ad uno assoluto e tirannico," so that "quando Roma divenne libera, . . . non fu innovato alcun ordine dello antico, se non che in luogo d'uno Re perpetuo fossero due Consoli annuali"); I 55 (". . . quelle republiche dove si è mantenuto il vivere politico ed incorrotto, non sopportono che alcuno loro cittadino né sia né viva a uso di gentiluomo").

[17] This is what J. H. Whitfield maintains in his papers "On Machiavelli's use of *Ordini*," *Italian Studies* 10 (1955): 33–39, and "Machiavelli e il problema del *Principe*," in *I Problemi della Pedagogia* 4, no. 1 (1958). The same identification is found in the chapter on Machiavelli in R. von Albertini's *Das Florentinische Staatsbewusstsein im Übergang von der Republik zum Prinzipat* (Bern, 1955), where it is said, confusingly, that *The Prince* offers the hope that a

this, what in practice are these *ordini* for which Romulus—along with Moses, Cyrus, and Theseus—is made to serve as a patron saint? The *principe nuovo* is asked to imitate "the new institutions and forms of government which men [who like those legendary heroes rose to princely power through their *virtù*] have been forced to introduce in order to establish and secure their regimes."[18] Subsequently, the nature of the *ordini* that give "security" is explained by more mundane examples. Hiero, the tyrant of Syracuse, first dissolved the old citizen army and assembled new troops, then changed the alliances of the city and made everything in the state dependent on himself. Other model founders of new *ordini* are Francesco Sforza, the *condottiere* who destroyed the republic in Milan and made himself duke; Cesare Borgia; and a modern counterpart to the great malefactor Agathocles of Sicily, the tyrant Oliverotto da Fermo, who rose to power by murdering the leading citizens after inviting them to a banquet. "When in this fashion all had died who could offend him, Oliverotto da Fermo strengthened his position with *nuovi ordini civili e militari*," with the result that within a year he had secured his regime.[19] One wonders how anyone can regard these *nuovi ordini civili* for the rule of tyrants as the counterparts in spirit to the *ordini* of the nascent Roman commonwealth for which Romulus is praised in the *Discourses*.

The inclusion of a chapter on the *principatus civilis* in *The Prince* (ch. IX) does not mean that we have at last found a parallel here to Romulus' *vivere civile e libero*, praised in the *Discourses*. In *The Prince*, the *principatus civilis* refers to one-man rule established with the consent of the citizens of a former republic, and the chapter discusses not the harmfulness of absolute rule but the suitable moment for its introduction. There

---

riordinatore will establish a *vivere politico* and *libero* through "restoration of the *ordini antichi*," whereas the *Discourses* provides a "theoretische Fundierung" for this policy (p. 69f.).

[18] ". . . da' nuovi ordini e modi che sono forzati introdurre per fondare lo stato loro e la loro securtà" (*The Prince*, ch. VI).

[19] Ibid., chs. VI–VIII.

will be trouble, we read, when a prince in such an environment wants to advance from an *ordine civile* to *autorità assoluta* and, in order to strengthen his control, tries to do so at a time when the political situation is still in flux, instead of waiting for a moment when the personal interest of every citizen makes him dependent on the new regime. And what about the references to the Parlement of Paris? The *Discourses* praises the right of the Parlement to pass judgment even on the king. *The Prince*, too, praises the existence of "countless good ordinances" in the kingdom of France, first among them the great authority of the Parlement of Paris. But the Parlement promotes *libertà e sicurità* not for the subjects but for the king. In any kingdom or principate, the great nobles must be restrained, the people befriended, and each balanced against the other. Thus the wise lawgiver of France established the Parlement as a judge and buffer, "to relieve the king of the dissatisfaction he might incur among the nobles by favoring the people, and among the people by favoring the nobles." This was the most prudent measure ever devised, and it teaches the lesson "that princes should let the carrying out of unpopular duties devolve upon others and bestow favors themselves."[20]

The closer the comparison of the two works, the more absurd seems the idea that they should be two harmonious halves of one and the same political philosophy, applicable under different conditions.[21] The author of *The Prince* does not

---

[20] *Disc.* III 1; *The Prince*, ch. XIX.

[21] A growing number of scholars apparently doubt this alleged harmony. In addition to Garrett Mattingly (see above, note 14), one may refer to J. H. Hexter, whose paper "*Il principe* and *lo stato*," *Studies in the Renaissance* 4 (1957): esp. 133f., has drawn attention to an unnoticed difference in language and terminology between the two works: Whereas the conception of the state as "a political body transcending the individuals who compose it" is central to the *Discourses*, it does not exist in *The Prince*; terms that are frequent in the *Discourses*, such as *il vivere civile* or *politico*, or *il bene commune*, have no equivalent in *The Prince*. Again, Ernst Cassirer, in his *The Myth of the State*, pp. 145–48, has spoken of a "bewildering" contrast in the political attitude of the two works; but Cassirer's comment—that in Machiavelli's opinion a chance for republican life had existed only in Antiquity and did not exist in his own time—is the old, perilous oversimplification of a much more complicated sit

favor restrictions on a ruler in the name of liberty; he does not think of the people as an active force—the central concern of the author of the *Discourses* when leadership is the issue. So the puzzle of the relationship between Machiavelli's two works remains, and unless we are prepared to return to the eighteenth-century suspicion that *The Prince* has a hidden meaning which differs from what it appears to say, there is only one alternative: in the time which elapsed between the creation of these two profoundly divergent views of the political world, something in the author's thinking must have changed. It appears, therefore, that the process must again be reversed: instead of trying to harmonize Machiavelli's thought, we need to confront the obvious differences within it and explore whether they may not after all be the consequence of a change of mind.

II

One school of thought in present Machiavelli scholarship has already taken the next logical step—at least to an extent. In

---

uation. Among Italian writers, a helpful protest against the traditional tendency to harmonize the views of the *Discourses* and *The Prince* has come (besides from Chabod and his school, about whom we shall have more to say presently) from Carmelo Caristia: cf. his strongly polemical *Il pensiero politico di Niccolò Machiavelli*, 2d ed. (Naples, 1951), 57ff. Similar protests have come from a group of Swiss scholars, who gave added significance to the noted difference by proposing that the true and lasting convictions of the Florentine citizen Machiavelli must be sought in the republican *Discourses*, his "life-work," whereas *The Prince* was "written for a special occasion" (*Gelegenheitsschriftchen*) and was the "fruit of a few summer weeks": cf. W. Kaegi, *Historische Meditationen* (Zurich, 1942), vol. 1, pp. 107–109 (a mere episode thrown in between the writing of the *Discourses*); and L. v. Muralt, *Machiavellis Staatsgedanke* (Basel, 1945), 103f., 162. Essentially the same argument reappears in A. Renaudet's *Machiavel* (see note 9, above), where we read (pp. 175f.) that whereas "les *Discours* . . . expriment la pensée qu'il a véritablement soutenu jusqu'à la mort, . . . le *Prince* . . . ne représente que l'occupation de quelques mois, consacrés à l'étude d'une hypothèse illusoire." The contrast thus suggested does not stand the test, as we shall soon see: the ideas of *The Prince* did have an incubation period of many years, and they were not preceded by any of the republican considerations found in the *Discourses*.

Italy, where scholars have always been more inclined than in other countries to pay attention to the biographical aspects of Machiavelli's relationship to his Italian and Florentine environment, Federico Chabod wrote as early as 1926: "At one time the Machiavelli of *The Prince* was placed in grotesque opposition to the Machiavelli of the *Discourses*. Today . . . critics are too often led to minimize the differences that arise from his varying emotional outlook." We must not forget, Chabod insists, that "Machiavelli was not an abstract theoretician who developed, first in one sense, then in another, a concept that had been completely assimilated from the start; he was a politician and a man of passion, who gradually unfolded and defined his ideas. . . ."[22]

The heart of Chabod's thesis and that of the large Italian school under his influence is that the *Discourses* is a biographical document—like a diary, reflecting successive changes in a writer's outlook and evaluations. In the first half of the first book, Chabod argues, we encounter a strong republican confidence, the conviction that a vigorous state is the product of the collective action of its citizens; here we find the theory that civil strife between patricians and plebeians had a healthy effect on ancient Rome, evidence that all classes were free and held their own in the Roman state. When we read on, however, we encounter some chapters (I 16–18 and 26–27) in which concern for the people, "the animating spirit" of the previous chapters, is replaced by concern for the personal success of the prince. We now read (these passages have already been cited[23]) that if a "new prince" does not wish to found a legally ordered state but aspires instead to the kind of *potestà assoluta* called "tyranny," he must change every institution and authority in his new state; he must make the rich, poor, and the poor, rich, and shrink from no cruelty, because a new tyrant can hope for survival only when every subject has be-

[22] F. Chabod, *Machiavelli and the Renaissance* (London, 1958), 41, 117; Chabod, *Del 'Principe' di Niccolò Machiavelli*, Biblioteca della *Nuova Rivista Storica*, no. 8 (Milan, 1926), 8f., 67.

[23] Above, p. 113, note 15.

come his creature through patronage or fear. Chapters like these, in Chabod's eyes, are not digressions but suggest that in the course of writing, the republican confidence of the preceding chapters gave way to the mood in which *The Prince* was composed.

It is possible to identify the cause of this transformation, Chabod thought. After discussing Rome's foundation and the rise and fall of its civic energies, Machiavelli, in the seventeenth and eighteenth chapters of *Discourses* I, recalls the conditions of his own day, stating that in a phase in which civic virtue was totally corrupted, it would be very difficult, perhaps impossible, to "maintain or restore" a republic. Whoever wants to rebuild the state in such a phase "must of necessity resort to extraordinary methods, such as the use of force and an appeal to arms; before he can achieve anything, he must become a prince in the state." Thus, Chabod concludes, "we have *The Prince*." In other words, at this point Machiavelli must have interrupted his work on the *Discourses* and begun to write *The Prince*, until finally frustrated and disillusioned, he returned to the *Discourses*, completing it in accordance with the original character of the work.[24]

One might object to this ingenious construction by pointing out that in chapter eighteen, Machiavelli eventually reaches the conclusion that for many reasons, such a princely position would be extremely difficult, perhaps even impossible, to establish; but a book of Chabod's school, by Gennaro Sasso, has skillfully shown that the theory can be adapted to this objection: Although the skepticism of the eighteenth chapter is not in accord with the standpoint of *The Prince*, Sasso argues, it shows the writer in an immediately preceding phase; it gives us a glimpse of the doubt and despair that caused Machiavelli to excogitate the ruthless means by which

---

[24] "The Republic yielded place to the Principate; . . . the vision of past glory—a vision clouded by nostalgic regret—was replaced by the theoretical prospect of Italy's political recovery" (Chabod, *Machiavelli and the Renaissance*, 21 and 36–41; *Del 'Principe,'* 4–9).

one who is unafraid to commit crimes may achieve what seems virtually impossible.[25]

Do these speculations offer more than a barely conceivable possibility? Their wide acceptance by a large number of Italian students[26] and ever-broadening support in other countries[27] are due, it would seem, to several causes. Above all, this is the first clear acknowledgment of the great difference in spirit between Machiavelli's two works and the first attempt to trace its origin to a change in his experiences and evaluations. This method was bound to appeal to those who feared that we were losing touch with a man of politics whose values and passions changed, and who could not close their eyes to the shrill dissonances that set the two treatises apart.

Furthermore, the argument seemed to be confirmed by the text itself. At the beginning of the second chapter of *The Prince*, the author notes that he intends to omit the discussion of republics in this work "because on another occasion I have reasoned about them at length" (. . . *perchè altra volta ne ragionai a lungo*). We do not know of any work of Machiavelli's but the *Discourses* of which it could be said that he had "reasoned about republics at length";[28] and this characterization is

[25] G. Sasso, *Niccolò Machiavelli: Storia del suo pensiero politico* (Naples, 1958), 213ff., 357ff., esp. 218f.

[26] Three representative examples: V. Branca, "Rileggendo il *Principe* e i *Discorsi*," *La Nuova Italia* 8 (1937): 107f.; G. Prezzolini, *Machiavelli Anticristo* (Rome, 1954), 171; R. Ridolfi, *Vita di Niccolò Machiavelli* (Rome, 1954), 223ff., 254.

[27] According to Felix Gilbert's judgment in *Renaissance News* 12 (1959): 95, "it will be very difficult to disprove the validity of the analysis by which Sasso shows the close connection of the first eighteen chapters of the *Discorsi* with the *Prince*."

[28] Therefore, the only way to escape from the conclusions which follow is to hypothesize that the reference to "altra volta" was aimed at a lost work, of which no other trace or reference has survived. This is the thesis suggested, though hesitantly, by Felix Gilbert in 1953, "Composition and Structure of Machiavelli's *Discorsi*" (see note 1 above), 150ff. But the conjecture, daring under any circumstances, could qualify for consideration only if we had information that before or during 1513, Machiavelli was indeed occupied with the problems discussed in *Disc.* 1 1–18. However, the opposite is the case: we

particularly apt for the introductory part of the *Discourses*, where types of republics are distinguished according to their origins, and Roman liberty is traced from the times of the Roman kings. On the other hand, since later parts of the *Discourses* (the second and third books) contain three or four cross references to *The Prince*,[29] the situation, at first glance at least, seems eminently clear: the second and third books followed the composition of *The Prince*, but the first book, or at least its initial portion, must have preceded it, because it is referred to in *The Prince*'s second chapter. And since Chabod's awareness of the contemporary political scene allowed him to state that *The Prince* was written between the autumn of 1513 and early 1514, even though it was not dedicated to Lorenzo di Piero de' Medici before 1515–1516, we may feel compelled to conclude that Machiavelli wrote a substantial section of the first book of the *Discourses* by the summer of 1513, composed *The Prince* during the autumn and possibly the following winter, and soon afterwards—or a few years later—continued the *Discourses*, eventually dedicating them to Cosimo Rucellai, who died in 1519.

Most adherents of this theory have been guided not only by such biographical arguments but also by a more general historical consideration. The presumed development of Machiavelli appeared to crown a still widely accepted notion of the political course of Renaissance Italy. By Machiavelli's time, the argument runs, the city-state republic born of the Italian commune had become hopelessly outdated, owing to the efficiency of princely absolutism. It is a testimony to Machiavelli's perspicacity, and it was only natural that his way should

---

can establish with assurance that Machiavelli did not occupy himself with those problems before 1513; see below, p. 137. Furthermore, our argument against the possibility that Machiavelli referred in 1513, in *The Prince*, to an unpublished fragment of the text of the *Discourses* (p. 135) will implicitly also disprove the assumption that Machiavelli referred to the draft of a hypothetical work, unpublished and later lost.

[29] *Disc.* II 1, II 20 (undoubtedly referring to *The Prince*, chs. XII and XIII, not to the *Art of War*), *Disc.* III 19, III 42.

lead him from humanistic admiration of the Roman Republic to the insight that under the conditions of his own age, the absolutism of princes was a rational political expediency and would perhaps result in national unification. Even though Machiavelli's hope that a "new prince" would quickly restore Italy's national strength was utopian on the level of practical politics, Chabod argued, the notion that a "vigorous unitarian policy" would come from a government with "absolute supremacy" represented the quintessence of the political experience of Renaissance Italy. It was "unique good fortune" that Machiavelli's pamphlet, written at the time when Renaissance Italy suffered its tragic breakdown, "epitomized" the lessons of the Italian political catastrophe and handed them down to the age of absolutism.[30]

Here we see not only the ultimate reason for the long unchallenged dominance of the approach ushered in by Chabod's essay of 1926, but also its vulnerable point: the moment we doubt the premise that to be great, a political thinker in Renaissance Italy had to change his preference from the city-state republic to the efficient absolutism of the modern monarchy, we also have reason to doubt a reconstruction of Machiavelli's development that is tied a priori to this subjective view of the Italian Renaissance. But there is still another reason for doubt. Could Machiavelli really have had in mind the tyrannical solution offered in *The Prince* when he considered in chapter eighteen of *Discourses* I how the political health of a republic might be restored by a reformer in a time of decadence? It is argued there, to be sure, that when civic spirit has been corrupted, regeneration demands force and violence. A potential reformer, before anything else, would thus have to make himself a *principe* in his republic. Yet the aim of the chapter is definitely not to present the usurper prince as a sometimes necessary remedy in the history of a republic. The author of chapter eighteen of *Discourses* I is too firmly convinced that anyone ready to become an autocratic ruler in a

---

[30] Chabod, *Machiavelli and the Renaissance*, 41, 98ff., 104f., 121ff.

time of crisis will not act for the good of the people. "Reorganization of the constitutional life of a republic," he says, "presupposes a good man, and recourse to violence in order to make oneself prince in a republic presupposes a bad man. Hence, a good man will rarely be found who is willing, even with a good end in view, to use evil means to make himself prince, or a wicked man who is willing to act benevolently once he has become a prince." This is, of course, never a consideration in *The Prince*, where the *principe nuovo* is taught the art of "using the beast" in man whenever he so wishes.[31]

Moreover, in chapter eighteen of *Discourses* I, the argument is headed in an entirely different direction from that of replacing a republic by a *principe nuovo*, despite the fact that in both cases Machiavelli advocates recourse to force by the trans-

---

[31] ". . . è necessario venire allo straordinario, come è alla violenza ed all'armi, *e diventare innanzi a ogni cosa principe di quella città e poterne disporre a suo modo* [my emphasis]. E perché il riordinare una città al vivere politico presuppone uno uomo buono, e il diventare per violenza principe di una repubblica presuppone uno uomo cattivo, per questo si troverrà che radissime volte accaggia che uno buono, per vie cattive, ancora che il fine suo fusse buono, voglia diventare principe; e che uno reo, divenuto principe, voglia operare bene" (*Disc.* I 18). As for the striking formulation (in I 18) that the reformer must "diventare innanzi a ogni cosa principe" in his "città," in order to be able to "poterne disporre a suo modo," it would be quite erroneous to interpret this as meaning that he must destroy the republic and found a *principato*. It only means that he must make himself a dictator by force, and Machiavelli's problem is precisely whether a dictator who has used force will ever be ready to become a reformer of constitutional life instead of an absolute prince. That this is the correct interpretation is clear from the use of "principe" in *Disc.* I 26, where it is argued that anyone who becomes a "principe d'una città o d'uno stato" can follow three different paths: he can maintain "quel principato" as a "nuovo principe" by reversing every particle of the former order of the state, but he can also turn, either "per via di regno" or "per via di repubblica," "alla vita civile." Here the term *principe* is applied to someone who might employ his power for establishing constitutional government in the form of a legally limited monarchy (*regno*) or even a "republica." This use of the term must be borne in mind in any explanation of what Machiavelli, in I 18, did or did not wish to say with the statement that it was necessary to "diventare innanzi a ogni cosa principe di quella città." For the terminology of *vivere politico* and *vita civile*, cf. above, note 16.

former of the institutions of the state. Chapter eighteen of the first book of the *Discourses* ends, after all, with the counsel that those who "are called upon to create or maintain a republic" in a period of corruption should strengthen the authoritative, monarchical element within the constitution by modifying existing laws "in the direction of a regal rather than a democratic order."[32] Citizens unrestrained by law might thus be "curbed in some measure by an almost regal power" (*da una podestà quasi* [!] *regia*); that is, by a less than royal power, which Machiavelli regards as more strictly limited than the power of autocracy. "To try to restore men to good conduct in any other way," Machiavelli adds, "would be either a most cruel or an impossible undertaking."[33]

This clearly repudiates a program of salvation through the ruthlessness of a princely usurper in the manner recommended in *The Prince*. Resignation and relativism appear to be the gist of chapters seventeen and eighteen of *Discourses* I: although theoretically a determined statesman might rebuild a decadent state, it is unrealistic to hope for so much, given the nature of man; history teaches that when things have come to such a pass, the institution of a "quasi-regal power" within a surviving republic is the best remedy.

There is further advice in *Discourses* I helping us to understand the spirit of a reformer's work. Having pointed out in chapter seventeen (which is formally related to the eighteenth[34]) that after the expulsion of her kings, Rome,

[32] This is the meaning of the advice "sarebbe necessario ridurla [i.e., una republica] più verso lo stato regio, che verso lo stato popolare."

[33] "Da tutte le soprascritte cose nasce la difficultà o impossibilità, che è nelle città corrotte, a mantenervi una republica o a crearvela di nuovo. E quando pure la vi si avesse a creare o a mantenere, sarebbe necessario ridurla piú verso lo stato regio che verso lo stato popolare, acciocché quegli uomini i quali dalle leggi per la loro insolenzia non possono essere corretti, fussero da una podestà quasi regia in qualche modo frenati. E a volergli fare per altre vie diventare buoni, sarebbe o crudelissima impresa o al tutto impossibile" (*Disc.* I 18).

[34] Chapter 18 begins: "Io credo che non sia fuora di proposito, né disforme dal soprascritto discorso [that is, chapter 17] considerare se in una città cor-

which was then uncorrupted, remained free, whereas after Caesar's murder corrupted Rome could not preserve her liberty, Machiavelli defines his understanding of "corruption" and "incapacity for a free mode of life" with reference to modern Italy. The cause of such incapacity, chapter seventeen suggests, lies in the "inequality" inherent in feudal conditions. This is confirmed by the example of some contemporary Italian populations ("popoli conosciuti ne' nostri tempi"); he means those of Milan and Naples. Nothing, we are told, could ever bring a viable republic to countries like these. Florence is not mentioned here, but reference is made to a later chapter—*Discourses* I 55[35]—where the reason for this becomes clear: the presence of "gentiluomini" (gentlemen)—defined as lords who "live in idleness on the revenue derived from their estates," who own castles, and to whom people are subject—makes any form of free political life impossible in Lombardy and Naples, throughout the Romagna, and in the Papal State. In Tuscany, however, where there are few feudal lords, Florence, Siena, and Lucca have always been republics, every small country town strives to be free, and "a wise man familiar with the ancient forms of civic government should easily be able to introduce a civic way of life." But "it has been Tuscany's great misfortune that so far no one with the requisite ability and knowledge has ever attempted to do so."[36]

---

rotta si può mantenere lo stato libero, sendovi; o quando e' non vi fusse, se vi si può ordinare."

[35] The reference does not identify the chapter—"come *in altro luogo* [my emphasis] più particularmente si dirà"—but says that at that later point it would be shown that inequality can be changed into equality (the condition of republican freedom) only by such "extraordinary devices as few would know how to employ, or would be ready to employ." Precisely this is the object of *Disc.* I 55, where transformation of a country of equality into one of inequality, and vice versa, is said to be so difficult that there are "but few who have had the ability to carry it through, . . . partly because men become terrified and partly owing to the obstacles encountered"; wherefore the fitness of Naples, the Papal provinces, Romagna, and Lombardy for monarchy, as well as the fitness of Tuscany and Venice for republican life, must be looked upon as practically unchangeable.

[36] ". . . ma esservi [i.e., in Tuscany] tanta equalità che facilmente da uno

When Machiavelli wrote chapters seventeen, eighteen, and fifty-five of the first book of the *Discourses*, he was focusing, as we now see, not on the potential founder of a new *principatus* in the anarchic region of the Papal State (as envisaged in *The Prince*), but on a lawgiver who would maintain or restore some republican or civil form of life in Tuscany. And indeed, shortly after the completion of the *Discourses*, Machiavelli proved that he took his idea of the continuing fitness of Tuscany and Florence for republican institutions seriously. When in 1519–1520 Pope Leo and Cardinal Medici (later Clement VII) asked a number of Florentine citizens for counsel regarding Florence's government in the years to come, Machiavelli dared to propose in his *Discorso delle cose fiorentine dopo la morte di Lorenzo*[37] the point of view expounded in the first book of

---

uomo prudente, e che delle antiche civiltà avesse cognizione, vi s'introdurebbe uno vivere civile. Ma lo infortunio suo è stato tanto grande che infino a questi tempi non si è abattuta a alcuno uomo che lo abbia possuto o saputo fare." It might seem strange at first sight to read that "uno uomo prudente" should introduce, in Tuscany, "uno vivere civile," and not "uno vivere politico" as one would expect according to Machiavelli's normal usage (see above, note 16). This is particularly surprising in view of the fact that, in the same chapter, the problem had previously been stated in the normal fashion; namely that "republiche dove si è mantenuto il vivere politico ed incorrotto" do not admit "gentiluomini," whereas in those Italian regions that have feudal lords "non è mai surta alcuna republica né alcuno vivere politico; perché tali generazioni di uomini sono al tutto inimici d'ogni civiltà," and that in order to restrain (*frenare*) such lords "vi bisogna ordinare . . . maggior forza, la quale è una mano regia che con la potenza assoluta ed eccessiva ponga freno alla eccessiva ambizione e corruttela de' potenti." Although the phrases "inimici d'ogni civiltà" and "delle antiche civiltà" form a connecting link between the terminologies of the two parts of the chapter, the use of "uno vivere civile" instead of "uno vivere politico" in the application to the conditions of Tuscany remains an inconsistency, but is perhaps not impossible to explain. Only a few years later, in his *Discorso* of 1519–1520 on the Florentine constitution, Machiavelli was to suggest for Florence, for the time being, a quasi-monarchical government under Pope Leo X and Cardinal Giulio de' Medici, with so many features of civic participation in offices and city councils—i.e., a "vivere civile"—built in, that after the death of Leo and Giulio de' Medici, Florence would automatically return to its republican way of life, its "vivere politico." Cf. p. 127 below.

[37] Called "Discorso sopra il riformare lo Stato di Firenze" until R. Ridolfi,

the *Discourses*. He again argued, and this time as practical political advice, that since Florentine society was free of *gentiluomini*, the only workable and farsighted plan was to restructure the Florentine constitution under the overlordship of those two highly placed members of the Medici family in such a way that after their deaths the Florentine republic would be able to resume her normal functions. And so the gulf between the philosopher of *uno vivere politico e civile* in the *Discourses* and the analyst and advocate of unlimited power in *The Prince* remains as wide as ever—too wide for the bridge so ingeniously constructed between Machiavelli's two works by Chabod and his successors.[38]

III

We can prove in other ways the unlikelihood of the assumption that portions of the first book of the *Discourses* were written years before the remainder of the work. Two well-informed contemporaries of Machiavelli—Filippo de' Nerli and Jacopo Nardi—tell us that the *Discourses* were written at the request of the group of cultured citizens who met in the Oricellari Gardens;[39] but Machiavelli can hardly have been a visitor there before 1515, certainly not as early as 1513.[40] In the

---

in his *Vita di Niccolò Machiavelli*, 275, 450f., adopted the above title from an early manuscript. There (pp. 450f.) also persuasive reasons for the date 1519–1520.

[38] As for Chabod's related argument (see above, p. 119)—that in *Disc.* I 16–18 and 26–27 counsel for an absolute prince replaces the usual concern of the *Discourses* for a government built on the *virtù* and active participation of the people in the state—it has been shown (above, pp. 111f.) that the pertinent sections of those chapters are deviations from the main argument and lack perfect fusion with the context. The phrases Chabod has in mind, therefore, may have been written and given their place in the text at practically any time; they need not have been part of the first draft of the chapters in which they occur.

[39] For particulars, I refer the reader to my discussion of the chronology of the *Discourses* in *Bibliothèque d'Human. et Renaiss.* 18, quoted above, note 1; cf. esp. *Bibliothèque* 18, pp. 420f.

[40] See below, note 49.

preface to the *Discourses*, he himself thanks Zanobi Buondelmonti and Cosimo Rucellai, two principal members of that
group, "for having impelled me to write down what I would
never have written of my own accord."[41] To be sure, this does
not make it inconceivable that a portion of the work composed
for his Oricellari friends had been prepared earlier. Still,
if this were so, Nerli and Nardi would appear to have known
nothing of it, and Machiavelli would have kept it secret that
part of his book had lain in his desk for a number of years.
And why would he not then have thanked Buondelmonti and
Rucellai in his preface for having spurred him to resume and
save an interrupted work instead of thanking them for inducing him to "write" it?

More doubts arise when one realizes that in the synthetic
chapters at the beginning of the *Discourses*, Machiavelli dis-
plays a breadth and profoundness of historical vision and a
penetration in his analysis of social forces which in comparison makes the mere interest in governmental action characteristic of *The Prince* look superficial and immature. Chabod and
other students of his group have found this puzzling. In moving from the *Discourses* to *The Prince*, Sasso has remarked, one
finds not an expansion of Machiavelli's horizon but a process
of "impoverishment," which "reduces the power of historical
comprehension" found in the *Discourses* to "one isolated element"—a focus on power dependent on troops of the prince
and the ruler's diplomacy. Sasso, indeed, felt compelled to refer to the "lesser profundity of *The Prince* in comparison to the
Discourses"; *The Prince* "remains without doubt considerably
beneath the far-reaching analyses in the *Discourses*."[42] Those
who accept the sequence *Discourses–Prince* account for this
anomaly by pointing to the need, in a practical guide for
princes, to focus upon a few concrete and malleable factors.
But where else have changes in the thinking of great political

[41] ". . . che mi avete forzato a scrivere quello ch'io mai per me medesimo
non arei scritto."

[42] Chabod, *Machiavelli and the Renaissance*, 79f., 86, 96f.; Sasso, *Niccolò
Machiavelli*, 119, 223f., 227, 303.

and historical writers from one major work to another amounted to a narrowing of interest and a loss of profundity?

Even greater puzzles await us. In 1953, Felix Gilbert drew attention to the fact that whereas the introductory sections of the three books of the *Discourses* have been developed into a rounded treatise on politics (and into a rounded picture of ancient Rome, one might add), there are sections in the latter parts of all three books that look like simple commentaries, with each chapter centered on the discussion of one or a few important passages from Livy. Here, the chapters are not arranged according to the problems with which they deal, but according to the sequence of the selected passages in Livy's narrative. It would be difficult to imagine any other reason for this unusual arrangement but that Machiavelli began working up comments following the order of Livy's text, and subsequently divided this commentary into three books according to content, expanding the introductory chapters of each book into treatises no longer closely connected with Livy and relegating the unchanged, or little changed, bits of commentary to the latter portions of the books, often in their original order.

One need not agree with Gilbert regarding the exact boundaries between the transformed sections and those chapters which represent the initial commentary form, and one may disagree with most of his conclusions about the early history and date of the completion of the *Discourses*: all this will matter little so long as we assume—as we obviously must—that Machiavelli's efforts developed from a running commentary to a semi-systematic work. It was undoubtedly from his pedestrian commentation of Livy's history that he acquired the knowledge of Rome's religion, constitution, military order, and foreign politics necessary to construct the great syntheses at the beginnings of the three books.[43]

---

[43] Cf. Gilbert's "Composition" (note 1, above), esp. 147ff. It should be noted that Gilbert did not admit the validity of the above conclusions for the all-important first eighteen chapters; he thus deprived his argument of its greatest potential effect. Instead, he proposed what he called a "speculative"

If this was indeed the course taken by Machiavelli, the first eighteen chapters of the *Discourses* cannot possibly belong to an early phase of the work, and it is even less likely that they can have been the part of the *Discourses* written first. These chapters could have existed in 1513 only if most of the work on the *Discourses* had already been completed by the autumn of that year. But this is clearly an impossible assumption.

We would seem to be at the point where we have to reject the thesis that Machiavelli moved from the *Discourses* to *The Prince* and then back again to the *Discourses*, were it not for the stumbling block presented by the statement in the second chapter of *The Prince* that the author will not discuss republics "because on another occasion I have reasoned about them at length."[44] But is this passage really the final evidence it has been thought to be—documentary proof that a part of the *Discourses* already existed when *The Prince* was being written? If we had a manuscript of *The Prince* from 1513 or 1514 containing a cross reference to a former work dealing with republics, this would be conclusive proof. But all extant early manuscripts of *The Prince* are from a later period, since they include the dedication to Lorenzo de' Medici the Younger,[45] which for compelling reasons must have been written between the autumn of 1515 and the autumn of 1516, and most probably between March and October 1516.[46] The lack of earlier manu-

---

theory; namely, that when Machiavelli transformed his Livy commentary into the present three books, he used in the composition of *Disc.* 1 1–18 a lost work on republics which he had drafted before the composition of *The Prince*, and consequently several years before the beginning of his work on the Livy commentary (Gilbert, pp. 150, 152). For the fallacies inherent in this unacceptable hypothesis, see above, note 28, and below, p. 135. In Gilbert's eyes, therefore, *Disc.* 1 1–18, far from representing Machiavelli's thought during a phase subsequent to *The Prince*, shows an approach which—in contrast to the rest of the *Discourses*—"is very similar to that in the *Prince*" (p. 149).

[44] "Io lascerò indrieto el ragionare delle republiche, perché altra volta ne ragionai a lungo. Volterommi solo al principato. . . ."

[45] A. Gerber, *Niccolò Machiavelli: Die Handschriften, Ausgaben und Übersetzungen* . . . (Gotha, 1912), vol. 1, p. 82.

[46] Before 8 October 1516, when Lorenzo was made Duke of Urbino, because, as R. Ridolfi, *Vita*, 439f., and others have pointed out, after that event

scripts suggests that Machiavelli had not allowed his work to circulate in 1513–1514 and that in 1515–1516 he was still at liberty to adapt the text to changed conditions. Chabod's important demonstration that no political experiences or events later than 1513 have left their mark on the text of *The Prince* and that, as a reflection of Machiavelli's development as a political thinker, it is basically a document of the year 1513,[47] is not the same as concluding that nothing in the wording of the text was changed when the preface to Lorenzo was added. On the contrary, from a textual point of view, *The Prince* as handed down to posterity is a publication of about 1516, one in which no *visible* entries or changes postdating 1513 have been found (except in the preface), but in which many invisible changes may well have been made in 1514, 1515, and 1516. In fact, our greatest critical problem is not whether, in a publication of 1516, a passage according with conditions of about 1516 can be ascribed specifically to that year, but whether, in trying to reconstruct Machiavelli's thinking in 1513 from a text released about 1516, we are not unwittingly attributing some opinions or phrases of the Machiavelli of 1516 to the Machiavelli of 1513.

Machiavelli would have addressed Lorenzo in his preface as "magnificus" and Duke, not as "eccellenza." As for the *terminus a quo*, Ridolfi argued that Machiavelli could hardly have put so much hope in Lorenzo before Lorenzo's election as Florentine *capitano generale* in May 1515. (For this date, see the English translation of Ridolfi's *Vita* [Chicago, 1963], 163, and the 5th Ital. ed. of Ridolfi's work [Florence, 1972], 257: "Fattosi eleggere fino dal maggio 1515 capitano generale dei Fiorentini. . . .") Although this, too, is convincing as far as it goes, one should also consider the still more precise argument that Machiavelli's original intention had been to dedicate *The Prince* to Giuliano de' Medici; this plan cannot have remained secret after his letter to Vettori on 10 December 1513, and Giuliano died in March 1516. *The Prince* was thus most probably dedicated to Lorenzo after Giuliano's death and after Lorenzo had replaced him as Medicean pretender to a princely position in the Papal State, but before he became "magnificus" and Duke; that is, between March and October 1516.

[47] Cf. Chabod's statement in *Machiavelli and the Renaissance*, 36, with a reference to the observations he had made in a paper in *Archivum Romanicum* (1927).

The cross reference in *The Prince* to "another occasion" appears on the first page of the pamphlet; it virtually belongs to the introductory matter and follows the brief opening definition (the so-called Chapter 1) of "how many kinds of principates exist and how they are acquired." The context is not interrupted—rather, it becomes more logical—when the cross reference is omitted.[48] It is quite conceivable, therefore, that before sending *The Prince* on its way with an added dedication, the author inserted also a note of reference at the beginning of the second chapter in order to establish a link to the very different kind of work in which he had become engaged by 1516; there are no chronological obstacles to the assumption that work on the *Discourses* had sufficiently advanced by that time. Nor is the possibility to be excluded that an insertion was made as late as 1517 or early 1518. For after sending off the dedication copy to Lorenzo, Machiavelli could easily have waited for his reaction before allowing other copies to be made. The *Discourses* was essentially finished by 1517 or 1518, but even as early as the spring or summer of 1516 work on it must have been far enough advanced for his friends' knowledge of it to permit him the vague reference, "on another occasion [*altra volta*] I have reasoned at length."[49]

[48] Cf. my detailed demonstration in *Bibliothèque d'Human. et Renaiss.* 18 (as cited in note 1, above): 409f.

[49] The following three comments should further help to clarify the crucial point that Machiavelli could very well have joined the Oricellari circle and have finished the major part of his work on the *Discourses* by the time *The Prince* was dedicated to Lorenzo. In the first place, the period in which the dedication occurred can almost certainly be shortened from October 1515–October 1516 to March 1516–October 1516, as pointed out above, note 46. Second, Machiavelli's attendance at the Oricellari meetings early in 1516 is suggested by the conversation described in his *Art of War*. The debate there presented is supposed to have taken place in the Oricellari Gardens in Machiavelli's presence ("essendo con alcuni altri nostri amici stato presente," Lib. 1, beginning), and although the setting of a Renaissance dialogue can only in rare cases be used as testimony for biographical facts, Machiavelli's *Art of War* seems to be among the exceptions. The conversation, which according to the preface shows Cosimo Rucellai's excellence in debate, is identified with an historical event: the visit of the *condottiere* Fabrizio Colonna to Florence and to

To be sure, all these observations and conjectures do not yet provide certitude, but the situation is already changed if it can be considered an undeniable possibility that the reference in *The Prince* to the *Discourses* may have been written between late 1515 and early 1518, rather than in 1513. Moreover, the

---

Cosimo in the early part of 1516. The *Art of War*—written four years later, after Cosimo's death—claims that it is meant to keep Cosimo's memory fresh among all those who had been eyewitnesses to that event, and to show his great qualities to others. This does not necessarily mean that a great deal of the conversation as presented must have had a counterpart in Cosimo's and Colonna's actual encounter, but it is very unlikely that Machiavelli would have written that he drew upon his own observations in making the event of 1516 a memorial for Cosimo had he not attended the meetings in the Gardens together with "altri nostri amici" during Colonna's visit. This should allay Ridolfi's doubts (*Vita*, 252, 441) regarding Machiavelli's presence in the Gardens before the summer of 1517.

Third and finally, in spite of Sasso's and Whitfield's skepticism, the seven or eight visible hints to the year 1517 (or possibly 1518) in the text of the *Discourses* do reveal themselves as likely revisions of a previously written text. To recognize this, we must remove from our examination three that do not really refer to events of 1517. (In *Disc.* II 17 and III 27, two earlier events are said to have occurred fifteen and twenty-four years ago, which, it is true, takes us to 1517. But this does not mean that the passages in question were written in 1517; it would be quite natural that any references made in the text to events that occurred so and so many years ago would be brought up to date during a last revision before dedication and publication. A similar final correction, one would think, was due in *Disc.* I 1, where we read that the Mameluk militia in Egypt could have served as a good example until its recent destruction by the Turks early in 1517.) In these three cases, no textual analysis can reconstruct with certainty what changes the author actually made during the year 1517. But the remaining five examples testify to rather clumsy, and therefore detectable, insertions in an already finished and coherent text. Twice, a somewhat incongruous supplement appears to have been added to an original triad of references, which are complete without the supplement. In particular, in I 19 we find a comparison of three kings in Rome, Israel, and among the Turks, and this comparison is completed by the sentence: "Ma se il figliuolo suo Salì [Selim I], presente signore, fusse stato simile al padre e non all' avolo, quel regno rovinava." Yet this "but" sentence is supplemented by another, probably appended under the fresh impression of Selim's victory over the Mameluks early in 1517: "Ma . . . rovinava; ma e' si vede costui essere per superare la gloria dell' avolo." Similarly, in II 10 we find a sequence of one example taken from Greek history, one from Roman his-

knowledge that the disturbing citation in *The Prince* has no bearing in itself on the chronology of Machiavelli's two works has almost the same effect as would a definitive establishment of the date. For since this passage has long operated like a switch automatically turning the attention of students away from the possibility that the *Discourses* were begun later than 1513, recognition of the chronological ambiguity and, therefore, neutrality of the passage means that we are no longer bound by an old prejudice and can make a new start; we are now free to decide whether the notion of a meandering journey from the first eighteen chapters (or even a larger part) of Book I of the *Discourses* to *The Prince* and back to the rest of the *Discourses* retains any plausibility at all once we have the alternative of a more natural succession from the one work to the other.

IV

We have found that the hypothesis that the initial portion of the *Discourses* was composed a few years before the rest of the work is contradicted by much direct and indirect information on its genesis. The contradictions multiply when, with Chabod's hypothesis in mind, we examine Machiavelli's literary labors in 1513 and during the preceding years of his life. Indeed, the further we proceed the more implausibilities we encounter. All of them must be considered before we can rule out once and for all the possibility that part of the *Discourses* was composed in 1513.

---

tory, and one that had occurred "ne' nostri tempi"; but this last is followed by another that occurred "a few days ago" (*pochi giorni sono*), which is clearly an oddly appended event also from "ne' nostri tempi." In the last three phrases indicative of 1517, the references occur in places where they do not fit logically, or where an argument is suddenly split up and continued later. (This occurs in II 17, II 22, and II 24. I believe the results of my detailed analyses in *Bibliothèque d'Human. et Renaiss.* 18: 415–19, are convincing on this score.) Even the most insistent skeptic could not contend on the basis of five such suspiciously phrased hints at 1517, quite possibly mere changes in the text, that Machiavelli's work cannot in substance have been composed before 1517.

In the first place, the very phrasing of the reference to the *Discourses* in *The Prince* would give cause for wonder if it came from the year 1513. If the initial eighteen chapters of the *Discourses* existed that summer, they would have amounted, as I have already emphasized, to no more than a draft hidden away in the author's study. So if we insist on 1513 as the year of origin, we must be prepared to believe that when Machiavelli told his readers in *The Prince* that he had sufficiently reasoned about republics "on another occasion," he was referring to a discontinued draft, a draft which we have no reason to think would have been known to his friends, much less talked about in public; it was, indeed, unknown even to one of his most intimate friends, as emerges from his correspondence with Francesco Vettori.

For in December 1513, after completing the draft of *The Prince*, Machiavelli wrote to Vettori, then Florentine ambassador in Rome, telling him of his recent labors, their purpose, and their origin. The two friends had been in frequent correspondence during the month of August about the international political situation, but they had then ceased writing each other until late November when Vettori sent a detailed report of his life during that interval. On 10 December, Machiavelli reciprocated with an equally full account of how he had spent his time since September ("dirvi in questa mia lettera . . . qual sia la vita mia"). He begins with the famous description of his life among rude lumbermen and country people, neighbors of his tiny estate near S. Casciano—a life which changed at nightfall, however, when, putting on dignified clothes, he retired to his rural study where for four hours each night he forgot the misery of his life by inquiring into the teachings and deeds of the great men of Antiquity, "who out of humanity" received him well and satisfied his inquisitiveness. In those hours of close mental intercourse with the ancient writers, he says, "I completely give myself up to the ancients." He then adds: "And because Dante says that there is no knowledge unless one retains what one has read, I have written down the profit I have gained from this conversation and composed a little book *De Principatibus*. . . . If any of my trifles gives you pleasure, this one should not displease you."[50]

Although this elaborate report is on the genesis of *The Prince* and on Machiavelli's life from September to November 1513, we would be poor critics if we did not notice the light it sheds on a wider area of his occupations. From the report we may learn that the friend who more than any other was interested in Machiavelli's political ideas and writings knew nothing of the *Discourses* at the time *The Prince* was composed. For if Vettori had been aware that Machiavelli was occupied with a work on republics earlier in the year, Machiavelli could not tell him in December about the composition of a work *De Principatibus* without some mention of the former, because Vettori would have expected Machiavelli to produce that work and not *The Prince*. Furthermore, Machiavelli's report excludes by implication the possibility that he had pursued a study of republics before autumn. The purpose of his letter is to communicate something new and wonderful that had entered his life during the recent period of silence. If his spiritual communion with the great ancients, which necessarily must have preceded the *Discourses* as well as *The Prince*, had already been underway during the spring or summer, and if in September or October the earlier experience with the *Discourses* was renewed in the writing of *The Prince*, the phrasing and tone of the letter to Vettori would in all likelihood have been very different. One could hardly be more precise than Machiavelli when he wrote with respect to the autumn that his "little book *De Principatibus*" was *the*—not *a*—profit of his new experience. So the letter leads us much further than to a mere, inconclusive *argumentum ex silentio*;[51] its wording is explicit

---

[50] "E perché Dante dice che non fa scienza senza ritener lo havere inteso, io ho notato quello di che per la loro conversazione ho fatto capitale, e composto uno opusculo *De principatibus* [the oldest form of the title, also found in manuscripts], dove io mi profondo quanto io posso nelle cogitazioni di questo subietto, disputando che cosa è principato. . . ." On this letter as an historical source, cf. also *Bibliothèque d'Human. et Renaiss.* 18: 424ff.

[51] As G. Sasso, *Giornale Stor. della Lett. Ital.* 134 (1957): 509, has charged.

enough to tell us that during the autumn or the earlier part of 1513, neither the writer nor the recipient of the letter knew anything about the preparation of a work on republics. We are not at liberty to neglect the implications of Machiavelli's own report.

Moreover, if we were to accept the hypothesis that the first part of the *Discourses* was composed in 1513, we would have to assume that Machiavelli wrote its republican-minded opening during the very phase of his life in which he most eagerly craved a career in the service of the Medici. As his letters show, he was (rightly or wrongly) convinced that he owed his deliverance from imprisonment and torture in February to Giuliano de' Medici. For several months after his release from prison, we find him beseeching his friends to use their influence on his behalf with Giuliano and Cardinal Giovanni de' Medici. In March he celebrated the cardinal's elevation to the papal see as Leo X with a poem,[52] and in April he wrote with a sigh to Vettori that he wished Leo would use him in some office, in Rome or in the Papal State, if not in Florence. In June he tried "to put myself in the pope's place" and to work out an analysis of Leo's political interests in Italy and in Europe.[53] About five months later he decided to offer his services to Giuliano by dedicating *The Prince* to him. These anxious efforts clearly depict Machiavelli's state of mind during the period in which the *Discourses* would have been conceived if it had been begun in 1513.[54]

---

[52] As R. Ridolfi, *Vita*, 210, 431, has demonstrated.

[53] Letters to Vettori of 16 April and 20 June 1513.

[54] Nor can one overlook the fact that the dominant tone in all of Machiavelli's letters from March to June 1513 is one of utter personal despair; I have become useless to my friends, my family, and myself, he laments again and again. The puzzle which must be faced by those who believe in the composition of parts of the *Discourses* during those months has been put aptly and honestly by Sasso, *Niccolò Machiavelli*, 196: "It is indeed singular [è veramente singolare] that during the preparation . . . of his *magnum opus* . . . Machiavelli should have been able to express such limitless discouragement in his letters to Vettori and, above all, never hint at the great work on which he was engaged."

Finally, we would have to believe that the republican *Discourses* originated not only at a time when Machiavelli's faith in the Florentine republic was at its lowest, but when, as far as we know, none of the basic ideas of the *Discourses* were yet in his mind. We know his interests in the period from 1498 to 1512 from his letters and his political and historical writings.[55] It would be fair to sum up these years as a time of uninterrupted exercise in the kind of thinking which *The Prince* was to epitomize; nowhere do we find the slightest anticipation of the attention paid in the *Discourses* to the forces molding the social and constitutional life of the *Respublica Romana* or other republics. Indeed, students have noted with surprise that in the writings which concern the creation of a Florentine militia in 1506, Machiavelli did not allude to the Roman Republic as a model or counterpart.[56] Again, when, as late as about the middle of 1512, he worked out the final versions of his *Portraits* (*Ritratti*) of Germany and France[57] and noted that, in contrast to German cities, feudal nobility was excluded from those in Switzerland, he gave no indication that he already felt equality to be the foremost element in republican life.[58] And when he mentioned the Parlement of Paris in his portrayal of the French monarchy, he showed himself to be interested solely in the growing power of the crown; he failed to pay the slight-

[55] Three excellent and comprehensive analyses allow us to judge this point with great assurance: Federico Chabod, "Niccolò Machiavelli: Il segretario fiorentino," lectures of 1952–1953 on Machiavelli's writings, ideas, and practical political experiences from 1498 to 1512, published in Chabod's *Scritti su Machiavelli* (Turin, 1964), 241–368; Raffaello Ramat, "Vigilia Machiavellica," in *Studi Letterari: Miscellanea in onore di Emilio Santini* (Palermo, 1956), 197–213; and Gennaro Sasso, *Niccolò Machiavelli*, 7–181. Additional confirmation may be found in J. R. Hale's *Machiavelli and Renaissance Italy* (London, 1961), 28–140—the first biography of Machiavelli which, after tracing his experiences and writings during his youth, adopts the view that whereas *The Prince* originated in 1513, no part of the *Discourses* was written until several years later.

[56] Cf. Chabod, "Niccolò Machiavelli: Il segretario," 334–35.

[57] For the dates, see Ridolfi, *Vita*, 420f., and Sasso, *Giornale Stor. della Lett. Ital.* 134: 510.

[58] Sasso, *Niccolò Machiavelli*, 169f.

est attention to the institutions which guaranteed the rule of law over the king—the central point in his portrayal of the French kingdom in the *Discourses*.

Not that Machiavelli was still unfamiliar at the time with at least some of the ancient sources that were to play so decisive a role in the historical vision embodied in the *Discourses*. Livy, at least, appears to have been frequently read. His father had compiled the index of the first printed edition of Livy in Florence when Niccolò was seventeen, and a copy, fetched by the youth from the binder, found its way into the family library. But this early occupation with Livy did not prepare for the views which later were to make the *Discourses* primarily a treatise on republics. Wherever Livy's influence is perceptible in Machiavelli's writings during the years of his secretaryship, the Livian narrative is used not as a guide to the spirit and constitutional fabric of the *Respublica Romana*, but as a stimulus for the politics that appears in *The Prince* and in related "Machiavellian" chapters of the *Discourses*. The first precept drawn from Livy's history is encountered in a letter written on the occasion of Machiavelli's first legation to France in 1500, when Florence attempted to dissuade her French ally from compromising with Spain. In her north Italian politics, Machiavelli advised, France should "follow the procedure of those who in the past have aimed at the possession of foreign provinces." The Roman method had been "to humiliate those with power, to pamper subject peoples, to give help to friends, and to be wary of those who want to have equal authority in the same place."[59] A warning against half measures and indecision is the theme on the next occasion when Machiavelli's preoccupation with Livy becomes manifest. After a

[59] ". . . che questa Maestà doveva . . . seguire l'ordine di coloro che hanno per lo addrieto volsuto possedere una provincia esterna, che è diminuire e' potenti, vezeggiare li sudditi, mantenere li amici, e guardarsi de' compagni, cioè da coloro che vogliono in tale luogo avere equale autorità." From the letter of 21 November 1500, in Machiavelli's *Legazioni*, to Cardinal D'Amboise. The same ideas on the treatment of a new province recur later in *The Prince*, ch. III.

brief defection by Arezzo in 1502, Machiavelli advised Florence, in one of his best-known early writings, that she should respond either with deliberate cruelty or with such great clemency that Arezzo would be won over. The Romans, he contended, had always judged the "middle way" injurious in their dealings with their subjects.[60] After the fall of the Florentine republic in 1512, Machiavelli again had recourse to Livy when he reflected that the gonfalonier Piero Soderini, honest and well-meaning statesman that he was, had perished and ruined his state, which he had maintained for so many years, by refusing—or being unable—to resort to cunning and cruelty in a time of emergency. The solution to this typically "Machiavellian" dilemma was sought in Livy's account of how Hannibal and Scipio, the one by cruelty and perfidy, the other by compassion and faithfulness, for many years achieved equal success.[61]

Until 1513, no political or historical viewpoint other than a "Machiavellian" one, ever seems to appear. Perhaps one should not expect anything else in view of Machiavelli's occupations and experiences from the day of his entrance into the Florentine chancery until the fall of the republic. With hardly any pause, his diplomatic missions had taken him not only to France, Germany, and the papal see but to the countless cities and lordly domains in the almost lawless region of the Romagna and the State of the Church, as well as to places within the Florentine territorial state. He helped to suppress revolts, mediate conflicts with neighboring Tuscan city-states, conduct difficult negotiations with treacherous merce-

[60] "Puossi per questa deliberazione considerare come i Romani nel giudicare di queste loro terre ribellate pensarono che bisognasse o guadagnare la fede loro con i benefizi o trattarli in modo che mai più ne potessero dubitare: e per questo giudicarono dannosa ogni altra via di mezzo che si pigliasse." "I Romani pensarono una volta che i popoli ribellati si debbano o beneficare o spegnere e che ogni altra via sia pericolosissima." From the pamphlet *Del Modo di trattare i popoli della Valdichiana ribellati* (1503).

[61] In the letter (so-called *Ghiribizzi scritti in Raugia*) to Piero Soderini, late 1512. The same comparison between Hannibal and Scipio recurs later in *Disc.* III 21.

nary *condottieri*, and establish a Florentine territorial militia. In the course of these duties, he observed the superior power of the large nation-states and their oppressive impact on weak Italy, as well as the efforts of tyrannical rulers in central Italy, a region of constant change and without traditions, to build a "new principate" by shrewdness, ruthlessness, and crime—from Alexander VI and his *nepote* Cesare Borgia, to Julius II and his *nepote* Francesco Maria della Rovere, to Leo X and his *nepote* Giuliano de' Medici. At home, he was in close contact with the problems of Florence's military defense and her difficult rule over often unwilling subjects in the Tuscan territories. In brief, the Florentine secretary had served his republic with total fidelity for fourteen years, almost never emerging, in action or thought, from the endless stream of power politics.[62]

Such was the only life Machiavelli had known before the winter of 1512–1513, when he suddenly found himself condemned to live in solitude, leisure, and penury. The letters of 1513 allow us to observe the influence of this change on his state of mind. For several months, until in the autumn he discovered a new life in his study of the ancients, his every thought was bent on regaining a place in the world of action, and his attention was focused on the rapid changes in the contemporary scene. Gradually, by applying his knowledge of the nature of the power struggle to the events unfolding before his eyes, the problems of *The Prince* emerged. As early as April, when he discussed with Vettori the annexation of the Duchy of Milan by France or Spain, he mentioned the "ways in which new states are retained"; in mapping an unscrupulous policy for the king of Spain, he remarked that "good faith and obli-

---

[62] That Machiavelli, in addition to being "second chancellor" of the chancery, also ranked as "secretary" (the term used throughout this essay) and was employed in this capacity outside his chancery office, for instance as a member of missions to foreign powers, has been shown in N. Rubinstein's "The Beginnings of Niccolò Machiavelli's Career in the Florentine Chancery," *Italian Studies* 11 (1956): 76, 78, 85.

gations are not taken into consideration today."[63] But even if the psychological and factual evidence from documents were lacking, it would be fantastic to conjecture that Machiavelli sat down almost immediately, between March and August, to write a book based on ideas and studies unrelated to the former direction of his life and interests. This is the very assumption we would have to make, in defiance of all rules of historical plausibility, if we were to cling to the hypothesis that the *Discourses* originated in 1513; and we would have to add this contradictory assumption to the many other implausibilities that come to the surface on reading Chabod's theory: that Machiavelli could have claimed he had already said enough about a subject discussed only in an unfinished and unpublished manuscript; that his claim that he would never have composed the *Discourses* without the inducement of his friends in the Oricellari Gardens could have pointed to a time when he was not yet frequenting the gardens; that he could have described the progress of his work on *The Prince*, as he did in his letter to Vettori, if he had had to interrupt work on another major project in order to begin the pamphlet; and finally, that the republican-minded chapters of the first book of the *Discourses* were conceived in a period when he was making daily efforts to reconcile himself to the overthrow of the Florentine republic and win a place in the service of her new rulers. It seems to me that no critical reader can acquiesce to any of these improbable assumptions.

[63] "Et uno de' modi con che li stati nuovi si tengono . . ."; ". . . et della fede et delli obblighi non si tiene hoggi conto." We can be sure of the date of this letter—29 April 1513—owing to manuscript findings already known to P. Villari, *Niccolò Machiavelli e i suoi tempi*, 2d ed. (Milan 1897), vol. 3, p. 416, and O. Tommasini, *La vita e gli scritti di Niccolò Machiavelli* (Rome, 1911), vol. 2, pt. 1, p. 86. The latter already called the interest in the "modi" of preserving "stati nuovi" shown in the letter a testimony "that the substance of the pamphlet on the *Prince* was developing in Machiavelli's mind as early as that time." Sasso, *Niccolò Machiavelli*, pp. 208–10, interestingly shows that some basic ideas found in *The Prince* appear in other writings by Machiavelli early in 1513, but he does not draw the obvious consequences from his observations.

Moreover, our reexamination of the structure and genesis of the *Discourses* has had the negative result of calling in question the raison d'être of the thesis that Machiavelli went from the *Discourses* to *The Prince*. As we have found, there is no bridge between the model of a *principe nuovo*, as pictured in *The Prince*, and the intentions of chapters seventeen and eighteen of *Discourses* I. The latter (like Machiavelli's memorandum of 1519–1520 on the Florentine constitution) take their orientation not from the founding of a new princely state in the territories of the Church but from his conviction that Tuscany, a country with few feudal lords, was suited in the long run only for a republican way of life. We have further been forced to conclude that the introductory chapters of the *Discourses* cannot have been composed in the same year as *The Prince* because they are the product of a late phase of Machiavelli's work on the *Discourses*. Thus all indications, without exception, point in one direction: no part of the *Discourses* was written as early as 1513. As far as I can see, this is an inescapable conclusion, and the unhappy nineteenth- and early twentieth-century notion that *The Prince* and the *Discourses* are indissolubly joined Siamese twins can at last be dismissed in favor of the idea of a natural succession and a development of the author's thinking from one work to the other.

Instead of looking at the *Discourses* as a hodge-podge from two periods of Machiavelli's life, we would indeed do better to reconsider what to earlier generations had seemed manifest: that his two major works are different in basic attitudes and that the *Discourses*, though serving various purposes, includes a republican message irreconcilable with *The Prince*. This does not, of course, suggest a return to the judgments of eighteenth-century authors. The evolutionary understanding at which we have arrived will of necessity remain close to the genetic approach proposed by Italian scholars since Chabod. Yet now that we have strong evidence that *The Prince* and the *Discourses* were composed in different phases of Machiavelli's development, the period in which our awareness of the individual character of the *Discourses* was dimmed may at last come to an end.

V

What the new view will eventually turn out to be is perhaps not yet clear in every detail, but a fresh look and interpretation is promised by at least three avenues of approach.

In the first place, it now becomes possible to reconstruct a more intelligible pattern of Machiavelli's growth as a political thinker. Work on *The Prince*, we begin to see, did not compel the author to leave the paths he had previously trodden; nor was the mental preparation of the pamphlet merely the work of a few summer weeks or a contraction of initially broader historical and philosophical horizons.[64] What Machiavelli intended to offer to a Medici prince late in 1513 was a synthesis of his experiences and reflections during the fourteen years in which his world had witnessed the power struggle for Italy and the fight for survival of the Florentine dominion in northern Tuscany. What he had learned about diplomatic technique and administrative efficiency while serving the republic could help to establish the rule of a new prince. He made use of this expertise because after the frustration of his previous career, his burning desire for an active place in the world of politics and his wounded Italian feelings caused him to hope that a powerful ruler would found a new state.

But although the views and counsels given in pamphlet form in *The Prince* were the fruit of many years, they represent merely the first phase of Machiavelli's development as a writer. We could hardly imagine a greater contrast than that between his active political existence prior to 1513 and his life between about 1515 and 1520 when he wrote in leisure as a member of the educated circle of citizens who met in the Oricellari Gardens. There he formed closer contacts with the tra-

[64] See the assumptions mentioned above, note 21 and pp. 118f., 127.

ditions of civic Humanism than he had been able to establish during the busy years of his absorption in diplomatic and military affairs.[65] These traditions included an historical outlook that for several generations had centered on an admiration for Antiquity as an era of city-states and institutions based on the life of a free society. Even though Machiavelli had previously studied Livy and other Latin and Greek authors (the latter in translation), it is clear that in his changed intellectual climate the ancient world revealed another dimension to him.[66] This is not to suggest that the *Discourses* can or should be appraised solely on the strength of its relationship to a republican-minded Humanism. Not a few of its chapters, as we have seen, are intended to apply the methods and conceptions of "Machiavellianism" to both principates and republics. Yet the

[65] On the reemergence in the Oricellari circle of some of the central concerns of the civic humanists (though after a hundred years, the answers to the old questions were not, of course, always identical), cf. D. Cantimori, "Rhetoric and Politics in Italian Humanism," *Journal of the Warburg Institute* 1 (1937–1938): esp. 94ff., and R. von Albertini, *Das Florentinische Staatsbewusstsein*, passim, esp. 76ff.

[66] If J. H. Hexter's reasoning in his study on "Seyssel, Machiavelli, and Polybius VI," 75–96, is correct, we may even assume that one of the chief inspirations for the introductory part of the *Discourses*—the fragments of the sixth book of Polybius—did not become available to Machiavelli in Latin until the time of his contacts with the circle in the Oricellari Gardens. In that case his inability to read Polybius VI before 1515, because of his ignorance of Greek, would give us a further weighty argument against the composition of *Disc.* I 1–18 before 1515. However, Sasso (*Giornale Stor. della Letteratura Ital.* 135: 242ff.) and Whitfield (*Italian Studies* 13: 31ff.) have suggested that there were chances for Machiavelli to procure a Latin version of Polybius VI, other than that by Janus Lascaris (to which Hexter has pointed), as early as 1513 or even earlier, although we do not know whether Machiavelli took advantage of these opportunities. As a consequence, we had better not use Hexter's discovery of a plausible late channel for Machiavelli's knowledge of Polybius VI as proof of the late composition of *Disc.* I 1–18 (as I did in 1956, *Bibliothèque d'Human. et Renaiss.* 18: 408). On the other hand, since the present essay establishes by other means that the section of the *Discourses* which depends on knowledge of Polybius VI was not written before 1516, the probability that Polybius VI did not become known to Machiavelli until 1515 is now increased.

Discourses developed as it did only because the comments on the rule of republics already planned at the time of *The Prince*[67] were eventually joined by a politico-historical philosophy firmly based on a new vision of the life of nations, on a reassessment of the reasons underlying the rise and fall of their freedom and vigor—the legacy of fifteenth-century Florentine Humanism. Although a central problem for Machiavelli remained that of winning and defending political power, its source was no longer sought exclusively in diplomatic craftsmanship but also—and primarily—in the creation of a social and constitutional fabric allowing civic energies and a spirit of political devotion and sacrifice to develop in all classes of a people. A revived and strengthened republicanism helped Machiavelli to arrive at a more profound answer to the questions he had so passionately been asking since his early years.

Not that Machiavelli ever became a steadfast republican with regard to the practical problems of Florence's future and his own. He continued to waver between his certainty that a republic was needed under Tuscan conditions of civic equality and his lingering hope that some new *principatus* in the provinces of the Papal State might create a power nucleus strong enough to make possible the establishment of peace in central Italy and, perhaps, a successful resistance to the foreign invaders of the peninsula. When, after Giuliano de' Medici's death, Lorenzo de' Medici seemed on the verge of erecting in the tyrant-prone territory of the Papal State the principality vainly aspired to by the *nepoti* of Alexander VI and Julius II, Machiavelli, in the midst of his preparations for the *Discourses*, took his old guide for princes out of his desk and dedicated it to Lorenzo. When a few years later death brought an end to this hope as well, he inscribed his *Discourses* to Buondelmonti and Rucellai, two Florentine citizens from the circle of the Oricellari Gardens, thereby, as he said, "departing from the usual practice of authors . . . of dedicating their works to some

[67] This seems to follow from the phrase "dove si trattassi delle republiche" at the beginning of chapter VIII of *The Prince*, discussed above, note 15.

prince, and . . . of praising him for all his virtuous qualities when they ought to blame him for all manner of shameless deeds." In 1519–1520 he dared to recommend the practical advice offered in the *Discourses* to Leo X: that only a republican way of life could endure in Florence under Tuscan conditions of civic equality. But soon his restless mind began to explore yet another approach to the past and the present. During the 1520s, in his *Florentine History*, a third Machiavelli appeared— the first Florentine writer to view Florence's development in the melancholy light in which it was to appear as the sixteenth century advanced, and to judge that the energy generated by freedom had gradually been consumed in the course of Florentine history, until finally all partisan passions were extinguished and a stable order was established under the Medici.

From the viewpoint of Florentine republicanism, therefore, Machiavelli was certainly not a good and faithful citizen, despite his great love and inspired teaching of civic liberty—as Giovanni Battista Busini observed. The story of his life will always have to be presented as a delicate tissue of sometimes conflicting motivations, not simply as a neat succession of distinct phases. Yet for all his fluctuations, the history of the development of Machiavelli's thought and its shaping forces looks profoundly different when we take into account the new experiences that entered his life on the way from *The Prince* to the *Discourses*—when we have recognized that his horizon expanded with the years, like that of every great creative thinker.

Moreover, and here a second new avenue of approach presents itself, since we now know that, from another point of view, this expansion was a development from realistic pragmatism to civic Humanism, the problem of Machiavelli's "realism" and "humanism," debated under erroneous assumptions in recent years,[68] can also be viewed from a fresh

---

[68] According to Chabod, *Machiavelli and the Renaissance*, 37f., "the ancient world was gradually obliged [i.e., during Machiavelli's presumed development from the first book of the *Discourses* to *The Prince*] to retreat before the modern world"; "the classical examples are replaced by men and events taken from contemporary history," and Machiavelli's "receptivity and imagination,

perspective. If we accept that all three books of the *Discourses* were written after *The Prince*, the political realism of the pamphlet, rather than being the second step in Machiavelli's development, much less its climax, actually represents an earlier phase; and what followed was by no means a mere return to a classicistic belief in the imitation of Antiquity but amounted to an historical "realism," the most mature expression of which we find in the synthetic chapters introducing the three books of the *Discourses*.

These introductions, continuing the line of historical thinking begun by Leonardo Bruni and Flavio Biondo a century before,[69] emphasize the point that the ancient world was full of independent states, most of them freedom-loving city-states, before its early vitality was largely extinguished by Rome's conquests. In the introductions, the Roman Empire is no longer viewed as a divine foundation, destined to last until Judgment Day, but as an historical phenomenon with a natural growth and decline followed by the emergence of new cities and states. And just as interstate struggle and change never end, these introductions inform us that there is no pattern in social and constitutional life, however perfect, that can endure without change and adaptation. Political *virtù* among a healthy people must continuously be renewed in all groups and classes. Even the political and military greatness of Rome was not the product of an ideal, perfect constitution but rested on an order permitting the constant regeneration of civic energy through free rivalry, even through civil strife among the Roman classes and estates.[70]

---

having been moulded and developed by the civilization of the Ancients, were being applied once more to present-day life. . . ." According to F. Gilbert (*Journal of the History of Ideas* 14: 148f., 153ff., 156) and G. Sasso (*Niccolò Machiavelli*, 374ff., 401f., 410ff.), *The Prince* and the opening part of the *Discourses* were "realistic," but Machiavelli's alleged subsequent return to the last two books of the *Discourses* reveals to a degree a backward trend, a return to "a traditional literary genre" and to a classicistic bias and imitation of Antiquity.

[69] For Flavio Biondo, see Denys Hay, "Flavio Biondo and the Middle Ages," *Proceedings of the British Academy* 45 (London, 1959), 97–128.

[70] *Disc.* I 1–6; II intro. and 1–4; III 1.

Clearly, this conception of Rome and the ancient world is not "classicistic" in contrast to "realistic." Rather, it provides a framework in which the sovereignty of each individual state, already taken for granted in *The Prince*, can be perceived as an innate quality of the body politic, which strives anew for independence after any bondage to empire or foreign rule. In other words, through an intensified contact with Antiquity, seen through the eyes of civic humanists, some of the implied premises of *The Prince* developed into an ever more distinctly modern approach to the political and historical world.[71]

The third and last, but not the least important, consequence of our new understanding of the growth of Machiavelli's thought concerns the balance in Renaissance Italy between the principality and the city-state republic. Early in the twentieth century, as we have noted, the great persuasiveness of the thesis that some of the basic ideas in the *Discourses* were followed and superseded by those in *The Prince* had much to do with the then prevailing opinion that the inherent trend in Renaissance Italy was away from the commune and republic, and toward the principality; it was further posited that by Machiavelli's time, the perspicacity of a political thinker would show itself in his ability to understand the principality as a modern, progressive element and the city-state republic as a thing of

---

[71] Machiavelli's relationship to Humanism was, of course, not altogether positive. His pessimistic view of man and explicit subordination of the pursuits of culture to those of power and military efficiency make him in some respects one of the first great antipodes of the humanistic attitude in Italy, as has been convincingly pointed out by August Buck, "Die Krise des humanistischen Menschenbildes bei Machiavelli," *Archiv für das Studium der neueren Sprachen* 189 (1953): 304–17, republished in Buck's *Die humanistische Tradition in der Romania* (Bad Homburg v. d. H., 1968). But this need not prevent us from recognizing that certain other humanistic tendencies are basic to Machiavelli's thought and that he is one of their most important representatives. This is not only true of his classicistic belief that contemporary Italy could be regenerated through a "rebirth" of the political wisdom and the military organization of ancient Rome, but applies also to his relationship to the historical—and even political—outlook of Florentine civic Humanism in pre-Medici Florence, in particular to that of Leonardo Bruni. Cf. my *Crisis*, 2d ed., 70, 428f., 431, 481, and Sasso, *Niccolò Machiavelli*, 285ff., 316ff., 333ff.

the past. During the last decades, however, this one-track notion has been increasingly replaced by an awareness that the transition from the republic to the principality was less ubiquitous and uniform. The civilization of the Quattrocento depended on the confrontation and interaction of both elements, and one may question which was the more intellectually creative of the two.[72] Similar questions have been asked about the Florence of Machiavelli's generation. Thanks to the rediscovery and reinterpretation of a great number of vital testimonies on Florentine political ideas during the first decades of the sixteenth century,[73] we have become more aware that although some members of the Florentine aristocracy at that time decided for the Medicean principality, in other social classes republican ideals gained a new momentum, drawing partly from fifteenth-century Humanism and partly from the constitutional thinking of the period of Savonarola. This strong current was eventually to play its part in the last Florentine republic of 1527–1530.

Today we are, indeed, beginning to realize that before the final triumph of absolutism, vigorous forces were at work throughout the late Italian Renaissance to develop—and sometimes even realize in actuality—some of the ideas of freedom on which life in Renaissance Italy had largely depended

[72] For the new view of the political balance in the Quattrocento—initiated in Italy especially by Nino Valeri—cf. the appendix, "Interpretations of the Political Background of the Early Renaissance," to *Crisis*, vol. 2, pp. 379–90, and my paper "Die politische Entwicklung der italienischen Renaissance," *Historische Zeitschrift* 174 (1952): 48–54. For the more recent view of a cultural balance, see W. J. Bouwsma's *The Interpretation of Renaissance Humanism* (New York, 1959), 14ff.

[73] In particular by Felix Gilbert, through the reconstruction of the political ideas discussed in the meetings in the Oricellari Gardens ("Bernardo Rucellai and the Orti Oricellari," *Journal of the Warburg Institute* 12 [1949]: 101–31) and by the authors quoted above, note 65. Much of the earlier picture has been replaced by the fundamental synthesis in Rudolf von Albertini's *Das florentinische Staatsbewusstsein im Übergang von der Republik zum Prinzipat*, which traces the political and historical thought of the various Florentine groups and parties from ca. 1500 to 1550. Cf. my note on von Albertini's work in *American Historical Review* 62 (1957): 909–11.

until the end of the fifteenth century. Not only in Florence—although it was and remained the focal point—but elsewhere on the Italian peninsula as well, more instances of such reactions to princely absolutism have come to light. They form an indispensable part of the picture, and of the legacy, of the Italian Quattrocento.[74]

It is against this knowledge of Machiavelli's age and the preceding century that we shall have to appraise the course of his development, not from the *Discourses* to *The Prince* but from *The Prince* to the *Discourses*, from a pamphlet on the Renaissance principality to the most penetrating Renaissance treatise on the republic.

[74] To mention only the most obvious one from the area with which Machiavelli students are immediately concerned, one cannot fully weigh the growth of Machiavelli's mind in its twofold response to his Florentine environment and the impact of the contemporaneous events in Rome and the State of the Church, without remembering the influence the experiences of the same years had on the mind of the Roman jurist and statesman Mario Salamonio degli Alberteschi. This Roman contemporary, who had served as *capitano del popolo* in Florence under the Savonarolan republic in the year in which Machiavelli entered the Florentine chancery, inscribed to Leo X, almost simultaneously with Machiavelli's *The Prince*, a Latin treatise, *De Principatu*. Besides a preference, reminiscent of Machiavelli, for a native militia (*arme proprie*) over mercenary troops, we encounter there an historical interpretation of the ancient Roman imperial monarchy that endeavors to present the Roman *princeps*, viewed in the light of Augustus' *principatus*, as a contractual representative of the Roman people. This is another example from Machiavelli's time of the use of history against rising absolutism—an attack against the notion of "princeps legibus solutus"—in a work still read by late sixteenth-century *monarchomachi*. Cf. Marius Salamonius de Alberteschis, *De Principatu Libri Septem, nec non Orationes ad Priores Florentinos*, ed. M. d'Addio (Milan, 1955); and M. d'Addio, *L'idea del contratto sociale dai sofisti alla riforma, e il 'De Principatu' di Mario Salamonio* (Milan, 1954).

A helpful synopsis of "The Survival of Republican Values" in Italy during the late Quattrocento and early Cinquecento may now be had in Quentin Skinner's *The Foundations of Modern Political Thought*, vol. 1., *The Renaissance* (Cambridge, 1978), 139ff.

PART III

Historiographical and Autobiographical Commentaries

SIXTEEN

The Limits of the Notion of
"Renaissance Individualism":
Burckhardt After a Century
(1960)*

S EPTEMBER 1960 marked the hundredth year since the appearance of Jacob Burckhardt's *Kultur der Renaissance in Italien*. No other work has had a comparable influence on the formation of the historical concept of the Renaissance, and during the last four decades before its centenary it became a classic read in all western countries. Since the republication of Burckhardt's original text by Walter Goetz in 1922,[1] one German reprint has followed another. After the Second World War, the early Italian and English translations began to share in this ever-growing popularity (America has seen about half a dozen editions recently), while the first Spanish translation came out in South America in 1942.

How is the Renaissance scholar to evaluate this late triumph of a book whose slow acceptance by his contemporaries brought bitter disappointment to its author? About 1900, when a "revolt of medievalists" against the nineteenth-century conception of the Renaissance was in full swing, the usual

---

* Under the title "Burckhardt's *Civilization of the Renaissance* a Century after Its Publication," this essay was written for the *Renaissance News* of the Renaissance Society of America (vol. 13, 1960) as an anniversary reflection on Burckhardt's *Kultur der Renaissance in Italien*. An Italian translation, essentially unchanged, appeared in *Il Pensiero Politico* 2 (Florence, 1969) as "Critica dell'*individualismo* Burckhardtiano: Elementi politici e sociali nel concetto di Rinascimento." In 1973, the essay was substantially revised and the concluding part (sections IV and V) enlarged. It is now presented for the first time in the unpublished version of 1973.

[1] Between the third and twelfth editions, the editor, L. Geiger, transformed the book into an increasingly enlarged, two-volume handbook.

reaction of scholars to Burckhardt's work was fear that an apparently irrepressible product of a period of historiography long passed might perpetuate an antiquated bias against the Middle Ages through a false image of the unscrupulous, ruthless and lusty "superman" of the Renaissance. Today, at a longer distance in time, little of that suspicion has survived. Many, of course, disagree with some aspects of Burckhardt's views, but few still think they are confronted with a work disfigured by strong prejudices against the medieval past. The reason is both a keener awareness of the role in modern historiography of the phenomena described in the *Civilization of the Renaissance* and a better knowledge of the mind and motives of its author.

I

To begin with the second point, in several respects our judgment of Burckhardt as the first historian of the Renaissance can be quite different today from what it was around 1900. There is no doubt that we see more clearly the injustice of too closely identifying the positions of Burckhardt and Jules Michelet, the two authors who first entitled books "The Renaissance"—even though it is true that Burckhardt borrowed the famous formula "the discovery of the world and of man" from Michelet. For whereas the latter, as heir to eighteenth-century attitudes, saw the Middle Ages as a time of "proscription" of nature and science, of "abdications successives de l'indépendance humaine," one finds no trace of such a disparagement in Burckhardt. That his work could at all be considered to reflect an antimedieval prejudice is explainable only by the circumstance that the terse and pointed comments of the *Kultur der Renaissance* cannot be read together with the originally planned companion volumes on the culture of the Middle Ages, which were never published (except for the previously written *Age of Constantine the Great*).

As an academic teacher in Zurich and Basel, Burckhardt often lectured on medieval history, and the carefully prepared manuscripts of these lectures, preserved in the Burckhardt archives in Basel, have been consulted in recent decades for the reconstruction of his historical ideas, particularly by Werner Kaegi for his fundamental biography of Burckhardt. In his courses in Zurich at the very time when he was working out the guiding principles of his *Kultur*, we find Burckhardt apologizing to his listeners for the adoption—"for want of something better"—of the fashionable term "Renaissance," even though the word sounded "as if during the Middle Ages all cultural life had been sound asleep." He talked about the "undying sympathy" that moves anyone who has grasped the spiritual harmony of medieval art, and even after the appearance of his book he never retracted in his lectures his positive approach to the Middle Ages.[2] Although from the 1850s on, classic art became his greatest love, and although he now discovered the emergence of a new world of culture in the background of the art of the fifteenth and sixteenth centuries, he did not lose his responsiveness to medieval values. Rather, he set an example of empathic flexibility, thereby becoming one of the founding fathers of historicism.

There has been a corresponding change in appraising the precise nature of Burckhardt's influence on Renaissance historiography. When at about the turn of the century scholars began to criticize and repudiate the late nineteenth-century notion of the uninhibited, secular, and even pagan "man of the Renaissance," little distinction was made between John Addington Symonds' glorification of the fifteenth and sixteenth centuries,[3] the effects of Nietzsche's teaching of the superman, and Burckhardt's own preceding ideas. Since World War II, however, a number of investigations, especially in Germany, have sharply brought out the difference in spirit that separated Burckhardt's attitude from Nietzsche's, a difference clearly noticed by Burckhardt himself. Wallace K. Ferguson's history

[2] W. Kaegi, *Jacob Burckhardt: Eine Biographie* (Basel, 1956), vol. 3, pp. 325f., 586, 590.

[3] J. K. Symonds, *Renaissance in Italy*, 7 vols. (London, 1875–1886).

of the interpretations of the Renaissance has also shown in detail that the presumed Burckhardtian elements which were attacked and pruned after 1900 were to a large extent not actually Burckhardt's own but modifications of his conception by late nineteenth century writers.[4]

This sharper definition of Burckhardt's perspective has in turn influenced the long-standing controversy over his treatment of religion in Italy during the centuries of the Renaissance. To be sure, the religious attitudes of the fourteenth, fifteenth, and sixteenth centuries have remained a moot problem of Renaissance historiography, but the anti-Burckhardtian asperity of the time about 1900 has disappeared from most of these discussions. We have become more aware of Burckhardt's tendency to give due place to Christian devotion, and even to the impact of traditional medieval religion, alongside the agnosticism, skepticism, and disbelief which are stressed in his book. If these latter received more emphasis than most historians today assign to them, it is not so much, we now realize, because of any bias on Burckhardt's part as of his need to spell out, in his section on religion, the consequences, good and bad, of "Renaissance individualism." The challenge to traditional religion, which Burckhardt believed to be evident in the lives of many highly developed individuals, had to be put into proper focus by abundant illustration; but the reasoning he drew from it was hardly strained. If the astrological superstition which he considered a sign of growing religious disbelief in Renaissance Italy has turned out to be more typical of the late Middle Ages in general than he realized, it is easy enough to play down the effects of individualism in this one case without touching the core of his argument; and if today we know even more than Burckhardt did about the remarkable part played by the urge for a more spiritual religiosity in the cultured Italian society of the Renaissance, most of the re-

---

[4] Alfred v. Martin, *Nietzsche und Burckhardt: Zwei geistige Welten im Dialog*, 3d ed. (Basel, 1945), passim; Edgar Salin, *Jacob Burckhardt und Nietzsche*, 2d ed. (Heidelberg, 1948), passim; Wallace K. Ferguson, *The Renaissance in Historical Thought* (Boston, 1948), 204f.

cent corrections of Burckhardt fit quite well the picture offered in his book, which is highlighted by a sympathetic reference to the emergence of "theistic" tendencies among the
Florentine Neoplatonists, "one of the most precious fruits of
the discovery of the world and of man." Here again one has to
conclude that the imperfections of Burckhardt's concept of
the Renaissance are not so difficult for us to overcome.

Finally, criticism of Burckhardt has subsided markedly because of a growing realization that the idea of an Italian Renaissance was not contrived by him suddenly—and, therefore,
perhaps rather willfully—but had been taking shape for generations before its mature formulation in his book. Many
studies have established[5] not only that the term "Renaissance"
was already in wide use, especially among French scholars,
when Burckhardt adopted it, but also that the view that Humanism represented the beginning of a stage of culture no
longer medieval had, in essence, been championed by the
Renaissance humanists themselves. And when, a century before Burckhardt, the historians of the Enlightenment began to
argue that the resumption of neglected classical studies and the
influx of Greek scholars into Italy after the Turkish conquest
of Constantinople could not by themselves have caused an intellectual revolution, they were in fact continuing to make a
generations-long assumption that it was in fifteenth- and sixteenth-century Italy that the decisive intellectual breakthrough to the modern age took place. As Voltaire put it, during the age of the Medici "the Italians alone had everything."
Voltaire differed from the humanistic writers of the later Renaissance only in his two conclusions that it was, to a large extent, "le génie des Toscanes," and not only the spur of the
revival of Latin and Greek letters that made such a unique
flowering possible in Medici Italy, and that Humanism contained an element of rational enlightenment that was to blos-

---

[5] Especially Ferguson, *The Renaissance*. On the conception of the Renaissance among the writers of the French Enlightenment, see also Franco Simone, *Studi Francesi* 9 (1959): 399–411.

som into a "sound philosophy" and "la raison humaine per-fectionnée" in the France of Louis XIV.

After Voltaire, the views of the Renaissance humanists and of the eighteenth-century *philosophes* could mingle and rein-force each other. Gibbon, appraising in the epilogue to his *De-cline and Fall of the Roman Empire* the reemergence of familiar-ity with Antiquity in fifteenth-century Italy, described the humanistic erudition of the Quattrocento as the "celestial dew" that helped to prepare the ground for the rise of modern vernacular idioms and letters and eventually for speculative philosophy and experimental science. In Burckhardt's own time, Jean-Pierre Charpentier published a two-volume *His-toire de la renaissance des lettres en Europe au quinzième siècle* (1843) in which the Middle Ages and the Italian Quattrocento were recognized as two different worlds, the Humanism of the Quattrocento opening the way to modern national litera-tures and to the skeptical, anti-authoritarian spirit which cul-minated in Erasmus and Montaigne.

An evolutional scheme of modern history that included bas-ically what, since Burckhardt, we have come to call the Ren-aissance in Italy had, therefore, been in preparation for several centuries. What was new and important in Burckhardt's work was the degree of maturity and the profounder meaning he gave to an already established tradition. Having followed Ro-manticism in his youth, he was, unlike his predecessors, no longer ready to identify the spirit of Renaissance Italy with the infancy of the thought of the Enlightenment. Nor was he will-ing to agree with the neoclassicists, past and present, in ac-cording the most important role to the revival of ancient let-ters, not even to the degree to which this opinion was still usually accepted after Voltaire. Burckhardt's book, in fact, abounds with rebuttals of the classicists' beliefs. The "rebirth" of Antiquity, he objects, "has been arbitrarily chosen as the name to sum up the whole period"; yet the deliverance of the state and the individual in Italy from medieval ties "would have sufficed, apart from Antiquity, to shake and mature the national mind; and most of the intellectual tendencies . . .

would be conceivable without it. . . . We must insist, as one of the chief propositions of this book, that it was not the revival of Antiquity alone, but its union with the genius of the Italian people, that achieved the conquest of the Western World." As for the exceptional influence of the Italian Trecento, Quattrocento, and Cinquecento in the history of European culture, Burckhardt saw eye to eye with his humanist predecessors and maintained their attribution to Italy of a unique and highly advanced position at the beginning of the modern age.

Some of Burckhardt's other guiding ideas were equally far from being personal idiosyncracies. They were borrowed from nineteenth-century literary movements in which he found support for his revolt against the romantic view of history to which he had adhered in his youth. The notion that at the end of the Middle Ages there occurred a "discovery of the world and of man" was shared by many who, after abandoning their romantic attitudes, wondered about the nature and origin of the world that had succeeded the age of feudalism and religious asceticism. While the succinct and elegant formula "la découverte du monde et . . . de l'homme" came from France, a similar leitmotif was used in Germany. There Hegel and historians like Karl Hagen, who was influenced by Hegel, had begun to define the tendencies initiating the modern world in terms of a new self-respect, a vindication of family life and material goods, the dignity of labor, and a new interest in "man's inner life" and in "external nature."

Other parts of Burckhardt's key tenet of "the development of the individual" were derived from Goethe. To his German translation (published in 1803) of Benvenuto Cellini's sixteenth-century autobiography, Goethe had appended a sketch of Cellini and his world that turned the old, time-honored accusations against the wickedness and depravity of the sixteenth-century Italian into a searching psychological analysis. While studying Cellini, Goethe had conceived the notion of an age that brought forth men of rare passion, marked by gross sensuality and feverish, brutal vindictiveness, but also by higher yearnings: a sincere respect for religious and ethical values, for the genius of great men, and for noble enterprises. In Goethe's depiction, Cellini's impulsive nature yields to a thousand temptations but does not succumb in the end to lowly pleasures. The force of this psychology—as well as of some comparable portrayals of the sixteenth-century Italian by two other recent poets, Alfieri in Italy and Stendhal in France—is felt throughout Burckhardt's analysis of the development of the individual.[6]

The fact that Burckhardt wove these various strands of thought into his *Kultur der Renaissance in Italien* does not detract from the originality of his vision. It is high praise to say of any historian's work that it has succeeded in making some of the most fruitful philosophical and psychological insights of his own period effective aids in the discovery and interpretation of a past age. In Burckhardt's case, this age comprised the Italian Trecento—especially from the generation of Petrarch onward—the Quattrocento, and the early Cinquecento; in other words, roughly the stretch of history to which the historiography of the humanists and of the Enlightenment had drawn attention long before Burckhardt.[7]

Thus, Burckhardt's decisive step was to focus some of the basic historical queries of the early nineteenth century upon a long-favored portion of Italian history. In order to realize the originality of his conclusions, one needs to recall that Hegel, in attributing the beginning of the modern age to the German

---

[6] Stendhal's influence on Burckhardt's conception of Renaissance individualism has long been well known. The stimulation given by Alfieri emerges from Burckhardt's reference to Alfieri's dictum "La pianta uomo nasce più robusta in Italia che in qualunque altra terra—e che gli stessi atroci delitti che vi si commettono ne sono una prova." Cf. Kaegi, *Jacob Burckhardt*, vol. 4, p. 468, and E. M. Janssen, *Jacob Burckhardt und die Renaissance* (Assen, 1970), 244.

[7] As for Burckhardt's inclusion of Petrarch's generation in the "Renaissance," and at times Dante's and even that of Frederick II of Hohenstaufen, it should be said that there is no consistency in his practice. He did not draw any clear chronological boundary line between the Middle Ages and his newly established period—a major imprecision which has proved a stumbling block in discussions of the Burckhardtian conception of the Renaissance.

Reformation, and Michelet, in placing the dividing line between the Middle Ages and the modern world in the sixteenth century and chiefly outside Italy, had both expressly disparaged the civilization of Quattrocento Italy.[8] The psychological observations and *aperçus* of poets and writers like Goethe, Alfieri, and Stendhal, on the other hand, had tended to concentrate upon sixteenth-century Italians and their characteristic state of mind, and none of them had paid attention to the consequences of the appearance of the new individualism for the historical concept of the transition from the Middle Ages to the modern age. Although Burckhardt adopted some of the queries of previous historians and of contemporary thinkers, it was only when three Italian centuries were systematically reviewed by him through the prism of early nineteenth-century ideas that the concept of those centuries changed from the long-familiar one of "a renaissance of the arts and letters in Italy" to the period concept of "the Italian Renaissance."

A laborious process of reading and reinterpreting the historical sources was needed for this metamorphosis. Burckhardt began with an awareness of a new spirit in the art of the Quattrocento,[9] but before his observations could develop into a statement on Renaissance or even Quattrocento culture in general, he had to assimilate a world of chronicles and sources of information available in the tales and other literature of those centuries, which had never been exploited in detail for "Kulturgeschichte." From Kaegi's biographical narrative we learn that Burckhardt accepted the call to Zurich for the half decade preceding the publication of his *Kultur der Renaissance* in part because an important collection of editions of fourteenth- and fifteenth-century sources existed there. He took home one by one the huge eighteenth-century tomes of Muratori's *Rerum Italicarum Scriptores* and all the rich material that came to light in his own time, laying a foundation broader

---

[8] On Hegel, cf. Delio Cantimori, in *Annali della Scuola Norm. Sup. di Pisa*, 2d ser., vol. 1 (1932), 235–39.

[9] See notes 20 and 21, below.

than any one previous for reconstructing the age of humanistic literature and culture.

The discovery that the historical conception set forth in Burckhardt's book had been elaborated by the generations before him and by certain of his contemporaries appears to be the main reason why the negative judgments current about 1900, and still in circulation in the 1920s, have finally given way to a wide reliance on Burckhardt and his scholarship. No one with sufficient knowledge of the antecedents and genesis of Burckhardt's work can still ask sarcastically whether Burckhardt's claim to have described a new period profoundly distinct from the Middle Ages may not, after all, have been an illusion springing from ignorance of the Middle Ages—as was suggested during the first decades of the twentieth century by such scholars as Étienne Gilson and Lynn Thorndike.

II

Does the consensus about the solidity and scope of Burckhardt's attainment mean that his view of the place of the Italian Renaissance in European history has now, after a hundred years, finally won out?

Burckhardt's thesis, we must understand, is not identical with the notion that some basic elements of modern civilization and, in particular, of the modern mind, appeared in a rudimentary form in Italy during the fourteenth, fifteenth, and sixteenth centuries and afterwards spread through the northern countries. This was how humanistic scholars had always viewed the progress of their cause, at least from the Italian Quattrocento onward, and how eighteenth-century writers had conceived the course of history from the Medicean age to the French and English Enlightenment, with its "sound philosophy." But to the nineteenth-century generation that had abandoned Romanticism, the cardinal point seemed to be in what form, where, and when, after the decay of feudalism and a hierarchical order of life, there first appeared a type of society in which the social function of the individual, his sense of values, and his perceptive powers differed from those of men in the medieval centuries. Burckhardt was searching not so much for the roots of a gradual evolution toward the modern world as for the first appearance of a clearly modern pattern of culture and thought within the framework of a modern state and for the emergence of the psychological and intellectual characteristics of modern man. "The Renaissance will be presented," he explained during the preparation of his work, "in so far as it has become the mother and home of modern man"—that is, through the molding influence of the period on subsequent centuries; his book would point out, for Renaissance Italy, "a number of phenomena of the modern mind."[10] No other leitmotif occurs as often in his text as the contention that the Italians of the Renaissance were the "first-born among the sons of modern Europe," that "the Italian Renaissance must be called the leader of modern ages," and that "the first truly modern man," "a wholly recognizable prototype of modern man," appeared in the period of Petrarch and the Quattrocento.[11] Only two other points are made as frequently, and these are always closely interrelated with the first. One is that the classical revival in literature and art was not the *cause* of the new culture, although it was only in the revived classical form that the new intellectual tendencies could find a means of expression capable of influencing and changing the course of Western culture as a whole. The other

---

[10] From Burckhardt's letters during his work on the *Kultur der Renaissance*, quoted by Kaegi, *Jacob Burckhardt*, vol. 4, pp. 664 and 673. Cf. also the comments by Kaegi, 674, and Janssen, *Burckhardt und die Renaissance*, 82.

[11] *The Civilization of the Renaissance in Italy* (New York: Modern Library, 1954), 100, 416, 219, 249. In the only available, continually reprinted translation, by S.G.C. Middlemore, the last quotation, in German "ein ganz kenntliches Urbild des modernen Menschen," reads: "a significant type of the modern spirit." "Significant," "type," and "spirit," are all inaccurate and misleading renderings—a warning against the use of Middlemore's text without consultation of the German original. Incidentally, this specific reference to the "Urbild des modernen Menschen" was later canceled, presumably because of objections raised by Wilhelm Dilthey; cf. Kaegi, *Jacob Burckhardt*, vol. 4, pp. 719–22.

point is that a new cultural growth took place in Italy because, as the book states on its first page, there, in contrast to all other European countries, "the feudal system" did not survive long but was transformed at an early date into the society of the modern world. Already by the end of the struggle between the popes and the Hohenstaufen emperors, feudalism "had been shaken off almost entirely." This made it possible, only a few generations later, for a new type of state to emerge in which the individual was delivered from his former bonds, and this, in turn, transformed secular values and generated critical thought to a degree unknown outside Italy until the sixteenth century or even later.

Couched in these precise terms, the Burckhardtian concept of the Renaissance is far from being on its way to unanimous adoption by present-day scholars. At least two other notions of the historical development of Europe at the time of the Renaissance, both intrinsically antagonistic to that of Burckhardt, have also made headway since the late nineteenth century. First, the classicistic view of history returned in a new guise, in spite of Burckhardt's caveat against treating the revival of classical studies as *causa prima*. As the role of classical models in medieval literature, philosophy, and art became better known, the history of European culture began to be viewed by some, especially literary scholars, as a continual oscillation between periods of greater or lesser influence of classical elements. In this view, Italian Humanism from the fourteenth to the sixteenth centuries occupies a position between a medieval phase and a modern phase of humanistic classicism, both under French leadership; and thus Renaissance Italy loses much of the newness which the Burckhardtian perspective gives to it. In France, and wherever interest in the medieval humanism of the twelfth century or in the humanistic aspects of Thomism during the thirteenth has been strong, the work of Burckhardt has not held much attraction for the general reader, nor has it had much effect on scholars.

At the opposite end of the spectrum are those who, instead of attributing more influence to the ancient heritage than

Burckhardt would allow, wonder whether our standard for what was "modern" after 1300 has not, on the contrary, remained too close to the classicistic point of view; whether we are not wrong to exclude from our concept of the Renaissance the realistic, individualistic, and urban movements outside the classical tradition. Should we not include such European-wide currents of the fourteenth and fifteenth centuries as philosophical "nominalism" and Occamistic science, the naturalism inherent in the political philosophy which sprang from the clash between papal and secular powers, the mystical movements of the late Middle Ages, and the realism of Flemish art? Within this larger framework, can we attribute to the course of events in Italy more significance than that of a merely local or national variation of a European development?

This is not the place to attempt to weigh the relative merits of the three approaches, each representing a partial truth. The point here is that we have every reason to expect that they will be in vigorous contention for decades to come, and perhaps forever. What I wish to explore is to what extent those who believe that the Italian Renaissance can be considered a "prototype" of the modern age will still be able to rely on Burckhardt's book as a sufficient foundation. In order to answer this question, we must try to find any symptomatic lacunae in his definition of Italian culture during the fourteenth, fifteenth, and sixteenth centuries.[12]

III

From the vantage point of present-day scholarship, Burckhardt's picture of the Renaissance and Humanism is, of course, incomplete because of his ignorance of countless facts, writings, and queries brought forward in recent years. But this is bound to be true of any historical work more than a

[12] The only omission in the *Civilization* which is usually mentioned is the neglect (originally not planned) of Renaissance art; cf. Kaegi, *Jacob Burckhardt*, vol. 4, pp. 665f., 689f. There are, however, other omissions with graver consequences, as will be seen.

hundred years old. A deeper problem raised by his book is whether, despite its many great qualities, it was sufficiently inclusive with respect to the historical questions that could be posed—and were posed—in its own time. The fact, already stressed, that Burckhardt's presentation shows an unusually broad response to the philosophical and literary issues of his generation and those immediately preceding would make any serious omission all the more remarkable and in need of explanation.

There have not been many investigations of how complete Burckhardt's reconstruction was relative to the scholarship of his own age. Nevertheless, one gap in his work is strikingly obvious. One would think that nothing would have appealed to Burckhardt as much as the idea, already formulated in the eighteenth century, that the vitality of the Italian communes was stimulated by their successful defense of political independence and republican freedom during the eleventh, twelfth, and thirteenth centuries, and that it was owing to this political stimulus that the arts and letters later matured so rapidly. Even before 1800, philosophers and historians in Europe had sought to identify the factors in Italian society that might have been responsible for the distinctive flowering of culture on the peninsula; and by the early nineteenth century, two main complementary theories had gradually emerged to account for it.

One ascribed it to the invigorating power of competition within and between free city-states; this was an English eighteenth-century idea traceable to Hume (who applied it to Antiquity but was too prejudiced against Italian politics and literature to apply it to the Italian city-republics of the late Middle Ages). It was proposed most maturely in Adam Ferguson's *Essay on the History of Civil Society* of 1767, where it is argued that when in free societies many different types of men react to a common challenge, every conceivable form of human energy is released, and engagement and "exertion" become the major stimuli for culture. Ancient "Greece, divided into many little states, and agitated beyond any spot on the

globe by domestic contentions and foreign wars, set the example in every species of literature. The fire was communi-
cated to Rome; not when the [Roman] state ceased to be war-
like and discontinued political agitations, but when she mixed
the love of refinement and of pleasure with her national pursuits, and indulged an inclination to study in the midst of fer-
ments occasioned by the wars and pretensions of opposite fac-
tions. It was revived in modern Europe among the turbulent
states of modern Italy. . . ."

The second approach was stimulated by Rousseau's praise
of popular sovereignty and direct democracy in small local
states. Under the influence of his early life in Geneva, the participation of a full-fledged citizen in the government of his city
patria had seemed to him an even more effective spur to civic
vigor than "turbulence." At the time of Geneva's subjection to
Napoleon, Rousseau's countryman Simonde de' Sismondi
drew upon Rousseau's ideas for a comparative study of the
effects of the ancient Greek and medieval Italian city-states on
the behavior and outlook of their citizens. Sismondi's multi-
volumed history of the Italian republics of the Middle Ages
was, it is true, strongly disfigured by a passionate, rationalis-
tic, and democratic bias, often obtrusive and anachronistic,
which caused his books, after an enormous success during the
first decades of the nineteenth century, to fall into relatively
early obscurity. But this does not detract from the fact that he
was the first to weigh seriously the consequences of participation by all full-fledged citizens in the sovereignty and government of the Italian as well as the Greek city-states. A man
who has once had a share in the exercise of public power, Sismondi argued, "est une créature plus noble, plus relevée, que
celui qui n'en exerce aucun," for his horizons have widened
and his powers of critical reflection have grown. "Instead of
being occupied solely with himself, he has occupied himself
with others for their greater good. He has thus opened his
heart to more noble feelings, he has formed a higher idea of
his own dignity." Sismondi maintained that "Liberté politique"—that is, active participation in the life of the state—

"est la plus noble des éducations qu'on puisse donner à l'homme"; a citizen who has tasted this divine food "disdains all human nourishment." Despite its rhetorical garb, this might be called the first theory of the historical consequences of city-state life; it is an effort to explain its vigor in late medieval Italy by drawing a parallel with polis life in ancient Greece.

In the works of Adam Ferguson and Sismondi we find the seeds of an interpretation[13] that intimately connects psychological and intellectual change with a citizen's political life. Some historians of the subsequent romantic period carried this approach still further. In 1844, the *Storia delle belle lettere in Italia* by Paolo Emiliani Giudici (like Ferguson's and Sismondi's works, a book that should have been known to Burckhardt) made a special plea for "a political interpretation of literature [*spiegazione politica della letteratura*]." Political and literary ideas were to be considered in conjunction because of the interrelationship that exists between political independence and "independenza mentale." Even in the sixteenth century, Emiliani Giudici endeavored to show, there was a profound difference in intellectual attitude between the writers of Machiavelli's generation—"who had all been educated to think freely while the heart of the republic still palpitated"— and the courtiers of the subsequent period under Duke Cosimo I; any understanding of the Florentine Cinquecento depended on clearly differentiating the climate of the first thirty years from that of the rest of the century.[14]

[13] Hardly more than seeds, because Ferguson's *Essay* does not elaborate upon conditions in Italy, and Sismondi condemned the Quattrocento as the period of tyrants too passionately to search for any survival of *liberté politique* after the fourteenth century.

[14] On Hume, see John R. Hale, *England and the Italian Renaissance* (London, 1954), 46f.; Adam Ferguson, *Essay* (Edinburgh, 1767), 271f.; Sismondi, in his *Études sur les constitutions des peuples libres* (Brussels, 1836), and *Histoire des républiques italiennes du moyen âge* (Paris, 1809–1815); also H. R. Felder, "Simonde de Sismondi: Gedanken über Freiheit" (diss., University of Zurich, 1954), 11, 25, 29. For Emiliani Giudici, see Giovanni Getto, *Storia delle storie letterarie* (Milan, 1942), esp. 239f.

Against this background one realizes that some approaches which had been taken long before 1860 were overlooked or quietly excluded when Burckhardt undertook to describe "the development of the individual" in Renaissance Italy. In the chapter so titled, after insisting on the disappearance of medieval cast distinctions, he analyzes the growth of many new fields of knowledge, the changes in the evaluation of life, and especially the appearance of uniquely "rounded" personalities. All these—to him, outstanding—characteristics of the period he traces back not to the molding influence of a society in which citizens were exposed to competitive conditions and allowed to be rulers as well as ruled, but rather to the impact of the life of those who through avoidance of public duties gained leisure for cultural pursuits. The type of "private man, indifferent to politics and occupied partly . . . with the interests of a dilettante," is said to have developed primarily in those states in which despots had taken the burden of government and administration upon themselves and thus relieved their subjects of participation in the common pursuits.[15] But similar conditions existed also in republics, where men in power often had "to make the utmost" of a short period of triumph and afterwards, defeated or exiled, found themselves "involuntarily at leisure." Like the subjects of despots, such citizens, recognizing "the dangers and thanklessness of public life," learned to prize "a developed private life" as the necessary basis for cultural pursuits.

Why did Burckhardt limit his interest to this one aspect? Why did he not make use of the rudimentary sociology of city-state life already prepared by historians of the Enlightenment and Romanticism? Certainly not because he misjudged the continued importance of the republics of Florence and Venice during the Renaissance. His book includes some of the most impressive and sympathetic pages ever written on

[15] "Despotism fostered in the highest degree the individuality not only of the tyrant or condottiere himself, but also of the men whom he . . . used as his tools: the secretary, minister, poet, and companion" (*Civilization*, Modern Library ed., 101).

achievements in the Florentine republic: the spread of political *raisonnement* and a keen sense of calculation among an entire people, and the priority in time of the patronage of Florentine citizens over that of the princes. He described the difference between Florentine historiography—written "by citizens for citizens, as the ancients did"—and the work of official, paid historiographers in most principalities, from whose propensity for the "servile citation" of ancient parallels to the actions of the prince "the great Florentine historians and statesmen are completely free . . . , because the nature of their political life necessarily fostered in them a mode of thought with some analogy to that of Antiquity"; and he cited the last, heroic defense of the city in 1529–1530, without which Florentine history "would have been the poorer by one of its greatest and most enobling memories."

The reason why Burckhardt did not develop any such observations for his general conception of the period must be sought, rather, in the peculiar bent of his personal relationship to culture. During the mid-1840s, when he was not yet thirty years old, he had turned with abhorrence from the rising democratic trend, which seemed to him to represent a fatal peril to civilization, heralding an upsurge of the masses, brutal wars, and despotism. He felt that he himself in such an iron, barbaric age should lead a life of privacy and withdrawal, by which he might best help to preserve the old, aristocratic traditions of European culture. It is not a question here of how good a judge of his time and prophet of the future Burckhardt was, or how valid his appraisal of Europe's aristocratic past. What matters to us is the impact these passionate convictions had on his views and historical methodology. Although his political outlook was far from the "liberalism" of German *Neuhumanisten* like Wilhelm von Humboldt, whom he admired, in effect he adopted Humboldt's belief that true individual culture could develop only in separation from the state. It is true that Burckhardt feared the further rise of the nineteenth-century state, shocked as he was by the revolutions of the 1840s, while Humboldt had been afraid of the absolutist

monarchy of the eighteenth century; but for both, the ultimate goal was the harmonious growth and training of all the
potentialities of the proud, autarchic individual.[16]

Because Burckhardt judged life and culture from the position of individualistic nineteenth-century liberalism, he did
not fully grasp that delicate balance between unusual stimulation and unusual violation of individual privacy typical of
civic life in city-state societies. When in his later years he defined the relationship between the Greek polis and Greek culture in his imposing *Griechische Kulturgeschichte*, he expounded, more than is today normally considered justified,
the thesis that the individual was forced by the Greek city-
state, after having come to maturity in the hothouse atmosphere of the polis, to "flee" its despotic pretensions and create,
like Diogenes, a humane culture apart from the state. On the
whole, post-Burckhardtian scholarship has gradually expanded the positive role assigned to the participatory life of
the polis in the creation of Greek ideas and ideals, and Burckhardt's concept of the "free individual," initially bred by the
city-state but subsequently forced, and glad, to nurture his
cultural life independent of the demands of the polis, has retained only a very partial validity.[17]

There is a similar divergence between the views of many
present-day scholars and those of Burckhardt on the relationship of Renaissance culture to the Renaissance state. Even
though no one denies that the "private man, indifferent to politics and occupied partly . . . with the interests of a dilettante"
became a factor in Renaissance life, especially during its later

[16] K. Löwith, "Burckhardt's Entschluss zur Apolitie," in his *Jacob Burckhardt: Der Mensch inmitten der Geschichte* (Lucerne, 1936), 152–88, 363–71. For
Cantimori on Burckhardt's *apolitismo*, see *Rivista Storica Italiana* 66 (1954):
532f., 536.

[17] See Rudolph Stadelmann's keen, though occasionally overstrained, analysis in "Jacob Burckhardts griechische Kulturgeschichte," *Die Antike* 7 (1931):
esp. 57–62; and we should keep in mind the many editons of Alfred Zim-
mern's *The Greek Commonwealth: Politics and Economics in Fifth-Century Athens*, a work of 1911, as well as Werner Jaeger's *Paideia: Die Formung des griech-
ischen Menschen*, a work of the 1930s.

stages, a good deal of recent study has focused on situations in which new values and ideas were created by men who, emotionally and intellectually, were deeply involved in the political struggles and public life of their age. Something similar applies to Burckhardt's attitude toward the new political science and its practical application—those subtle designs for constitutions (true Renaissance "works of art") which, drawing on the experience of generations, tried through an elaborate division of power to ensure efficiency and the fair participation in government of rival political groups and social strata. Burckhardt, in the way of the romantics, simply decried "the great modern fallacy that a constitution can be manufactured by a combination of existing forces and tendencies"; all he had to say on this score was that Renaissance thought had to be considered "the pattern" for the defects—not the achievements—of the modern world.[18]

No greater sympathy is shown by him for the forces that shaped the Renaissance philosophy of history. One of the central problems in post-Burckhardtian scholarship has been the interminable controversy among Renaissance humanists over the respective merits of the *Respublica Romana* and the subsequent monarchy of the Roman emperors—a controversy that focused on the well-known confrontation between Cicero, the defender of the *Respublica*, and Caesar, the founder of imperial monarchy. We probably have no better means than this controversy for studying the basic differences between the politico-historical outlook emerging in the city-republics and that of the tyrant courts; yet here again the *Kultur der Renaissance in Italien* has provided no point of departure for later scholarship. From the manuscripts in the Burckhardt archives we have learned that only a few years before beginning preparations for his book, Burckhardt had commented at length in his lectures upon Caesar and Caesar's assassination. One is amazed to find that the great master of objective historicism was unable to recognize that two ages and Weltanschauungen had

---

[18] *Civilization*, Modern Library ed., 68.

clashed. To Burckhardt, all truth and historical justification were on the side of Caesar; his murder had been perpetrated by "real criminals"; it was "the greatest stupidity" recorded in the annals of Roman history.[19] Thus, still another door to understanding the reciprocity of thought and political experience in the Renaissance was closed to the author of the *Kultur der Renaissance*.

IV

These blind spots also affected Burckhardt's appreciation of Humanism. If it is true that the political thought and historical outlook of the Renaissance can be appraised only in the context of the feud between city-state republics and Renaissance despotism, our understanding of humanistic pursuits will suffer if they are viewed, in isolation from the vital struggles of the age, as contributions of self-sufficient dilettantes or scholars.

Here again Burckhardt's conception of the period offers little guidance to attempts to view Renaissance Humanism as an evolving movement reflecting various political and social structures. Moreover, although Burckhardt had parted with the view that ancient literature was the major spur to Renaissance culture, he basically accepted the traditional opinion concerning the nature of humanistic contacts with the classical heritage. The idea of a renascence of something past remained at the heart of his conception of the work of the humanists, and in his book he made use of the vague *Volksgeist* notion of romantic historiography to explain the re-emergence of ancient literature and culture. The essence of the revival of classical Antiquity and the explanation for the Italian origin of this revival, we read in the *Kultur der Renaissance in Italien*, was "an alliance between two distant epochs in the civilization of the same people," a "partial reawakening of the old Italian genius."

[19] Kaegi, *Jacob Burckhardt*, vol. 3, pp. 308f.

By this token, those features of the humanistic movement which Burckhardt continued to call the "reproduction of Antiquity" remained in the foreground. While emphasis was put on neo-Latin poetry and Latin oratory and epistolography, composed in rivalry with the classical models, Latin treatises, dialogues, and works of historiography were given only a few pages or even paragraphs. This order of emphasis has practically been reversed in the study of Renaissance Humanism during the twentieth century. Most of the interest—amounting to an entirely new branch of intellectual history—has been devoted to the latter. This has happened precisely because these genera of humanistic literature, while probably the least successful as imitations, testify to the originality of the Renaissance, since representatives of diverse intellectual and political tendencies managed to express their own particular convictions through treatises, dialogues, and historical works. By revealing their authors' minds, these branches of humanistic literature often allow us deeper insight than any other source into the differences in outlook and sentiment that existed among humanists in various regions and states, specifically between writers in civic and courtly surroundings. Indeed, it is largely because of the transference of scholarly attention to these formerly neglected areas of literature that Burckhardt's estimation of the contribution of private life has now become a matter of doubt.

We have, thus, come to recognize that in the long period from the fourteenth to the sixteenth centuries, Humanism was a far more profoundly variable historical trend than Burckhardt knew, differing in structure and creativity, in ideas and values, and in political and social background. In fact, despite temporary setbacks, scholarship after Burckhardt has on the whole moved steadily in the direction of a conception of the Renaissance which recognizes—for Humanism as well as for art—two fundamentally different periods: the "Trecento" and the "Quattrocento," the first still basically medieval, the second the true beginning of the Renaissance. This important distinction had to be worked out in detail almost without the help of Burckhardt, who instead of differentiating the successive phases of the Renaissance, presented a comparatively static picture in which the rise of "individualism," "the discovery of the world and of man," and related themes are presented as features common to three centuries.

Does this criticism mean that our perspective of the Renaissance has so changed that we can no longer call ourselves "Burckhardtians"? Before drawing this conclusion, we should remember that as a young art historian, prior to writing his *Kultur der Renaissance*, Burckhardt had strongly emphasized the profundity of the changes at the beginning of the Quattrocento. In his *Cicerone*, a "Guide to the Art Treasures of Italy" written five years before the *Kultur*, he had dated the onset of "the true Renaissance" (*eigentliche Renaissance*) in architecture "about 1420,"[20] and had magnificently described the rise of "the new spirit" of Renaissance painting "during the first decades of the fifteenth century."[21] Thus, Burckhardt was actually the provider of two heterogeneous period concepts, one of which brings out the crucial role of the first decades of the Quattrocento in the breakthrough of "the new spirit" that guided and animated the mature Renaissance in art.

We do not know whether he himself was aware of the antithetical character of his approaches to art on the one hand and to culture in general on the other when, five years later, he drew his picture of Renaissance culture. But even if he was aware of the inherent antagonism between the period divisions set forth in his two books, he could not reconcile them in his *Kultur der Renaissance* by pointing out the chronological parallel between the emergence in art of the "true Renaissance" and the emergence of "true" Humanism. For it is only thanks to post-Burckhardtian insights into the history of Humanism—the emergence among Italian humanists not only of philological studies and rhetoric but also of a "new spirit" in their outlook on life, history, and politics—that students have

[20] Burckhardt, *Gesamtausgabe*, vol. 3, p. 153.
[21] Ibid., vol. 4, p. 186.

become aware of the parallelism of the two revolutions in art and in Humanism.

The recognition of the beginnings of the *eigentliche Renaissance* in these two areas during the early Quattrocento cannot be separated from the observation that in both the decisive steps were nearly always taken first by Florentines, or at least so often that for two crucial generations the city-state republic of Florence (and not merely individual Florentines) played the role in the history of Renaissance culture and thought that Athens had played in the culture and thought of Greece. But here again the obvious historical problem was not really tackled by Burckhardt; it was left to later historians, and it is one of the main propositions of the present essay that if one takes Burckhardt's point of departure—his one-sided emphasis on the "individualism" of the Renaissance, to the exclusion of nearly everything already proposed in the historiography of the Enlightenment and of Romanticism concerning the crucial role of city-state life for culture and thought—one cannot give a fully satisfying account of the position of Florence in humanistic culture. On the other hand, since Burckhardt's greatest contribution was not his stress on individualism but his attempt to prove that the culture of Renaissance Italy was a "prototype" of life and thought in the modern world, it does no damage to the heart of the Burckhardtian thesis if one tries to establish a better balance between city-state society and "the private man" in our picture of the Italian Renaissance.

Today it may be easier to accomplish such a shift in emphasis than it was for Burckhardt, because a belief in the great cultural creativity of city-state societies is in obvious harmony with some of the general historical assumptions of the century that has passed since his time. Increasing familiarity with the preceding civilizations of the ancient East has only helped to strengthen the conviction that Greek and Roman culture was different from that of the Orient because it was founded on the political liberty existing in city-states; that much of what was to remain the political, ethical, and cultural heritage of the Western world was first developed in the bracing atmosphere

of small commonwealths. The more fully, therefore, we recognize the significance that city-state society had for the Italian Renaissance, the more the relationship of Renaissance culture to modern life is seen to be part of a wider manifestation:
the unique affiliation of Western history with traditions inherited from poleis of some sort. With the growing attention paid
to this historical phenomenon, the essence of the Burckhardtian conception—the "prototypical" character of the Renaissance in Italy—may carry even greater conviction in years to
come.

V

This does not mean, of course, that we should visualize Italy
during the Renaissance exclusively as a country composed of
city-state republics. For although it is impossible to understand how fourteenth-, fifteenth-, and sixteenth-century Italy
could push ahead of the rest of late-medieval Europe without
a keen awareness of the climate prevailing in Italian cities, the
role of city-state society and republican freedom in Italy must
be appraised within another context as well.

This context is inseparable from the fact that the world of
semisovereign Italian city-states after 1300 was more or less
restricted to northern and central Italy. In one and the same
epoch the peninsula not only saw the despotic governments of
"tyrants" replace the liberty of most of the communes, especially north of the Apennines, but also experienced two other
unusual forms of government: the Papal State and, from the
early Middle Ages on, the first large monarchies in Europe
managed by efficient bureaucratic administrations. Ever since
Norman and Hohenstaufen times, the southern half of the
peninsula had been united in one or two monarchical states
(Naples and Sicily) which were in part the direct successors to
the Byzantine provincial government; and by the fourteenth
century, a north Italian counterpart to the southern monarchy
or monarchies had been established in the Duchy of Lom-
bardy-Milan, the successor to many of the local tyrant states

that had emerged in the north Italian communes from the early thirteenth century onward.

In a word, not only did the Italian peninsula contain within its borders the outstanding city-states of late medieval Europe, but at an early date Italians became familiar with virtually every form of feudal and postfeudal political life. For centuries, a large variety of governmental systems—a variety found nowhere else in Europe—vied with, learned from, and propelled each other: city-states and large regional states, republics and principalities, and the first international institution of European scope, the Papal Curia and Papal State.[22] Moreover, until the beginning of the Renaissance, the German emperors, as nominal heirs to the ancient Roman Empire, exercised a measure of supremacy over this diversified political world, at least during their military expeditions to Rome for imperial coronation. Out of the ensuing confrontation of the medieval empire with many of the Italian communes, there developed among the early humanists of the Renaissance a long-lived controversy over the historical significance of the ancient *Respublica Romana* and the *Imperium Romanum* that was seminal in the eventual rise of a secular, no longer medieval outlook on history. After 1400, alongside the civic society led by the patriciate of the republics—which in important cities, and especially Florence, anticipated in some respects the openness of modern society—there arose at the princely courts a new courtly society, no longer feudal, which was to serve as a model for European courts during the first modern centuries. This immense diversity of social and political experiences in the Renaissance helps to explain why Italy showed Europe the way from the Middle Ages to the modern world; why, in Burckhardtian terms, it became the"first-born" member of the modern European family of nations.

The conception of the Italian Renaissance suggested in this

---

[22] The reader will especially remember what the diversity of the Italian regions and states meant for the shaping of the minds of Bruni and Machiavelli and for the maturation of the new values during the Quattrocento.

essay undoubtedly amounts to a metamorphosis of some of Burckhardt's basic ideas. But it is in this revised form, it seems to me, that Burckhardt's perception of the historical impact of Renaissance Italy on modern Europe will have a chance to survive among the competing notions of the passage from the Middle Ages to the modern age.

SEVENTEEN

The Course of My Studies in Florentine Humanism (1965)★

I T IS impossible for me not to feel pleasure at today's recognition of my labors. But this does not put a nagging doubt to rest. More than a few students in my generation have experienced a troubling disproportion between the broad new horizons opened by the impact of their agitated lives, and a failure to produce full and comprehensive presentations of their new visions. War, exile, migration, and repeated changes of the language in which I set down the results of my studies had the effect that only too often I had to be content with writing essays or suggestions instead of rounded books. I cannot help wondering whether so fragmentary a life's work deserves the honor offered me today.

★ The following pages reproduce a speech given on 23 August 1965 on the occasion of the conferment—under the auspices of the Italian Rotary and the University of Pisa—of the "Premio internazionale Galileo Galilei, Forte dei Marmi" for work in the field of "Storia italiana." The speech was to be printed in the periodical *Critica Storica* in 1966, but for a number of reasons it did not appear until 1972 (as "Uno storico del Novecento in cammino verso l'Umanesimo civile fiorentino," *Critica Storica*, Anno 9), with a preliminary note stating that "the text appears here in the form in which it was originally read with only minor changes, but with the addition of a number of notes that refer to some of my more recent writings. The Italian version of the speech is owed to Professor Aldo Scaglione." In preparing the English version for print, I have limited changes primarily to those of style and formulation. Where alterations from the perspective of the 1970s and 1980s instead of 1965 seemed indispensable—mostly through references to publications after 1965—these have been made in the notes. On the first and last pages I have omitted some references to the external circumstances in which the speech was given. Readers wishing to learn as exactly as possible how I expressed myself in 1965 should consult *Critica Storica*.

However, most of my scattered publications have revolved around a common center. Their raison d'être has been a distinctive approach to the early Renaissance in Italy to which I have remained loyal even though it led to controversy with some of my seniors and coevals. Today I would like to say a few words about the nature of this approach and how I came to it, hoping that it will help to explain how works which, in my view, were often incomplete and largely confined to one locality, Florence, have nonetheless contributed to the understanding of broad issues in the study of Humanism and the Renaissance.

Let me begin with a personal recollection from my student years. It was in one of the first seminars I took at the University of Leipzig with my unforgettable teacher, Walter Goetz, that I came upon the prevailing theories of those years, according to which Humanism north of the Alps, and in particular in Germany, developed from a native, late medieval background essentially independent of any—at least any salutary—influence from the south. I was given the assignment of forming my own opinion on the basis of a good many original sources, and after concentrated study I formulated a statement that eventually proved convincing to our small group. I concluded that all the current theories were to a degree prejudiced and that the change in the intellectual climate in the rest of Europe would not have been possible without the changes in interest, education, and thought discernible in Italy during the Quattrocento. That seminar was held in 1920, and a caustic critic might say that all my later studies have been an effort to prove that my first impression was correct. In my defense, however, I plead that in an era of frequently adverse scholarly trends it may have been a merit to make my point tenaciously and try to bring out all the supporting facts.

When, at the end of my student years, I attempted seriously to define the relationship between the humanistic aspirations south and north of the Alps, I thought (as others then did) mainly of the impact the Florentine Neoplatonists might have had on Erasmian humanism.[1] It was with a stipend for research on Ficino and Pico della Mirandola that I crossed the Alps in 1925, and my first objects of study in the Florentine libraries were Ficino's early letters, his commentary on St. Paul's epistles, and some texts revealing Ficino's and Pico della Mirandola's divergent attitudes toward astrology. But the miscellaneous manuscripts, once owned by Florentine citizens, that contained these writings of Ficino's—mostly in the Volgare—frequently included other writings, which had circulated in Florence since the first half of the Quattrocento: speeches by citizens in public office, ancient Roman orations translated into the Volgare, and often works and translations of the chancellor Leonardo Bruni. Compared with these older writings, which expressed the views and values of a politically active, patriotic citizenry, the works produced by the Neoplatonic generation seemed abstruse and removed from the daily life of the city—material for students of philosophy rather than for historians eager to grasp the guiding ideas and emotive and moral forces that helped Florence to remain a vital political and cultural center during the Quattrocento. So after some minor publications on the Neoplatonists,[2] I gave my Platonic material to Paul Oskar Kristeller for use in his *Supplementum Ficinianum* and turned to the then much less-known early Renaissance generation whose intellectual leader had been Bruni. In that new study perplexing surprises awaited me.

It had long been rather generally assumed that by the late Trecento the time of freedom and republicanism in the communes had passed; that in the so-called *età delle signorie e dei principati* Humanism was being shaped primarily in the environment of the courts. But in Bruni and his Florentine followers, political thought and the evaluation of life were being

---

[1] Cf. my paper "Zur Frage des Ursprungs des deutschen Humanismus und seiner religiösen Reformbestrebungen," *Historische Zeitschrift* 132 (1925).

[2] See in particular my paper "Willensfreiheit und Astrologie bei Marsilio Ficino und Pico della Mirandola," in *Kultur- und Universalgeschichte. Walter Goetz . . . dargebracht* (Leipzig, 1927).

shaped by public spirit, by a full engagement in the life of the community, and by a firm republican idealism. These Florentine humanists were guided by uncompromising ideals of active participation in the state, believing that without a practical commitment to the community human nature cannot really fulfill itself.

Historians of philosophy around 1900 had often referred to Bruni erroneously as one of those advocates of a humanistic Stoicism who taught the sage to follow reason and suppress the passions.[3] Yet Bruni clearly represented an all but forgotten type of early humanistic Aristotelian; he had the outlook of one who had learned from Aristotle that a citizen's life ought to be devoted to his commonwealth; that strong emotions—both love and hate—are necessary if a man is to live up to his political commitments; and that wealth need not be contemptible in the eyes of wise men, because without riches no commonwealth can flourish.[4] Although Cicero had presented the Stoic view in his *Tusculan Disputations*, in his way of life and in many of his works he was evidently far from being a "Stoic sage." In the decades before and after 1400, I came to realize, Bruni and various other humanists of Salutati's school began to rediscover the Roman aspects of Cicero's life and thought, and it was from the vantage point of Cicero's civic interests that Bruni later also enlarged upon the views of the moral philosophy of Aristotle. For the first time since the beginning of the Middle Ages, a powerful intellectual influence was exerted by the specifically Roman and civic quality of Cicero's writings.

The discovery that Bruni and his generation were capable

[3] This explains my ambivalent position toward Wilhelm Dilthey, whose "Geistesgeschichte" (along with Benedetto Croce's works on historiography) was probably the greatest inspiration of my formative years but failed to grasp Bruni's role. The other major influence on my formative years, incidentally, came from Ernst Troeltsch, whose *Aufsätze zur Geistesgeschichte und Religions-soziologie* and *Deutscher Geist und Westeuropa* I was privileged to edit in 1925.

[4] First summarized in the introduction to my collection of Bruni's works, *Leonardo Bruni Aretino: Humanistisch-philosophische Schriften* (Leipzig, 1928).

through Cicero of seeing Roman life in a more genuinely historical light led to another surprise. The usual assumption had been that Quattrocento Humanism was responsible for a rhetorical, classicistic imitation of ancient historiography—the very opposite of any true historical thinking. Yet it turned out that Bruni and his contemporaries made history an indispensable part of the citizen's outlook and education; that they were the first to view the rise and fall of Rome and the later growth of the Italian states as natural phenomena to be explained by secular causes; and that these insights were the source of many of Machiavelli's ideas as well as the earliest instance of modern thinking about history.[5] Even the often heard accusation that the humanistic classicism of the early Quattrocento was blind to the possibilities of the Volgare required modification in the case of Florence. For the esteem of their native tongue remained alive among the Florentine civic humanists, and their growing historical-mindedness, at least since the 1430s, provided the foundation for Bruni's claim that every language had its own peculiar perfection and that the language of Dante would have its day in history, as the languages of Homer and Virgil had had theirs.[6]

I had to find the causes of this unexpected pattern of thought. It is certainly true that new conceptions and values are not created overnight, and once modern eyes became focused on what was ascendant in the intellectual world after 1400, they discovered that many of the new trends had had a kind of prehistory in the Trecento. But before 1400, whatever of later Renaissance attitudes already existed in rudimentary form was not yet linked by a coherent vision of human nature and history, and virtually every cautious new step was fol-

[5] Emilio Santini's helpful and securely based monographs, of course, introduced me to this aspect of Bruni's work, in addition to what I had already learned from Paul Joachimsen's *Geschichtsauffassung und Geschichtschreibung in Deutschland unter dem Einfluss des Humanismus* (Leipzig, 1910).

[6] As the chapter "Florentine Humanism and the Volgare in the Quattrocento" in my *Crisis of the Early Italian Renaissance* later tried to prove for Bruni and Florentine civic Humanism.

lowed by a retreat or even by a recrudescence of medieval convictions. Why, then, was there such an upsurge of creativity in so many fields, especially in Florence, once the threshold of the new century was crossed? Why did thought that had refused to thrive in the Trecento crystallize after 1400 and become permanent?

My answer was that events occurred in the relationship between the Italian states about and after 1400 that were to be decisive for the future of Italy. At that time the Florentine republic resisted, eventually with success, the efforts of the Visconti of Milan to build a north and central Italian monarchy—a resistance, the Florentines believed, carried out in defense not only of Florence's independence as a city-state but indirectly of the survival of republican freedom in Italy. The war with the Visconti brought to the surface both the glories and the problems of city-state life, including many of the uncertainties and contradictions in the politico-historical outlook of the Trecento humanists, especially when, in the 1410s, the Visconti efforts to build an empire were succeeded by those of the Kingdom of Naples. Together these developements were the catalyst in the rapid transformation of the moral, political, and historical outlook of the first three or four decades of the Quattrocento, the period of Florence's repeated, and at times single-handed, opposition to a forced unification of the peninsula; and the rising political status of Florence in this period goes far toward explaining its simultaneous ascent to the position of leader in Italian Renaissance culture.

Something like this picture was finally drawn in my *Crisis of the Early Italian Renaissance*. This book's appearance (first published in 1955), more than fifteen years after most of my discoveries in Florentine civic Humanism had been made, was due less to the difficulties of my life (although these were real enough) than to the problems inherent in the final stages of my work on the *Crisis*. Unusually lengthy investigations and critical revaluations of the sources were required in order to ascertain that, indeed, none of the Florentine writings exhibiting the new ideas of the Quattrocento was composed before the impact of the struggle between the Florentine republic and the Visconti despots could have been felt; and the exacting work of correcting a maze of chronological errors, which had prevented awareness of the relationship of the Florentine conceptions to the reality of the Visconti wars, took up many of my best working years. But this price had to be paid if the hypothesis of the impact of the war was to be well founded.

When my idea of "civic Humanism" and of the causes of Florence's primacy in culture and politics during the first decades of the Quattrocento reached maturity about the end of World War II,[7] I discovered to my delight that I was not alone on the road I was then traveling as a scholar in the United States. During the war, similar approaches had been tried in Italy, especially by three eminent scholars. Eugenio Garin had viewed with kindred eyes the Florentine humanistic philosophy which called for participation of citizens in the "vita civile" and defended the passions and "bona externa" as indispensable for an active political life.[8] He had read and agreed with my publications of the twenties and thirties[9] and proceeded to make the vital discovery that, in the latter half of the Quattrocento and during the Cinquecento, the major elements of the early Quattrocento Florentine view of life were widely circulated in Italian humanistic philosophy and literature. In my youth, Italian students of the history of Renaissance philosophy (especially the followers of Giovanni Gentile) had freshly appraised the philosophy of the Florentine humanists of the early Quattrocento, but only as preparation for the philosophy of the "dignitas hominis," which culmi-

[7] Cf. my essay "Articulation and Unity in the Italian Renaissance and in the Modern West," written in 1942 and published in 1944, in *The Quest for Political Unity in World History*, ed. S. Pargellis (vol. 3 of the Annual Report of the American Historical Association for the Year 1942).

[8] The first synopsis of Garin's reappraisal was his *L'umanesimo italiano: filosofia e vita civile nel Rinascimento*, published originally in a German version entitled *Der italienische Humanismus* (Bern, 1947).

[9] In 1941, in *La Rinascita* 4: 409ff., he had already referred to my interpretation of the civic spirit of the Florentine humanists, calling it a new and persuasive thesis.

nated with the Neoplatonists of the second half of the century. Today, thanks mainly to Garin and his school, the early Quattrocento, a time when ideas emerged in close relationship with the vicissitudes of civic society and republican life in Florence, is usually evaluated as a period in its own right, and scholars talk of loss as well as gain when they proceed from the early Quattrocento to the ascendancy of Neoplatonism and the culture of the princely courts. Given this new conception of the course of Quattrocento philosophy, my findings on early Quattrocento Florence no longer appeared strange.

Equally congenial to my views were those of Federico Chabod. Chabod's perception of the emergence of a causal and natural understanding of life as part of the transition from the Middle Ages to the Renaissance[10] was in striking accord with what I had learned about the rise of historical thinking in early Quattrocento Florence. His writings helped exceedingly to elucidate my conclusion that the few decades around 1400 were decisive in transforming a humanistic outlook still half medieval to one fully Renaissance and even modern.

Third and last, there was Nino Valeri, who described the Milanese–Florentine wars as the crucible in which Florentine civic spirit was regenerated. Like myself, he insisted that behind the conflicting aims of the contestants—a conquering but unifying monarchy or a rich variety of independent states, including republics—lay a genuine alternative for the Renaissance and the political future of Italy.[11]

Let me emphasize how much it has meant to me that during the middle years of my life I was fortified by the existence of these congenial trends in Italian scholarship. I have witnessed, and been fortunate to participate in, a profound transforma-

[10] Especially in his well-known essay of 1942, "Il Rinascimento," translated under the title "The Concept of the Renaissance" in his *Machiavelli and the Renaissance* (London, 1958).

[11] The details of my relationship to Valeri were discussed in my review essay, "Die politische Entwicklung der italienischen Renaissance," in *Historische Zeitschrift* 174 (1952), and briefly in *Crisis*, vol. 1, Appendix 1, "Interpretations of the Political Background of the Early Renaissance," 388–90.

tion of the picture of Humanism and the Renaissance in Italy—perhaps its most profound transformation since Burckhardt's masterpiece. As for the early Italian Renaissance, a vast quantity of unexpected information in a great variety of fields has by now emerged, and since this information contradicts former assumptions about the nature of the Quattrocento, it is difficult to believe that the simple facts will not continue to force changes in our explanation why the Quattrocento deviated so profoundly from the Middle Ages, transforming the outlook of the following centuries.

I do not want to say with this that the final effect of all these shifts can be foreseen, but a number of basic questions can and should be raised. One wonders, for instance, if closer familiarity with the situation of Humanism in early Quattrocento Florence will not show that some or all of the factors present at that time also played a role in the sixteenth century, when the Renaissance was spreading through Europe. Recent research—to the best of my knowledge, particularly by American scholars—has already begun to reveal that not only Venetian culture in the sixteenth century but also certain formerly neglected aspects of the French and English renaissances can be illuminated by the Italian Quattrocento model.[12] Even when we are dealing to some degree with parallels rather than influences, the fact remains that once a convincing new pattern has been established for the Italian Quattrocento mind, its use can in many ways further understanding of the structure of the later Renaissance, including Humanism in other European countries.[13]

[12] I am thinking of William Bouwsma's *Venice and the Defense of Republican Liberty: Renaissance Values in the Age of the Counter Reformation* (Berkeley, 1968), Eugene Rice's *The Renaissance Idea of Wisdom* (Cambridge, Mass., 1958), and other works named in Essay Thirteen.

[13] For the aftereffects of (or important parallels to) the Florentine Quattrocento during the sixteenth century, I remind the reader once again of the summation given in Essay Thirteen. Cf. also the striking example of connecting links established between Florentine civic Humanism, Machiavelli, and English political thought of the mid-seventeenth century—a line of development rather different from the one suggested in the *Crisis* and the present book but

Consideration of the pattern of Humanism in early Quattrocento Florence can be equally valuable in understanding
what preceded and what followed in the Florentine development itself. The foremost beneficiaries here should be the
great predecessor and the potential heir of early Quattrocento
Florentine thought, Petrarch and Machiavelli. To begin with
Petrarch, since we now know that the maturation of Renaissance ideas about 1400 was largely the result of a union between new humanistic values and the way of life led by city-
state citizens, we should ask whether the familiar irresolution
characteristic of Petrarch (and other Trecento writers) was not
due largely to the fact that Petrarch's way of life was still to a
high degree contemplative in the medieval sense and relatively
disengaged from the society and the *vita activa* of his day.
There is, to be sure, much merit in attempting to explore Petrarch's inner struggles; but this does not tell the whole story.
A more historical explanation may be found if Petrarch's
sometimes amazing contradictions and retroversions are seen
in the context of the profound differences between Trecento
life and life in Florentine humanistic circles a generation or
two later.[14]

And what about Machiavelli? Is not the discovery that more
of the politico-historical outlook of the *Discourses* was anticipated by the civic humanists of the early Quattrocento than
has been assumed in modern historiography and that the republic continued to play a fundamental emotional and intel-

---

built on an equally positive appraisal of Florentine civic Humanism—by
J.G.A. Pocock, *The Machiavellian Moment: Florentine Political Thought and the
Atlantic Republican Tradition* (Princeton, 1975). For the early circulation in
Great Britain of interpretations kindred to mine, cf. Denys Hay's *The Italian
Renaissance in Its Historical Background* (Cambridge, 1961).

[14] I later ventured upon comparisons of Petrarch and Florentine Quattrocento Humanism in Essay Seven, above, pp. 185–90; in "The Evolution of
Petrarch's Thought," in *From Petrarch to Leonardo Bruni* (Chicago, 1968); in
"Petrarch: His Inner Struggles and the Humanistic Discovery of Man's Nature," in *Florilegium Historiale: Essays Presented to Wallace K. Ferguson* (To-
ronto, 1971); and in *Petrarch's "Secretum": Its Making and Its Meaning* (Cambridge, Mass., 1985).

lectual role for him and for many members of his generation, bound to influence the perspective from which he is viewed and appraised? More precisely, will not greater recognition of Machiavelli's debt to the humanistic tradition of Florence—not merely at marginal points but wherever his civic outlook and historical realism are concerned—modify our conception of his thought? In Machiavelli's case even more than in Petrarch's, path-breaking investigations and controversies have been in full swing for years, and we have become aware that after the period of *The Prince*, Florence did not totally reject Humanism and republicanism. In a word, the gradual reconstruction of the early Quattrocento world of civic Humanism has assured us that the Florentine environment was capable of producing a far more genuinely "republican" Machiavelli than his traditional image seemed to admit. It was this realization that led me to work, after composing the *Crisis*, on the problem of the long-accepted chronological order of Machiavelli's literary writings. For it became obvious that *The Prince* could hardly have followed and, as it were, superseded those parts of the *Discourses* which might be called the major monument to Machiavelli's republicanism and indebtedness to Florentine Quattrocento Humanism; that since the republican-minded and humanistically oriented *Discourses* represent the more mature part of Machiavelli's work, it probably replaced the teachings of *The Prince*. Admittedly, this chronological revision of the succession of Machiavelli's writings has not as yet resulted in major biographical reconstructions of his life and thought. But the transformation which has taken place in our concept of the Quattrocento is clearly a prerequisite for future reappraisals.[15]

This allusion to what will be needed in future reinterpretations of the development of Machiavelli's thought brings me back to the regrets with which I began my remarks on the course of my scholarly efforts: that my work on some essen-

---

[15] See Essay Fifteen, above.

tial components of my field of study has remained preliminary or incomplete. As far as Machiavelli is concerned, I hope I have at least spurred scholars on to pursue with more open mind the intrinsic consequences of the change in the image of the early Renaissance that has come about in my lifetime.

EIGHTEEN

A Defense of the View of the Quattrocento First Offered in *The Crisis of the Early Italian Renaissance* (1970)*

I

IT MAY be helpful to readers of the *Crisis* to learn which guiding principles I followed when the book was written, and why I still regard them as crucial. Let us begin with some general remarks.

A complaint made by some critics is that the *Crisis* fails to live up to its claim that it views the ideas of the Quattrocento wherever possible from a sociopolitical angle. How can this intention have been carried out, it has been asked, if less than major attention was paid to the question how far the *libertas* on which the Florentine ideas ultimately focused was shaped according to the interests of a restricted ruling group, and without a systematic analysis of how the values proclaimed by Florentine humanists were translated into the reality of Florentine life? We are more sensitive today to questions of this sort than historians were at the time the *Crisis* was conceived. But even if the book were written today, these problems, though stressed more strongly, would remain marginal, because the limits to democracy and equality we encounter in Florence about 1400 were typical of political life in most city-states throughout history.

In fact, however, the new ideas of the Florentine Quattrocento could not have been characterized in the terms set forth

---

* First printed under the title "Presentazione al lettore italiano" in Renzo Pecchioli's Italian translation of the *Crisis* (Florence, Sansoni, 1970), x–xxxi. I am publishing here my original English draft with some deletions, many changes, primarily stylistic, and a few bibliographical additions to the notes.

in the *Crisis* if they had not, in some way, been viewed in their sociopolitical setting. One component of Quattrocento thought described in the *Crisis* was a new appreciation of what in the fifteenth century was called the *vita activa* and *civilis*. Nothing quite like it is found in medieval city-states, because in the Middle Ages the *vita contemplativa* of the monk, pregnant with religious meaning, took precedence over the admittedly indispensable active and civic life. In the society of the Renaissance after 1400, the *vita activa*, with its driving passions, was increasingly respected as a precondition for the full realization of human nature; action and political engagement, therefore, seemed to represent the only truly humane way of life. After I had proposed in various essays that early Quattrocento thought in Florence was characterized by this emphasis on the *vita civilis*, Eugenio Garin pointed out, and rightly so, that a similar tendency prevailed in later fifteenth- and sixteenth-century philosophy and literature throughout Italy.[1] But as the *Crisis* reminds us, for two or three generations it had been almost exclusively Florentine.

In order to appraise this no longer medieval Florentine train of thought, the *Crisis* viewed it together with the simultaneous rise of a new type of historical thinking. Again, a strong difference from the preceding medieval mode of thought became evident. In earlier generations the concept of ancient Rome, so important to Humanism, had not been free of the theological assumption that, in its dominance over the world, it represented the last of those universal empires through which Divine Providence had given human history an order unintelligible in merely secular and causal terms. It was this intrusion of theology into history and politics which had caused Trecento thinkers, including Dante, Petrarch, and even Salutati, to ignore the lessons of experience and look upon the German emperors as the predestined restorers of peace. Soon after 1400, in contrast, a conception of history came into being by means of which the *Imperium Romanum* of

[1] In his *Der italienische Humanismus* (Bern, 1947).

Antiquity came to be viewed in a more modern light. The empire, it was now believed, had indeed come to an end when the Roman people lost its natural strength, and it was followed by new states, the Italian heirs to those independent regions and city-states which had flourished on the peninsula before Roman domination. Among the new medieval states were independent republics in which free men once again participated in self-rule and whose cultural and political promise was equal to that of the ancient *Respublica Romana* and the city-states of Etruria and Greece.

Both these lines of thought—esteem for the *vita activa* and the new perspective of history—unmistakably reflect a changed social and political environment after 1400. When I began my research on Florentine Quattrocento Humanism in the 1920s, the transition from the Trecento to the Quattrocento was still commonly explained in terms of a growing knowledge of ancient literature or of a gradual unfolding of Trecento ideas. Scholars had scarcely begun to make serious use of the fact that whereas the Trecento still conceived of a universal Christian empire as the counterpart to the universal Church, after 1400 new views concerning the political articulation or unity of the Italian peninsula emerged. This change was of no concern to the early twentieth-century historians of the Weltanschauung of the Renaissance—Dilthey, Cassirer, Croce, and Gentile—who in their respective appraisals of the period all found sufficient explanation in the Burckhardtian view that the rising ideas of the Quattrocento were a result of the increasing intellectual and ethical "autonomy" of the individual.

The observations I made during the years when the *Crisis* was in preparation did not essentially follow Burckhardt, nor did they confirm the overwhelming impact of tyranny on Renaissance thought and culture assumed by him. It is true of most of the Florentine Quattrocento ideas presented in the *Crisis* that they brought to greater maturity opinions which, in the hierarchically ordered outlook of the Middle Ages, had been considered valid only on a lower level, where they were not in the focus of observation and interest. The *vita activa* had

had its place in the medieval outlook, but since religious contemplation was set on a higher plane, there was no access to the later argument—so central to Quattrocento humanists—that virtue must be constantly tested and practiced and that contemplative withdrawal causes human nature to fragment. By the same token, the beginnings of a causal approach to historical phenomena had existed throughout the Middle Ages, but they had remained beginnings, because in the higher reaches where events became truly meaningful to medieval thinkers, history showed the hand of God and was not principally the work of man and a manifestation of his nature. Clearly, only when conditions emerged in which the actuality of life refuted the belief in a hierarchy of governments culminating in the Roman Empire could there finally develop an awareness that the rules of natural growth and decay applied even to Rome and that Rome could therefore be used as a model for modern states.

Why did these attitudes emerge during the first decades of the Quattrocento? The answers given in the *Crisis* again point to the changing socio-political background. Historical and political forces could at last be imagined as moving on one level when, about 1400, the purely secular hope or fear that large parts of the peninsula would be pacified through conquest by one of the powerful Italian monarchies—Milan or Naples—began to supplant the half-mystical dream of pacification by the ruler of the divinely ordained empire. Moreover, the importance of different forms of states could now be better recognized: monarchy might offer a more rational kind of government for a large state, but the city-state republic generated more political and cultural vitality, because its citizens could take an active, responsible part in communal life.

A second answer given in the *Crisis* also has to do with the influence of background changes: the same decades around 1400 saw the building of a Florentine region-state stretching from the Tuscan coast to the Apennines. This unexpected side effect of resistance to the territorial expansion of Milan made Florence and Florentine citizenship so important that historical comparisons of Florence with Athens and Rome finally became meaningful. When Florentine historians began to look upon their city as the protagonist of independence among the surviving Italian city-states, they also began to regard the freedom of the *Respublica Romana* and the autocracy of the Roman imperial monarchy as political alternatives. At that juncture the long, successful rivalry of the Etruscan city-state republics with early Rome was discovered; the constitutions of ancient and modern city-states alike were analyzed to determine what they contributed to freedom or to power. History became comparative and secular, and the vital foundations were laid for the later thought of Machiavelli and Guicciardini.

The chapters in the *Crisis* on Florentine resistance to Milan and Naples should be compared with Burckhardt's description of the Renaissance state. His view of the period, based as it was on the belief that the tyrant states and princely courts afforded fullest scope to the emancipated individual, ignored the fact that after 1400 city-state republics no less than tyrant states reached the stage where the experiences of generations were finally manifested in stated principles and conscious thought. If it is true that autocratic principalities could claim a more effective administration and the ability to fulfill the mission of bringing unity and peace to the peninsula once attributed to the empire, it is also true that city-state citizens had become aware of a mission of their own: to keep alive the values and traditions of the medieval communes and also, through the medium of civic Humanism, the heritage of the *libertas* of ancient city-state republics. In short, the outcome of Burckhardt's insistence on the effects of tyranny was that only half the story of the humanistic outlook and the sociopolitical challenges after 1400 was usually told.

II

It is one of the unstated premises of the *Crisis* that Burckhardt's view of the Renaissance, though valid as far as it goes, needs to be complemented by approaches which may not be in easy harmony with his stress on tyranny and individualism, and it is this need that largely determined the structure of my book. It gathered together a body of evidence from formerly neglected sources showing that the cultural and political role of the city-state republic was not as fully played out after 1400 as Burckhardt thought. The *Crisis* attempted to give this source material its due place and urged the need for a multi-dimensional approach to the Quattrocento. Nevertheless, its introduction expressly states that "an estimate of the bearing of these findings on our total view of the Italian Renaissance is not the burden" of the book; it was hoped, rather, that "readers will pose this wider problem to themselves."

Even today, many years later, the time may not have come for a final weighing of the accumulated evidence. Although the strong impact of the city-state ideal of the *vita activa politica* on the literature of the fifteenth and sixteenth centuries has become increasingly evident, we perhaps do not yet have enough information to judge the extent to which Humanism was permanently altered by that early Florentine Renaissance ideal. It is quite possible that the face of the period will change still further as our view of Quattrocento life and thought broadens.[2]

It was not my intention in the *Crisis* to pronounce former scholarship wrong, but merely too narrow. In particular, I did not attempt to deny that from its medieval beginnings until the late Renaissance, Humanism was steeped in the rhetorical tradition of Antiquity; nor did I intend to minimize the part played by the birth of humanistic philology in the transition from medieval to modern thought. The decisive question, rather, was whether rhetoric and the new philology were the only essential, or even the foremost, humanistic contributions to the making of the modern mind; whether Humanism could have played its fundamental role in the fifteenth and sixteenth centuries if it had not also offered a new vision of man's nature

---

[2] As I believe it has been changed through the space accorded to the Quattrocento defense of wealth in the present book. Note also that Lauro Martines' *The Social World of the Florentine Humanists* (Princeton, 1963), passim and esp. 271–302 ("The Genesis" and "The Decline of Civic Humanism"), provides a very substantial complement to the *Crisis* in all matters concerning the socioeconomic structure and political role of Florentine Humanism.

and of history, a new estimate of human values. The *Crisis* tried to show that Florentine humanists of the Quattrocento not only were continuers of the rhetorical tradition and pioneering contributors to the new philology but also originated the philosophy of the active political life and a secularized conception of history and culture, the two leitmotifs of the school of thought analyzed in the *Crisis*. As is stressed in its epilogue, it cannot be claimed that every humanist of the fifteenth and sixteenth centuries shared this particular outlook; but neither can it be said that rhetoric and philology were the only important aspects of Humanism in that time. Although the later structure of Humanism is rarely mentioned in the *Crisis*, because its focus is entirely on the early Quattrocento, the picture presented there should be evaluated with a view to the total history of Humanism.

As many recent studies have disclosed, emphasis on the *vita activa* and *civilis* and the secularization of historical conceptions were to reappear whenever Humanism became a trend in the remaining Italian city-state republics—as late as the sixteenth century in Genoa and Lucca and even later in Venice, where we still encounter a pattern of civic Humanism toward the very end of the Renaissance, about 1600, as has been pointed out by William Bouwsma.[3] North of the Alps, where a politically oriented Humanism comparable to the civic Humanism of the Italian city-state republics appeared less frequently and was more limited in scope, other humanistic schools of thought confirm that Renaissance Humanism cannot be characterized in terms of rhetorical motivation and the new philology alone, or even preponderantly. As an example, wherever Humanism coincided with new inventions in the mechanical arts, in which the moderns definitely surpassed the ancients, the humanistic propensity for the active life assumed yet another dimension: a view of man as *homo faber* (the craftsman and inventor), the greatest proponent of which was the early sixteenth-century humanist Luis Vives. There were

---

[3] In *Venice and the Defense of Republican Liberty: Renaissance Values in the Age of the Counter Reformation* (Berkeley, 1968).

other, differently structured, humanistic trends in the later Renaissance. For many humanists of the sixteenth century there could be no proper outlook on life without freedom from dogmatism. The disputatious obstinacy of scholars and their claims to authority were feared as threats to true culture, which required a large measure of skepticism and even agnosticism. One need only recall Montaigne to be aware of the immense contribution made by this strain of humanistic thought to the modern world. In Montaigne's work, agnosticism stops short of the Catholic tradition; it has entered into a union—in typically sixteenth-century fashion—with religious fideism. But the humanistic rejection of philosophic dogmatism also lessened the dominance of dogma in religion. There is no need to elaborate the fact that this type of humanistic outlook, which appeared in the work and school of Erasmus, was one of the most significant and widespread developments in modern Western thought, rivaled in its influence perhaps only by civic-political Humanism. In none of these cases was the thinking of the truly great humanists shaped primarily by rhetoric or philology.

I do not doubt that the history of Renaissance Humanism will ultimately have to be presented in terms of a comparative phenomenology of the aforementioned (and possibly other) humanistic outlooks on life and the successive views of man, history, and politics. When I wrote the *Crisis* I hoped that a fuller understanding of the type of humanistic outlook encountered in early Renaissance Florence might prove effective in expanding Renaissance Humanism beyond its "rhetorical" and "philological" dimensions into a more complex phenomenon.

III

A misinterpretation of the attempt in the *Crisis* to bring the background of early Humanism into sharper focus led some of my critics to charge that the book is overly partial to Florence. To some, the *Crisis* is apparently a descendant of that questionable branch of historiography which carried forward the parochial struggles of the cities and regions of earlier Italian history.

This could hardly be more contrary to the objectives of the *Crisis*, which aimed on the basis of neglected sources to reestablish an historical balance. The fact is that, even before Burckhardt, a one-sided emphasis had been placed on the courts of princes and tyrants. In the historiography of the Enlightenment these courts, as early counterparts of the court of Louis XIV, already seemed to overshadow everything else in the fifteenth and sixteenth centuries. Even Quattrocento Florence—"the Florence of the Medici"—was regarded as a Renaissance principality. In his reconstruction of the history of the Italian city-state republics of the Middle Ages, shortly after 1800, Simonde de Sismondi, the republican-minded historian of Rousseau's school, was convinced that by the end of the Trecento, time had run out for the republics. He believed that republican liberty was dead and that only princes still counted in Italy. With the establishment in the mid-nineteenth century of an Italian monarchy, the expansionist policy of the strongest of these princes, the Visconti of Milan, was often viewed as a harbinger or forerunner of the later achievements of the House of Savoy.

The first lesson taught by the sources on which the *Crisis* is based was that the Florentine war of ideas carried on against the Visconti in the name of liberty and with the ancient city-state republics constantly in mind, was not merely a matter of propaganda. Private and public utterances during the wars with Milan show a rapid growth of Florentine political self-awareness. The new political and historical ideas make their appearance more or less simultaneously in personal *ricordi* and letters, in the memoranda of Florentine officeholders and the minutes of city councils, in literary writings and, last but not least, in Florentine chronicles and humanistic histories, which were not composed by paid and supervised writers.[4]

---

[4] A source not to be ignored is the public correspondence of the republic with other states. But whereas these letters give basic information about the

In the *Crisis*, I would claim, equal attention is given to the manifestations of the new spirit in Florentine literature and to the voices heard in the camps of the Visconti and the kings of Naples. There, too, especially among the followers of the Visconti in northern Italy, firm and representative political convictions were coming to the fore after 1400. In the *Crisis*, in fact, respect for the superior efficiency of tyrannical autocracy was traced, for the first time, in the writings of such north Italian humanists of the early Renaissance as Giovanni Conversino, Uberto Decembrio, and Pier Candido Decembrio. Thus in the *Crisis* a hearing is given to both sides, and the conclusion is drawn that the ideas of both republics and principalities have to be taken more seriously than had hitherto been the case. In the final analysis, the political struggles of the early Renaissance were not mere quarrels between local neighbors equal in the pettiness of their aims, as is often taken for granted; rather, the encounters of the time involved basic

---

practical policies and prevailing mood of the heads of state, they usually reveal little, or even mislead the recipients intentionally whenever they refer to alleged general political convictions or adduce historic models or events. For nowhere would an official or humanist be more reluctant to honestly express his personal political persuasions (or those of the government in whose name he is writing) than in a type of correspondence which had to be adapted to the needs of the occasion in order to achieve specific diplomatic ends. Thus, when a humanist in the Florentine chancery addressed a German emperor he would, of course, sound like an obedient servant of the empire, writing admiring things about its ceaseless mission to bring peace to the world—even if the writer was Bruni. Or again, when in 1395 Salutati, in the name of the republic, officially had to congratulate Giangaleazzo on becoming Duke of Milan, he did not hesitate to tell him that Florence could conceive of no more welcome government in Milan than that of this prince, who had become known as a man of peace and would undoubtedly work for peace in Italy. It would be odd, I think, to conclude from these and similar examples that the republican convictions of those who phrased the official letters were weak or merely rhetorical and that the *Crisis* must be blamed for not paying attention to this "conflicting" evidence. Such reasoning seems to me absurd, although it has been used by some of the critics of the *Crisis*. In any case, the cumulative testimony contained in the various types of sources referred to above is not weakened by the apparent inconsistencies found in documents phrased for transparent diplomatic ends.

principles and persuasions. The triumph of the *principatus* in the so-called age of the principalities was not a foregone conclusion. On the contrary, an historic choice had to be made between two potential systems: a single monarchy for large parts of the peninsula or an equilibrium between regional states, in which independence and republican life could continue. To analyze the impact of this background on Renaissance thought without bias toward either side is one of the tasks of the *Crisis*. In this I had no predecessor, though I found an ally in Nino Valeri who at roughly the same time arrived at a similarly complex view of the political scene in early Quattrocento Italy.[5]

It is true nevertheless that the emphasis in the *Crisis* is on Florence and Florentine achievements. There are two reasons for this. In the first place, since modern historiography had so long stressed the principality, the balance could be righted only by presenting the overshadowed, and even ignored, role of the Florentine republic in full detail. For this purpose, considerable space is allocated in the *Crisis* to a reconstruction of the conduct of Florentine citizens during the ordeal of the wars and to the exploration of Florentine literary documents connected with the struggle. Most of the chapters in my book thus undertake spadework rather than a comprehensive reconstruction of the early Quattrocento.

Secondly, it is not the principal intention of the *Crisis* to weigh the significance of ideas as political weapons; the book is primarily intended to determine the impact of ideas, in a crucial period of war, on the nascent Weltanschauung of the Quattrocento Renaissance. From this point of view, its major finding is that Florentine writers in Bruni's time prepared the way for Machiavelli and Guicciardini, much more incisively than has been thought, not only through their literary influence on later Florentines but also because they moved away so rapidly from the medieval aspects of the Trecento, forming

[5] See Valeri's *L'Italia nell'età dei principati dal 1343 al 1516* (Verona, 1950), and my appraisals of his work referred to in Essay Seventeen, note 11.

conceptions of history and politics that were in accord with much of the thought of the next few centuries.

If we compare this new intellectual climate of early Renaissance Florence with what contemporary humanists at north Italian tyrant courts and in the Visconti camp thought about history and politics or about the life of scholars and citizens under the efficient autocratic governments of princely states, we find that there, too, considerable strides away from Trecento thought were made about 1400. The writings of early Quattrocento north Italian authors like Giovanni Conversino in Padua and the elder and younger Decembrios in Milan, present themselves as guides ranging from idealized descriptions of enforced vocational instruction for adolescents in a strictly supervised society to realistic reports on the progress of order, hygiene, and city planning. In this matter, too, the *Crisis* was the first book to draw attention to some of the crucial texts. But how insignificant were these often utopian modes of thought in tyrant states when compared with the truly modern concepts of life and history that emerged in Florence at the same time! It is, indeed, their disproportionate historical significance that ultimately justifies the dominant position allotted to Florence in the *Crisis*. The reader must be judge of whether the conclusions reached in the course of my discussion of the opposing trends are convincing. But even if my conclusions should occasionally be not quite fair, it would be owing to my estimation of what were the most creative and relevant elements in the growth of Quattrocento thought, not to any pro-Florentine bias.

IV

In still another respect, the user of the *Crisis* should refrain from reading into the book a dogmatism that is alien to its intention. As an examination of the literature of the decades about 1400 proves, the secular and causal approach of Florentine humanists to history, which included a new sensitivity to the problems of empire and the independence of states, was

fundamentally influenced by Giangaleazzo Visconti's challenge to Florence's *libertas* during his final years. It has to be
acknowledged, therefore, that the genesis of Florentine historical thought was decided by the political and military events
of a very few years, essentially the brief climactic period of
1400–1402, which ended with Giangaleazzo's death. In the
eyes of some critics, however, this statement, which is often
repeated in the *Crisis*, appears to violate the continuity from
the Trecento to the Quattrocento. They insist that an analysis
which shifts emphasis from continuity to relatively sudden
change is suspect from the start.

Whoever reads the *Crisis* in its entirety will find that this
criticism, too, is based on a misconception. My insistence on
the crucial role of the years 1400–1402 is closely associated
with two other arguments concerning the genesis of the ideas
of the Quattrocento, arguments not only explicitly defined in
the book but basic to its analysis of the intellectual transformation on the threshold of the new century. One is that the
changing historico-political ideas had harbingers during the
Trecento but that they did not bear mature fruit until the political climate in Italy changed about 1400. The Giangaleazzo
wars and the Florentine reaction to their challenge were the
"catalyst," to use the word in the *Crisis*; they were not the
causes of an unexpected change. The second, related argument is that the experience of 1402 might nonetheless not have
been sufficient by itself to transform Florentine thought if
other events had not pushed in the same direction. On the one
hand, the pattern of Italian interstate relations in 1400–1402—
the drive of a major monarchical power to conquer central Italy and the resistance of the Florentine republic—although
suspended for half a decade after Giangaleazzo's sudden death
in 1402, was repeated several times before the middle of the
Quattrocento by Ladislaus of Naples and Filippo Maria Visconti, thereby giving further impetus to the new ideas. On the
other hand, having become a north Tuscan region-state and
member of a nascent system of larger states, Quattrocento
Florence found itself much further along the road toward sov-

ereignty and the modern state than it had been even shortly before 1400.

The history of Florentine Quattrocento political and historical ideas, therefore, is presented in the *Crisis* not as an unprepared-for upheaval but as a development in stages. Important discoveries in ancient thought, politics, and history—including Cicero's ideas concerning the *vita activa politica* and the historic role of the *Respublica Romana*—had already been made during the Trecento, but they had been too much at variance with the medieval cast of mind and were once again discarded or neutralized. After 1402, the Florentine republic could seem to reincarnate the spirit which had animated Athens and Rome. The historical image of the *Respublica Romana* finally came to the fore, and the Roman citizen Cicero, relieved of his medieval disguises, became the model for civic humanists. Even so, works composed immediately after the Giangaleazzo wars (especially Bruni's *Laudatio* and Dati's dialogue-discussion of the struggle), though seminal, were still relatively undeveloped. The maturation of the new thought could not occur until Florence had annexed the Tuscan coast, including Pisa and Leghorn. The result was a Florentine state essentially on a level with that of Venice and the great principalities, endowed with a territory in which citizen participation in the administration of subject areas resembled more fully than at any earlier time the kind of participation that had existed in the leading ancient city-republics. The simultaneous resumption by Naples and the next Duke of Milan, Filippo Maria, of a policy of Italian unification through conquest, as well as the emergent realization that Florence no longer stood alone in its defiance of monarchical expansion but was now allied with other surviving city-state republics, brought relations between the Italian states nearer to ideological conflict in the modern sense. Only then, twenty or more years after the crucial turning point of 1402, were the great political issues in both camps finally understood and defined by humanistic authors.

This description of the environment of Florentine Quattro-

cento ideas offers the prospect of moving the discussion beyond the vagueness of earlier arguments about the "continuity" of Trecento traditions. Thus, in the *Crisis*, the so-called
continuous process of growth is broken into a sequence of distinct phases, in each of which some new element can be seen
to emerge from changing political experiences; foremost, of
course, the gradual, irreversible reorganization of Italy, and
with it the emergence of the Florentine region-state. Whether
the stages have been defined convincingly is again up to the
reader to decide.

It is vital for another reason as well that we be aware of the
transformation that took place in humanistic thought after
1400 and the factors that influenced it. Burckhardt's description of the growth of the Renaissance fails to explain why profound changes should have occurred in Italian politics and
thought in or shortly after 1400; yet in the history of art (including Burckhardt's own contributions to art history), the
transition from the Middle Ages to the Renaissance has always
been described in just such terms: the emergence in Florence
soon after 1400 of a new relationship to reality and to Antiquity; the appearance, precisely in the first three decades of the
Quattrocento, of the earliest masterpieces of a new style; and
more specifically, the rise of the new art after a century (the
Trecento) in which some of the new tendencies were accepted, only to be rejected again.[6] The depiction in the *Crisis*
of a mutation in politics and humanistic thought after 1400
thus fills a gap in the Burckhardtian scheme. It describes a development much more in harmony with the changes in Renaissance art—provided, of course, that the chronology of the
humanistic writings upon which the reconstruction in the
field of literature ultimately rests is as fully reliable as that of
the new art.

---

[6] In the essay dealing with Burckhardt, I have drawn attention to the fact
that he advanced these arguments in other works than the *Kultur der Renaissance*. See Essay Sixteen, above, p. 177.

V

At this point I must turn to criticizing the procedure of not a few users of the *Crisis*, who have avoided coming to grips with the important philological problems involved in establishing the chronological infrastructure of the early Quattrocento development. Too many students of the period reconstructed in the *Crisis* seem to think either that when discussing the genesis of Florentine civic Humanism it is a matter of no great concern whether a work was written a few years earlier or later, or that such intricacies may be left to the attention of biographical specialists. This tendency is so strong that, because the *Laudatio* has sometimes been attributed to 1400 and sometimes to the years after 1402 (that is, either before or after the decisive war with Giangaleazzo Visconti), some recent analysts have been content to date it "about 1401." Others seem to feel that they have met their obligations to historical accuracy when they have told their readers passively that both 1400 and the time after 1402 have been proposed.

I do not mean to say, of course, that scholars ought not attempt to prove that the dates of Bruni's early works present an insoluble puzzle, if this is their opinion. I wish to draw attention, rather, to the widespread attitude that encourages historians to believe that they may leave the "trifles" and enigmas of chronology to "specialists" without jeopardizing their own judgments of the period in question. We must keep in mind that any attempt to relate the history of thought, and especially the history of social and political ideas, to a contemporary background of changing political experience depends on distinguishing the precise historical conditions in which our documents and sources were conceived. The definition of periods in the history of thought must be anchored in an understanding of the new ideas as they appeared at the moment of their birth, and this understanding will vary with the circumstances in which we assume the documents, works, or passages expressing those new ideas to have been written.

It is not too sanguine to believe that in many cases in which external evidence is lacking, we can nevertheless find objective methods yielding verifiable conclusions. Those methods need not be newly invented; their basic criteria were established long ago by classical philology, and sometimes all that is needed is their cautious application.

In the case of the *Crisis*, the assumption that a relationship exists between the rise of the Quattrocento view of politics and history on the one hand, and the defense and reorganization of the surviving Italian states on the other, is sharpened by our awareness that the traditionally accepted dates of a group of Florentine writings in which the new ideas appeared for the first time are not tenable. Opinions may conceivably differ in their details, but an important part of the historical picture drawn in the *Crisis* depends on conclusions regarding the dates of four major sources: two of Bruni's early pioneer works—his *Laudatio* and the second of his *Dialogi*—which, I maintain, were composed under the direct impact of the triumph over Giangaleazzo; Dati's account of the Florentine wars with him, which must have been written at a time when the political climate of the period immediately following Giangaleazzo's death had not yet changed; and that inveterate mainstay of so many reconstructions of the declining Trecento, Giovanni da Prato's *Paradiso degli Alberti*, which contains politico-historical ideas that could have been formulated only after the Giangalezzo period. Now, at the end of many years of critical endeavor to put the chronology of the literature of the period on a sounder basis, I feel reasonably certain that the revision of the dates of these four literary documents will prevail.

I am well aware that it would be psychologically wiser simply to say once more that the reader must decide how much of it to accept. But here the degree of certainty we can achieve is significant, and I feel obligated to state honestly what I believe that degree to be. Although it was impossible within the framework of an analytical historical work like the *Crisis* to present these critical problems with the methodological precision demanded by their nature, I have done my best to refine the new chronology[7] in two chapters of my book *From Petrarch to Leonardo Bruni: Studies in Humanistic and Political Literature* (Chicago, 1968): "Chronology and Historical Certainty: The Dates of Bruni's *Laudatio* and *Dialogi*" (especially pages 111–37) and "A Crucial Date in the History of Florentine Historiography: The Composition of Dati's *Istoria di Firenze* in 1409." These two chapters are meant to survey and integrate the results of my previous research and present them to the critical reader who wishes to determine for himself how much or little doubt remains about the chronological infrastructure of the decisive years at the beginning of the Quattrocento.[8]

[7] Initially proposed in my *Humanistic and Political Literature in Florence and Venice at the Beginning of the Quattrocento* (Cambridge, Mass., 1955).

[8] For the post-1402 dating of the *Paradiso degli Alberti*, see the first chapter of *Humanistic and Political Literature in Florence and Venice*. For a convenient introduction to the problem and importance of the dates of Bruni's *Laudatio* and *Dialogi*, I also refer the reader to my reply to J. E. Seigel, "Leonardo Bruni: 'Professional Rhetorician' or 'Civic Humanist'?" in *Past and Present* 36 (1967): 21–37. The essay, "Chronology and Historical Certainty: The Dates of Bruni's *Laudatio* and *Dialogi*," will appear in clearer, more succinct form in my forthcoming book, *The Life and Literary Work of Leonardo Bruni*.

INDEX OF NAMES